50 WEAPONS THAT CHANGED WARFARE

By

William Weir

Author of *50 Battles That Changed the World*

NEW PAGE BOOKS
A division of The Career Press, Inc.
Franklin Lakes, NJ

50 WEAPONS THAT CHANGED WARFARE
EDITED BY KATHRYN HENCHES
TYPESET BY EILEEN DOW MUNSON
Cover design by Foster & Foster, Inc.
Black Hawk photo credit: Richard Zellner/Sikorsky Aircraft Corp.
Printed in the U.S.A. by Book-mart Press

To order this title, please call toll-free 1-800-CAREER-1 (NJ and Canada: 201-848-0310) to order using VISA or MasterCard, or for further information on books from Career Press.

The Career Press, Inc., 3 Tice Road, PO Box 687,
Franklin Lakes, NJ 07417
www.careerpress.com
www.newpagebooks.com

Library of Congress Cataloging-in-Publication Data

Weir, William, 1928-
    50 weapons that changed the world / by William Weir.
        p. cm.
    Includes bibliographical references and index.
    ISBN 1-56414-756-8 (pbk.)
        1. Military weapons—History. I. Title.

U800.W395 2005
355.8'2—dc22
                                                              2004055961

Acknowledgments

Any work of history owes a huge debt to hundreds, perhaps thousands, of persons the author does not know and may not have even heard of. That's especially true if the subject is invention, even invention of weapons. And it should be noted that inventors of these bloody devices were not necessarily bloody-minded.

Many inventors of weapons, such as Hiram Maxim, with his machine gun, and Alfred Nobel, with dynamite, thought their inventions were so powerful they would make war too horrible, and the world would try to settle disputes in a more peaceful way. The inventor of the spear probably considered it nothing more than a way to bring more meat to the family cave. The inventors of riding and the composite bow aimed to make it easier to herd cattle and sheep and protect them from predators, not to make it easier for Genghis Khan to conquer most of the known world. Like the inventors of barbed wire, they were thinking of the cattle business, not the battle business. The Wright brothers were mainly interested in soaring through the air with wings, like birds. They may have had some thoughts about faster transportation, possibly also the use of planes in war. But it is most unlikely that they had any inkling of the way their invention would be used in World War II.

Other inventors, of course, knew very well what their innovations would do. Callinicus knew that his "Greek fire" would annihilate enemy fleets and enemy sailors, but his object was not killing people but saving Christian civilization. David Bushnell, who built the first submarine used in combat, was interested only in freeing his country from British domination.

It should also be said that new weapons have made war different, but not necessarily more horrible. Genghis Khan, in the course of a few years, managed to kill 20 million people, which in the 13th century was quite chunk of humanity. And he did this primarily with bows, arrows, and swords.

In addition to the inventors, anyone writing about the development of weapons over the last million or so years had to rely on the testimony of writers who have seen them and seen their effects. Finding those writers would have been impossible without the research staff at the Guilford, Connecticut, public library and their librarian colleagues around the country and around the world.

That's just the work involved in writing the book. To produce what you're reading took the efforts of another team: Mike Lewis, my editor at Career Press/New Page Books and his colleagues in the editorial and production departments. Mike had the concept of a list of 50 weapons that changed warfare, and my agent, John White, convinced him I could handle the project. Finally, and most important, there's my wife, Anne, who not only put up with me hogging the family computer, but read every chapter and contributed much helpful criticism.

If, after all this help, you find any mistakes, there's only one place to lay the blame: on the evil spirits that inhabit my computer.

—Guilford, Connecticut, November, 2004

Table of Contents

Introduction

For the last few thousand years, wars have been fought with weapons. For long stretches of time, they have been fought with the same, or similar, weapons. For example, flintlock smoothbore muskets were the basic infantry weapons for more than a century. When, in the early 19th century, they were replaced by percussion smoothbore muskets, soldiers got a more reliable weapon, but they didn't have to change their tactics. A little later, they were given percussion rifled muskets. The musket looked almost the same. It had a percussion lock, and it was a muzzle-loader. About the only difference was the rifling grooves in the barrel. Generals didn't see why they should change their tactics. That's why the American Civil War is the bloodiest war in our history.

Most of the weapons that change warfare eventually become obsolete. The weapons that replace them may further change warfare, or they may not. The muzzle-loading rifle was quickly replaced by the breech-loading rifle, and the breech-loading single-shot by the breech-loading repeater. The repeater let troops fire faster. The muzzle-loading rifle had taught infantry the need to disperse and take cover. The breech-loader made firing from cover much easier, which meant that infantry opposing it had to move faster and in smaller groups. That was a substantial change. When the repeating rifle replaced the single-shot breech-loader, soldiers could still fire from cover, but they fired much faster. That should have required infantry opposing them to move faster and in smaller groups. Troops in the Second Boer War and the Russo-Japanese War learned that the hard way, but most European generals at the beginning of World War I hadn't even learned the lessons of the American Civil War. But then the machine gun appeared as a major weapon. In World War I, Hiram Maxim's brainchild demonstrated that tactics needed a drastic revision. The machine gun is still with us, but thanks to the tank it no longer owns the battlefield. The tank and its aerial partner, the dive bomber, took over ownership of battlefields early in World War II, but the "blitzkrieg" they created was quickly countered by other new weapons such as antitank land mines and shaped-charge rockets and artillery shells.

One war-changing weapon that did not become obsolete was Greek fire. In the 7th, 8th, and 9th centuries, it was the ultimate naval weapon. Then it was lost. It didn't get a chance to become obsolete. While it was in use, though, it preserved the life of the Byzantine Empire, which profoundly changed the history of Europe, and the history of the world.

Most weapons that changed war were used over a long period of time. One was used only twice, but it has changed the way people thought about war and waged war for a long time. Whether nuclear weapons will continue to have this effect cannot be predicted, although it is certainly hoped for.

This book will look at how 50 weapons changed war in much the same way as my previous book, *50 Battles that Changed the World,* looked at the most important military encounters in history. Each of the following chapters will explain how the weapon in question changed war, usually through showing how it was used in battle. It will also describe, in easy-to-follow terms, how the weapon worked. The weapons are presented in roughly chronological order—roughly because, with many weapons, it's difficult to say exactly when they went into use. Not all are like the tank, the introduction of which can be pinpointed at September 13, 1916. Bows and arrows were in use by 9000 BC and probably had been invented thousands of years prior. And even with tanks, there are qualifications. They are the most powerful of a larger class of weapons: armored vehicles. Armored vehicles go back at least as far as the Hussite Wars of the 15th century. But when we discuss armored vehicles, we'll start with World War I, because that was when they began to permanently change warfare. The same is true of armored ships, which were first used by the Korean admiral Yi Sun Shin in 1592. Yi's armored ships foiled a Japanese invasion, but they played no further part in warfare. So we start our discussion of armored ships—which include cruisers, battleships, and aircraft carriers—with the era when the C.S.S. *Virginia* and the U.S.S. *Monitor* revolutionized naval warfare.

Their records of making major changes in warfare was the reason these 50 weapons were chosen. For instance, the revolver is one of the weapons listed but the semiautomatic pistol is not, although most modern handgunners agree that the "automatic" is a more efficient weapon. The reason is that the revolver permanently changed cavalry fighting, but by the time the semiautomatic pistol was perfected, cavalry had become obsolete.

At the end of the book, I've included a list of "honorable mentions," weapons that didn't make the list of the 50 most important, with explanations as to why they were not chosen.

1

Getting to the Point:
The Spear

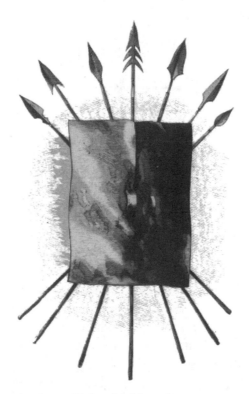

African elephant hide shield and an assortment of spears. The spear is still being used in some remote locations.

The first warriors probably used whatever weapons they could find on the ground. Sticks, stones, and bones have all been used to smash, pierce, or otherwise do in an enemy. Most likely it wasn't long before people began improving what they found. One of the earliest, and certainly the deadliest of these first purpose-made weapons, was the spear. The improved club may have been first, but there's not much you can do to improve a club as a weapon. In a battle, you'd use it the same way you'd use an unworked tree branch.

Some ancient warriors may have noticed that a partially burned stick tends to have a pointed end—the fire consumes the outer layers of the wood first. Then the warrior saw that if he scraped the charcoal off the stick, the point became even sharper. Better yet, it was much harder than the original wood. If he took a fairly long stick—a straight branch or a sapling—and sharpened one end with fire and scraping, he'd have a formidable weapon. A few years ago, such a weapon was found between the ribs of an elephant skeleton preserved in a German bog.

Perhaps about the same time, people began breaking stones to get a sharp edge for cutting meat and scraping hides. They quickly learned that the best kind of stone for this was flint or obsidian—hard, glassy minerals that could be given an extremely sharp edge by chipping. As they developed the technique of chipping, they produced thin, sharp-edged, needle-pointed blades. Then somebody tried mounting one of these blades on the edge of a pole to make a new and even deadlier type of spear. The next big step, of course, was the use of metals—first copper, then bronze, then iron—for weapons and tools. Bronze-tipped spears appeared in the Near East around 3500 B.C., and metal-headed spears continued to be the most important weapon of war in most armies until the late 17th century A.D.

The spear goes so far back in prehistory that there's no way to know exactly how it was first used in war. The most primitive people modern anthropologists study tended to use the spear as a throwing weapon. These people, like the very ancient spear-wielders, relied on hunting for a good share of their food. A human can seldom get close enough to a game animal to kill it with a spear thrust. A thrown spear is much more effective. So when hunters went to war, they used their spears the way they had learned to use them on their frequent hunting expeditions: They threw them.

Things were different when people gathered in towns and relied on farming for food. The proportion of people to game animals became so high that hunting could no longer be an important source of food. Townspeople got far less practice throwing spears, but they had many more activities that called for close cooperation and teamwork by many people—such things as building temples and digging irrigation canals. They developed a form of warfare that fitted their lifestyle. They appeared on the battlefield as a closely packed mass of spearmen, line after line of them. They charged, holding that formation, and were able to knife through more scattered opponents. This was the first appearance of the phalanx, a formation that made the Swiss infantry the terror of central Europe in the 15th century A.D. and didn't disappear until the invention of the bayonet at the end of the 17th century.

The phalanx prompted the invention of body armor. A mass of infantry made a good target for javelin throwers, or especially for archers. But an armored phalanx was more than a match for a larger number of archers, as the Greeks demonstrated at Marathon in 490 B.C. Greek phalangists became the most sought-after mercenaries in the eastern Mediterranean. Philip II of Macedon incorporated the phalanx into his military machine, and his son, Alexander, took that machine and conquered the world between Greece and India.

The Romans then modified the phalanx by organizing their troops into companies called maniples, which took the field in a checkerboard formation. Instead of a long thrusting spear, the first two lines of maniples had two new types of throwing spear, called pila. One pilum was lighter than the other. The Roman legionary threw that first, then, after he advanced a few steps more, they threw the heavy one. A pilum was about 6 feet long. About half of that length was wooden shaft, the rest was a long iron rod tipped with a small spear head. The Roman soldier's target, of course, was an enemy soldier, but he wasn't discouraged if the enemy caught his pilum on his shield. The long iron head made it impossible to chop the spear off, so the pilum, especially if it was the heavy one, tended to drag down the enemy's shield. The Roman then ran up to his enemy, stepped on the trailing spear shaft to pull the shield down entirely, then finished off the enemy with his sword.

The spear developed into a wide variety of weapons called pole arms. There were winged spears, with two projections on the blade to keep the spear from penetrating farther than necessary for a kill. (A spear that penetrated an enemy too far to permit its withdrawal could be a severe embarrassment in combat.) Some spears, such as the Japanese naginata and the European glaive, were cutting weapons—short, single-edged swords mounted on poles. A spear with an ax blade and a hook added became a *halberd*, and an extra-long spear was called a *pike*. The Swiss phalanxes of renaissance times used pikemen to stop enemy cavalry so the phalanx's halberdiers could close in and chop them up.

Those were infantry weapons. When horsemen carried a thrusting spear, it was called a lance. Alexander the Great relied on his lance-armed heavy cavalry to deliver the knock-out blow after his phalanx succeeded in holding enemy forces in place. The lance was the principal weapon of European cavalry from the Dark Ages through the 16th century. The use of the cavalry lance declined in western Europe after muskets became common, but Napoleon was so impressed by the Polish cavalry lancers he saw that he reintroduced the lance to his armies. The Poles and the Russians were still using lances in World War II.

Cavalry also used throwing spears at times. Greek cavalry in the Peloponnesian War used javelins instead of lances. They did not have stirrups, and without stirrups only the most skillful rider could use a lance without having his own weapon push him off his mount. The Libyan horsemen in Hannibal's army used short iron javelins, which they threw with both hands, while the Gaulish cavalry in the same army used a javelin that looked like the Roman pilum. In more modern times, the descendants of those Libyan cavalrymen, the Spanish jinetes, used javelins as their basic weapons.

In Europe, in China, and in Africa, the spear was the most common, most basic weapon of fighting men from the earliest times until the widespread use of gunpowder. In central and western Asia, another weapon was supreme for almost as long a time. For a very short time, it was also supreme in England. We'll discuss this in the next chapter.

2

Death at a Distance:
The Bow and Arrow

Tartar archers. One man is using the strength of his legs to help him string his powerful bow. The other uses two rope loops to train himself how to position his hands.

King Edward III had invaded France and was plundering the countryside. His army consisted of 10,000 men. About one third of them were armored knights or men at arms with almost all the rest infantry archers. King Philip VI of France intercepted the English near the town of Crecy. Philip had about 12,000 men, 8,000 of them armored knights and 4,000 Genoese mercenary crossbowmen.

When they were well within range of their weapons, the Genoese opened fire. The English replied with two surprises. The first was the fire of the three bombards Edward had brought across the channel. These small, primitive cannons did little damage, but their flashes and thunder were terrifying to men who had never faced gunpowder weapons before. The second surprise caused far more damage. The English archers rained arrows on the Genoese, who thought they were beyond arrow range. The English outnumbered the Genoese, and they could shoot five times as fast. Terrified by the cannons and the hail of arrows, the Genoese fled.

The French knights then charged, riding through the retreating mercenaries. The French aimed for the dismounted English knights, standing between wedges of archers protected by lines of sharpened poles. One could gain more honor, the French believed, by fighting knights than by cutting down infantry varlets. The archers turned their attention to the French horsemen.

Few of the French knights reached within striking distance of the English. The charge became a chaos of dead knights, dead horses, and wounded, maddened horses crashing into other horses. The first wave of French cavalry was almost destroyed, but successive waves kept galloping up from the rear. By the end of the day, one third of the French army was dead. The English losses came to about 100. The Battle of Crecy introduced the English longbow to the continent of Europe and made England, for the first time, a major military power.

The Longbow

There has probably been more nonsense written about the English longbow than any other weapon, with the possible exception of the Kentucky rifle.

First, the longbow had more range than the Genoese expected, based on their rather limited experience with other bows, but it did not outrange the crossbows. The Genoese did not open fire at extreme range, but at a range at which they could easily sight their crossbows. A crossbow, like a rifle or a longbow, gets maximum range when elevated about 43 degrees. Because of the way it is made, it's easier to aim a longbow at that elevation than it is to aim a crossbow. Around the turn of the last century, Sir Ralph Payne-Gallwey, using restored medieval crossbows, was able to shoot arrows up to 450 yards. A few years later, Dr. Saxton T. Pope, an expert archer and bowyer, used a replica of an English longbow to shoot 250 yards.

Second, the power of the longbow did not depend entirely on its length. The power of any bow depends on three things: (1) how much strength it takes to draw it, (2) how quickly it springs back to its original shape, and (3) over what distance the bow string is pushing the arrow. The old English war arrow was 28 inches long. To draw an arrow of that length to its fullest, the bow also had to be long. An old archers' adage holds that "A bow full drawn is 9/10 broke." A half round yew bow, with sapwood on the back and heartwood on the belly, had to be about 5 1/2 feet long to draw a standard arrow without breaking if its draw weight was 70 or 80 pounds.

Third, the longbow did not have a draw weight of 150 or 200 pounds and require a lifetime of training to use it. Dr. Pope made an exact replica of a longbow stave recovered from the wreck of the *Mary Rose*, an English warship that sank in 1545. The bow stave was 6 feet, 4 3/4 inches long. He made an exact replica of choice yew, strung it, and tested it. The bow had a draw weight of only 52 pounds and shot a flight arrow 185 yards. He cut the length to 6 feet. It now weighed 62 pounds and shot the flight arrow 227 yards. Pope again trimmed the bow, this time to 5 feet, 8 inches. It now weighed 70 pounds when drawn 28 inches and shot the flight arrow 245 yards. From Pope's experiments, it would seem that the average longbow had a draw weight of 70 or maybe 80 pounds. Most archers today would consider that a moderately heavy bow, but certainly not one that would require a lifetime of training.

Fourth, the longbow was neither a new weapon nor a particularly sophisticated bow. Longbows almost exactly like the English weapon have been dug out of European bogs and dated by radiocarbon technology to as early as 6000 B.C. In Neolithic times, the bow seems to have been the most important European weapon, perhaps because Neolithic people were primarily hunters. In the early Bronze Age, a people known to archaeologists as the "Beaker People" swept across Europe from Spain to central Europe. The graves of Beaker men contained bone or stone bracers, worn on the inside of the bow arm to prevent injury by the released bow string, and flint or bronze arrow heads. But the people of central Europe, after learning—often firsthand—of the effectiveness of the armored Greeks, had adopted the Greek tradition of shock warfare. In the densely forested central Europe of that time, shock warfare was probably more effective than mobile tactics based on the bow. The descendants of the Beaker People traded their bows for battle axes, spears, and, later, swords.

The bow continued to be an important weapon in Scandinavia, particularly in Norway, where almost all transportation was by boat or ship. Missile weapons have always been important in naval warfare. The descendants of the Northmen, the Normans, didn't lose their taste for archery during the time they stayed in France. Archery played a big part in Duke William's victory at Hastings over Harold Godwinsson. King Harold was even struck down by an arrow. A longbow was difficult to shoot from horseback, so the chivalry of England neglected the weapon until they invaded Wales, where the archery tradition was still strong. Welsh arrows perforated Norman armor and even penetrated a castle door made of seasoned oak 4 inches thick. The success of the Welsh archers led to the revival of the longbow by the English Infantry.

The English longbow was the simplest type of bow—a "self bow," one made of a single piece of wood. It was fairly sophisticated for a self bow, because the back—the part facing away from the archer—was the more flexible sapwood, which allowed the bow to be bent more sharply without breaking. More sophisticated than the self bow are: the laminated bow, composed of several layers of wood glued together; the backed bow, with animal sinew on the back to deter breakage and increase springiness; and the composite bow, a thin wood core backed with sinew and a belly—the part facing the archer—made of horn.

The Composite Bow

The composite bow was the reason the Hyksos conquered Egypt, the Romans failed to conquer Parthia, the Crusades failed, and the troops of Genghis Khan defeated every foe they met.

The manufacture of the composite bow was a long process, often taking a year or more, and one demanding a high degree of skill. The wooden core was first bent with the aid of steam so that it curved in the opposite direction from the direction it would be drawn. The back was covered with shredded sinew from the neck of a horse or bull that had been soaked in animal or fish glue and molded to shape. On the belly of the bow, the bowyer glued strips of previously bent horn. After a period of seasoning, the bow was strung—a difficult operation because some bows described almost a full circle, bent away from the belly. The result was a short bow flexible enough to shoot an extremely long arrow.

The composite bow was invented in central Asia and was the principal weapon of Asian nomads. With it, Scythians, Huns, Mongols, Turks, and other Asian nomads mowed down enemy infantry and cavalry from China to Gaul. It was the most powerful hand weapon before the introduction of gunpowder. Traditionally, all Turkish sultans had to learn one trade that involved manual labor. Most of them chose the bowyer's profession. The English longbow changed warfare in western Europe for a century or so. The composite bow changed warfare in Asia for at least four millennia. We'll discuss the composite bow further in the Chapter 6.

3

The Symbol of War: The Sword

A variety of swords. From top: Turkish yataghan, Philippine Moro kris, French naval cutlass, Japanese naval officer's sword, Indian Tulwar, U.S. Model 1913 cavalry sword.

"**M**asters of the sword are called strategists. As for the other military arts, those who master the bow are called archers, those who master the spear are called spearmen, those who master the gun are called marksmen, those who master the halberd are called halberdiers. But we do not call masters of the Way of the long sword 'longswordsmen,' nor do we speak of 'companion-swordsmen.' Because bows, guns, spears, and halberds are all warriors' equipment, they are certainly part of strategy. To master the virtue of the long sword is to govern the world and oneself, thus the long sword is the basis of strategy."

So wrote Miyamoto Musashi in 1645. Musashi was a *ronin*, a kind of Japanese knight-errant, and a master of the long sword. Shortly before he died, Musashi wrote *A Book of Five Rings: A Guide to Strategy*. Musashi was Japan's most celebrated duelist, a man who literally lived by the sword, so his estimate of the importance of his favorite weapon might seem to be somewhat prejudiced. However, his countrymen agreed with him. They continued to agree with him for the next three centuries—so much that in the 20th century they named the largest battleship ever built (and probably the largest that ever will be) after him.

The sword has had a unique place among weapons in many cultures beside the Japanese. It has been a symbolic weapon in the Islamic, Indian, and Western cultures. It has been part of the regalia of African kings, and it was the badge of a gentleman in Renaissance and early modern Europe.

Part of the reason for this is that, until the Industrial Age, the sword was hideously expensive. Only important people, and in the earliest times only rulers, could own a sword. In the Bronze Age, it used a lot of that costly metal (bronze would make many spears, axes, and daggers or scores of arrows). In the Iron Age, wrought iron had to be "steeled" before it could be an effective weapon. That took a long time and a skilled smith. Just tempering a long piece of iron or steel evenly was a tricky process. European and Indian smiths used "pattern welding"—braiding strips of hard steel and soft iron together and welding them to get a blade that was hard enough to take an edge and elastic enough not to shatter from a hard blow. Japanese smiths got these qualities by heating iron over charcoal, pounding it flat and folding it over, and welding again. They did this until the sword consisted of as many as 4 million layers of steel. Then they used a unique tempering process to make the edge and point harder than the rest of the sword. Even if the smith made a pittance per hour, making a sword took so long that one was extremely expensive. Swords were also handed down from father to son for this reason.

Men were willing to pay the very high price of these weapons because the sword had no equal as a weapon for hand-to-hand fighting. It was much longer than the dagger, but short enough to be far more maneuverable than a spear. It could be used to slash, parry, and thrust.

The first swords were long, thin bronze rapiers (straight, two-edged swords with narrow pointed blades) that were useful mostly for stabbing, because the blade was not securely joined to the hit. These early Bronze Age rapiers have been found everywhere from Crete to Ireland. That type was followed by a broader bladed weapon that had a tang that ran all the way through the hilt. The iron swords that followed them retained this cut-and-thrust style.

Swords were important weapons for the nobles of Mycenaean Greece, but to the Greeks of classical times they were merely last-ditch weapons. They would be used if the spear was broken and neither the point nor pointed butt of the spear was available. The Romans, however, made the sword a key part of their weaponry. The legionary threw his *pila* (spears) at the enemy, but he relied on his *gladius,* a short sword worn on his right side, to finish off his opponents. The gladius was worn on the right side so the Roman's enormous shield wouldn't interfere with drawing it.

The success of Greek and Roman armies established a tradition of close-range, shock warfare in all of Europe. It was a far different way of fighting than the mobile missile warfare practiced by the charioteers and later the horse archers of the Asian steppes. The European barbarians adopted shock warfare, whether they were foot warriors such as the Franks and Alemanni or cavalry suxch as the Goths. Among all of these peoples, from the Celts of Spain to the Teutonic tribes of Scandinavia, the sword was the most important weapon. The lance was good for a horseman's first contact with the foe, but, after that, the sword was supreme.

The sword was also highly esteemed by the Asian horse archers. The Huns would first open a fight with arrows, but after their enemies became weakened and demoralized, they charged with swords. The Turks were especially fond of swordplay, a characteristic that caused them a great deal of trouble when they met the more heavily armored crusaders. In Africa, the sword was also the principal weapon in the Sudan and the Sahara, among both the warriors of the great kingdoms of the Sahel or wandering nomads like the Tuareg tribes. British and French troops fighting in these areas in the 1890s found the natives still using their traditional swords as they charged the European machine guns.

In the Middle Ages, swords were almost as necessary to the knights as they were to Musashi and his fellow samurai. Infantry, too, carried swords. If anything happened to your spear or halberd, you had to have a "sidearm." Infantry were still carrying swords in the middle of the 18th century, although they also had muskets and bayonets. When infantry got muskets and pikes, western European cavalry adopted pistols instead of lances, but they kept their swords. Gustavus Adolphus, the great Swedish leader in the Thirty Years War, advocated a minium use of the pistol for his cavalry and charging the enemy with the sword. "Light Horse Harry" Lee, the American Revolutionary hero, said "...the fire of cavalry is at best innocent, especially in quick action.... The strength and activity of the horse, the precision and celerity of evolution, the adroitness of the rider, boot-top to boot-top, and the keen edge of the saber...constitute the vast power so often decisive in the day of battle."

Today, the sword is merely an item of costume in the military units that still carry it. The exception is the machete, still used in jungle fighting as both a tool and a weapon. For thousands of years, however, from before the Romans until well after the American Civil War, the sword was a key weapon of war. The last users of the sword were the sword-worshiping Japanese. During World War II, there were many reports of Japanese officers charging with their swords and a few of them beating on the sides of tanks with swords.

4

The First Warship: The Galley

Galleys clash at Lepanto, the last major battle fought with these craft.

On September 13, 1569, the gunpowder factory at the Venetian Arsenal exploded. The Arsenal was the center of all Venetian military power. The gunpowder factory was only one part of it. Guns were cast there, warships were built there, galleys were docked there, and all kinds of weapons were stored there. Venice was one of the two great powers of the eastern Mediterranean. But the explosion, it seemed, had instantly rendered the republic helpless.

That blast was a disaster for Venice, but for the other great power of the eastern Mediterranean, it sounded like the knock of opportunity. Turkey, under its aptly nicknamed Sultan, Selim the Sot, began gobbling up outposts of the Venetian Empire. The Christian powers united in the face of the Turkish threat and assembled a fleet of warships. In addition to the ships Venice still had there were galleys from the Papal States, Austria, Naples, Sicily, and, especially, Spain. King Philip II of Spain used the gold and silver he got from his American colonies to pay half the costs of the entire expedition. Then he made his young half-brother, Don Juan of Austria, commander of the fleet.

Don Juan reorganized the Christian fleet. To eliminate national rivalries, with a consequent failure to coordinate with each other, he mixed the nationalities in the three divisions of his fleet. Augustino Barbarigo, a Venetian admiral, commanded the left. Giovanni Andrea Doria of Genoa commanded the right. Don Juan led the center, with the 75-year-old Doge of Venice, Sebasitiano Veniero, commanding the galley on the left of his flagship and Marco Antonio Colonna, the Papal admiral, commanding the ship on the right. Almost all of the ships in Don Juan's fleet were galleys, the traditional Mediterranean warships. Galleys, the long, narrow, oar-propelled warships, had dominated the Inland Sea for three millennia. Don Juan added two less traditional ships: galleasses. Galleasses were sailing ships with a high freeboard. They could use oars in a pinch, but they were slow and clumsy when rowed. Don Juan knew that the Portuguese had used similar high-freeboard sailing ships successfully in combat on the Indian Ocean. He thought there might be a place for them in this battle. Though slower and far less agile than the galleys, they had two advantages: their sides were too high for a galley's crew to board them easily, and they had many guns.

In ancient times, galleys had used bronze rams on their bows to crush the sides of opposing ships. Because cannons had been invented, they replaced the ram. The Turkish galleys had three cannons firing over their bows. The Christian ships had four.

The enemy fleets met in the Gulf of Corinth, the long, narrow bay that almost cuts Greece in two, near the town of Lepanto. In battle, galleys were handled as if they were soldiers in a land battle. They charged each other directly, blasting the enemy with their bow guns. Because their sides were lined with rowers and their sterns occupied by steersmen with huge steering oars, there was no other place for the guns. Like armies, galley fleets attempted to break through an enemy's line, or attack his flanks, or encircle him. The Christians may have had more guns, but the Turks had more ships. To avoid being flanked, Andrea Doria advanced obliquely to the right, so his division made contact later than the rest of Don Juan's fleet. The Turkish admiral commanding the Muslim right, Mohammed Sirocco Pasha, tried to encircle the Christian left. Barbarigo, unfamiliar with the waters, had stayed well off shore. When he saw Sirocco's ships trying to flank him, though, Barbarigo knew the water was deep enough. He had his ships swivel and charge, catching the Turkish column in the flank and rear. Barbarigo was killed. His nephew succeeded him in command but was killed almost immediately afterwards. But two other Venetian officers, Frederigo Nani and Marco Quirini, took over. They drove the Turks ashore and killed or captured them all.

In the center, Don Juan's galleasses demonstrated their worth. Their gunfire raised havoc with the Turkish galleys. The Turks saw that they were too high to board and rowed furiously away from them, disrupting their own formation. Then Don Juan and the Turkish commander-in-chief, Ali Pasha, exchanged salutes and closed with each other. In spite of the superior Christian gunnery, Ali drove his galley right up to Don Juan's while soldiers on the decks of both ships showered each other with arrows and musket bullets. The Turks boarded the Spanish ship, but were pushed off, and the Spanish boarded the Turkish ship. The Turks pushed the Spaniards back to their ship and followed them, only to be again pushed off and boarded again. Veniero, the Doge, and his men joined the melee. Ali was killed and his ship taken. Meanwhile, Colonna, on the other side of the flagship, burned a Turkish galley. The center division began taking or sinking Turkish galleys all along the line. The remaining Turks reversed their ships and fled.

Uluch Ali, the commander of the Turkish left, had been trying unsuccessfully to flank Andrea Doria. He suddenly changed course and darted through the gap between the Christian center and right. He managed to get behind Don Juan's formation, but the Spanish admiral cut loose the prizes he had been towing and turned toward Uluch Ali's unit. Caught between Don Juan and the Christian reserve, Uluch Ali fled to the nearest Turkish harbor. Some of his ships made it.

Lepanto was the greatest defeat the Turks had ever suffered in the Mediterranean. Selim the Sot built a new fleet, but his ships were built of green wood and manned by greener sailors. From then on the Turkish Navy studiously sought to avoid battle. The Turks would still threaten Christendom, but after Lepanto, they were a greatly diminishing threat. That's one reason Lepanto is a notable battle.

The other reason is that it was the last great battle between galleys. Don Juan's four-gun galleys were not the wave of the future; his big, clumsy, heavily gunned galleasses were. That had been demonstrated more than 60 years earlier when a handful of Portuguese sailing ships wiped out 200 Turkish and Egyptian galleys off the Indian port of Diu. (See Chapter 13, *The Sailing Man of War*.) After Lepanto, the galley would never again play an important part in naval warfare, but it had had a long and honorable career.

As did the spear and the bow, the origins of the galley are lost in the mists of prehistory. The first boats were probably dugout canoes, propelled by paddles. They were followed by lighter boats with a covering of leather or bark stretched over a framework of wood. Someone discovered that rowing provided more powerful propulsion than paddling, and, probably about the same time, someone learned that fixing a sail to the boat made rowing unnecessary if the wind was right. From there, developing the galley was merely a matter of making a bigger row-or-sail boat with wooden sides.

One of the earliest accounts of a galley and its crew is the legend of Jason and the Argonauts, who sailed from Greece to Colchis on the Black Sea in search of the Golden Fleece. According to the legend, the expedition took place a generation before the Trojan War. To see if Jason's voyage was even possible, Tim Severin, the adventurer who crossed the North Atlantic in a skin boat to retrace the legendary voyage of St. Brendan, the Irish monk who supposedly reached America in the Dark Ages, built a replica of Jason's galley, *Argo*. Severin consulted experts on ancient Greek shipping and had a galley built according to the ship-building methods of Jason's time. The craft was 52 feet long and seated 20 rowers. It took Severin and his crew from Greece to the site of ancient Colchis. The crew was even able to row against a head wind added to the ferocious currents of the Bosporus that have defeated many modern boats. All the modern Argonauts agreed, however, that sailing on that sort of ancient galley was no holiday.

As time went on, ancient ship builders improved their designs. The boat had to be light, so it could be rowed swiftly, but it had to be strong enough to be seaworthy. It had to be fairly low so the rowers could use their oars at the optimum angle. Before long, ship builders were using mathematical formulae. Within reason, the longer the ship, the faster it would be, but the ship should not be longer than 10 times its beam or it would be too fragile to take to sea. In his *Greek and Roman Naval Warfare*, Admiral W.L. Rodgers explains the many calculations the ancient ship builders had to make. Ships got bigger and got two or three rows of oars. They got still bigger and had two or three men on each oar, sometimes as many as five men on each oar. According to Rodgers, a small Greek trireme of the Peloponnesian War period would carry about 18 soldiers for boarding, about 162 rowers, and 20 more as officers, row masters, and seamen. All the rowers were free men (not slaves, as they were during renaissance times), and all had weapons and took part in any melee when their ship was boarded. The galley would be 105 feet long, displace 69 tons, and be capable of 7.8 knots (almost 9 mph) at top speed.

Galleys were extremely maneuverable. With the rowers on one side pulling normally and those on the other side backing water, the galley could almost swivel on the spot. Oars were arranged so the rowers could step over them and back up instantly. Rapid maneuvering was essential, because a galley captain aimed to ram the side of an enemy vessel while avoiding being rammed himself. Another favorite tactic in galley fighting was to brush close to an enemy's side, pulling your oars out of the way at the last minute. The intention was to catch the enemy's oars still in rowing position and break them off. Galley crews threw fire pots on enemy ships to burn them, tossed jars of soft soap to make enemy decks slippery, and sometimes threw jars of poisonous snakes to distract enemy crews.

In Hellenistic and Roman times, galleys, which had grown quite large, were often equipped with catapults to hurl such missiles. And in the 7th century, the Eastern Romans came up with the ultimate weapon in galley warfare: Greek fire. That's worth a separate chapter (see Chapter 8).

5

To Foil All Weapons:
Body Armor

Frankish warrior of the 10th century.

According to George Cameron Stone in his classic *A Glossary of the Construction, Decoration and Use of Arms and Armor in All Countries and at All Times*, "Armor has been worn by all nations with any pretensions to civilization...." It has also been worn by many nations with few pretensions to civilization. Armor has been made of many materials besides metal. Among the types illustrated in Stone's book are Aleut armor composed of Chinese coins sewn on a leather vest; the wood, steel, and leather armor of the Koryak tribe of western Siberia; the leather and wood armor of the Chukchi people of eastern Siberia; the armor of the Lolo barbarians of southeastern China; and the armor of the Gilbert Islanders of the South Pacific, consisting of coconut fibers and fish skin. Corselets made of many layers of linen have been worn in many places, including ancient Greece. Leather armor has also been popular. One of the earliest depictions of armor is on the "Royal Standard of Ur," a box covered with figures carved from shell and limestone, found in the royal cemetery of the ancient Sumerian city of Ur. It shows a phalanx of warriors wearing copper helmets and long leather cloaks covered with metal disks.

Armor, a defensive weapon, varies with the weapons it is intended to defend against. The thick layers of cord worn by the Gilbert Islanders would not have stopped a steel lance head, but they did deaden the impact of sling stones, one of the islanders' principle offensive weapons. The Gilbert Islanders specialized in mobile missile warfare. They'd run up to stone-throwing range, fire their sling stones, run away, and attack again. To guard against enemy sling stones when they were retreating, their armor had a tall square piece behind the head, rising well above a fish skin helmet. The ancient Celts invented mail—armor composed of thousands of interlocking rings. Mail was more flexible than most armors, and it protected the wearer very well against sword cuts. It was less protective against thrusts with a sharply pointed sword, but Celtic warriors usually relied on the edge of the sword, rather than the point. Roman soldiers were taught to use the points of their short swords; *"duas uncias in puncto mortalis est"* ("two inches in the right place is fatal") was a motto of the legionaries. That was one of the reasons the Romans conquered the Gauls. The barbarian tribes that overran the Roman Empire, however, were slashers, so mail became the uniform of European knights. The knights usually wore their mail over a padded garment called an *aketon* to soften the impact of blows. A stroke that could not penetrate the mail could still break a bone. During the crusades, Christian soldiers sometimes wore a jacket of felt *over* their armor. It must have been stifling in sunny Palestine, but its wearers thought its advantages outweighed its discomfort. Beha ed-Din Ibn Shedad, one of Saladin's officers, wrote: "I have seen soldiers with up to 21 arrows stuck in their bodies marching no less easily for that."

Slashing with the sword is a more instinctive action than thrusting, so mail became popular far from its Celtic homeland. The Arabs, Persians, and Indians adopted it early, but some of them also added small metal plates to the mail that would stop a sword or spear thrust. Warriors of such West African kingdoms as Bornu, Mali, and Songhai also wore mail. Mail-wearers in such hot places as Africa and Arabia covered their armor with cloth robes to keep the sun off the metal and keep from turning a suit of armor into an oven capable of literally burning flesh. European warriors who went on crusade adopted the surcoat from their enemies and brought it back to Europe. There, European knights found the surcoat ideal for displaying their heraldic arms.

The ancient Greeks favored bronze armor because bronze could be melted and cast in large pieces. No European furnaces at that time were hot enough to melt iron. Iron was extracted from the ore by a laborious process of heating and beating, and the smith was left with small pieces that had to be welded together to make a piece as large as a sword blade. So for centuries, iron armor was composed of small pieces. Mail, made of rings formed from bits of iron wire, was one example. *Scale armor* (overlapping bits of metal fastened to fabric or leather and arranged like the scales of a fish) was another. And yet another example was *lamellar armor* (bits of metal fastened to each other with cords or wires). Japanese armor is probably the type of lamellar armor most familiar to Americans, but the type was also extremely popular in Persia, Central Asia, and India. The Romans used a wide variety of armor, including solid breast plates and back plates of bronze, mail, scale, and a type with overlapping strips of iron called the *lorica segmentata*. In the later Middle Ages, when the crossbow began to make life dangerous for mail-wearers, European knights began to cover their mail with a "coat of plates." This was a vest of strong fabric with small, rectangular iron plates riveted to the inside of it. The plates were usually lined with another layer of fabric. A century or two later, a similar garment was used by infantrymen, usually as their sole armor except for the helmet. It was called "brigandine." People at that time, during the Hundred Years War with its rapacious mercenary bands, saw little difference between infantrymen and brigands.

European smiths became more and more skilled in metal working and were able to produce large pieces of mild steel by the 14th century. That was fortunate for the knights, because they were just beginning to face three new missile weapons: the longbow, the crossbow with a steel bow that had a draw weight of more than a 1,000 pounds, and the handgun. Plate armor could be made proof against these weapons. In fact, the word *proof* comes from the practice of firing a crossbow or a gun at a finished breast plate. If the shot did not penetrate, it proved that the armor was safe. But guns got more powerful. Armor got heavier, but it finally got so heavy it interfered with fighting. It began to disappear. Leg armor was replaced by heavy "jack boots," thick leather boots that covered the thighs, and by the 17th century much of the upper body armor was replaced by a "buff coat," a coat of heavy buffalo leather that was worn under a steel corselet. Sometimes it was worn instead of the corselet.

All of the preceding refers to armor that was worn like clothing. But for most of the same period, the most effective piece of armor was not worn but carried: the shield. At close range, the arrow from a longbow will penetrate a breast plate of the type worn in the 15th century. It may not pass all the way through, but if only half of it got through, half of a 28-inch arrow is more than enough to kill the man wearing the breastplate. If the arrow hits a shield and has the same effect, it might not even reach the body of the shield-holder. Even if it did, after passing through the shield, it wouldn't have enough power to penetrate any kind of armor.

The shield was so important in classical Greece that the heavy infantryman, the hoplite, took his name from the word for shield, *hoplon*. For a hoplite to lose his shield was the ultimate disgrace. European knights carried shields until plate armor was developed so heavy it could resist a lance thrust by itself. The Saxon "shield wall" at Hastings turned back the Norman knights for most of the day. Archers and crossbowmen could not hang shields on their arms for obvious reasons, but they had substitutes. Some crossbowmen carried large shields on their backs. When loading their weapons, they turned their backs to the enemy. That was a less than satisfactory alternative, because a shield on the back was too close to the body. A better substitute was the pavises, a large shield propped up on the ground. Both archers and crossbowmen used pavises. Shields were such such effective pieces of equipment that they were the only armor that has been used by many nations. The Highlanders of Scotland, the Zulus of South Africa, and the Plains Indians of North America, as well as hundreds of peoples between them, used no armor but the shield. The Spanish infantry swordsmen of the 16th century had shields that were proof against pistol shots.

From the late Middle Ages into the early modern period, a type of shield was frequently worn by civilians. In an era when every male with pretensions to manhood wore a sword, the more aggressive types hung small round shields on the hilts of their swords. This type of shield, called a buckler, was held in the left hand of a right-handed swordsman and used to parry an opponent's sword strokes. People wearing a buckler on their swords were presumed to be looking for a fight and called "swashbucklers."

Armor did not entirely disappear with the advent of gunpowder. Some French cavalrymen were still wearing breastplate and metal helmets in the Franco-Prussian War of 1870, and British horsemen of the same period and later wore mail *epaulets*. In the American Civil War, many soldiers privately purchased "bullet-proof" steel vests to wear under their uniforms. Some of these actually worked. In the 1880s, Wyatt Earp wore one and it was said to have saved his life on at least one occasion.

World War I saw a revival of officially issued armor. The most widespread item was the steel helmet, which was designed to protect soldiers in the trenches from overhead shrapnel bursts. The Germans issued special armor to many of their machine gunners and some snipers. It consisted of a steel corselet and a helmet that covered the entire head except the eyes.

In World War II, the crews of bombers often wore "flak vests" as protection from the fragments of bursting anti-aircraft shells. Infantry were given armor vests made of nylon in the later stages of the Korean War. These vests would stop shell fragments and bullets from a .45 caliber pistol, but not bullets from any service rifle. They continued to be used in the Vietnam War. Body armor has continued to improve. In the Iraq War, combat soldiers have helmets of Kevlar, a synthetic material that is lighter and stronger than steel, and armor vests of the same material. The Kevlar "soft armor" vests have pockets that contain "hard armor" plates of metal, ceramic, or plastic, which can resist penetration by most rifle bullets. The most generally-used forms of the new armor will stop bullets from the 7.62 × 39 caliber Kalashnikov rifles. Some troops, particularly those on riot control, wear Kevlar greaves.

The modern infantryman is as thoroughly armored as a 17th-century pikeman.

6

Horses Change the Battlefield: The Chariot

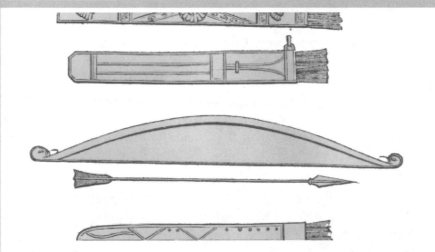

Assyrian bow, arrow, and quivers. With weapons like this, the charioteers of Assyria conquered most of the ancient Near East.

An army of enemies was approaching Egypt and they were coming from the northeast, not the south, the only direction from which enemies had come before. Nubians had occasionally marched north, along the Great River, but no large armies had ever come from either the east or the west. The barren, waterless deserts that stretched on either side of the Nile Valley had a way of discouraging invaders. The Pharaoh called up all the men of Lower Egypt to meet the invaders. They appeared with their copper axes, copper-headed spears, stone maces, and simple self-bows.

Egyptian weaponry was nowhere near as advanced as that of the people of Mesopotamia, where warfare was almost constant. The deserts had protected the Egyptians from all but occasional clashes with the Nubians, the black inhabitants of the much-less-populous kingdom on the Upper Nile. And if the Egyptians' military equipment and organization was primitive compared to that of the peoples in the valley of the Two Rivers, it was light-years behind what they faced now. The enemy, called the Hyksos, which has been variously translated as "Lords of the Uplands" or "Shepherd Kings," had sharp bronze weapons, including swords, bronze scale armor, and powerful composite bows. (See Chapter 2.) They also had something utterly unknown to the Egyptians: *horse-drawn chariots*.

Egyptian tradition says the Hyksos took Lower Egypt without a fight. That doesn't mean they slowly infiltrated. Archaeological evidence shows that they suddenly took possession of the Delta and all of Lower Egypt after thoroughly sacking it. "Without a fight" means that there was no toe-to-toe infantry slugging match—what the Egyptians meant by "fight."

On their light, fast chariots, the Hyksos literally rode circles around their enemies and shot them down. There were two men to a chariot: a driver and an archer. The Hyksos powerful composite bow easily outranged the bows of the Egyptians. The mobile Hyksos could concentrate on any part of the Egyptian line they chose and shoot down the unarmored Egyptian infantry with impunity. When at last the Egyptians broke and fled, the Hyksos charioteers rode them down, shooting arrows and slashing with their curved bronze swords. They stayed in the Delta and Lower Egypt for a century. They didn't try to conquer Upper Egypt, where the valley is narrow—not ideal chariot country—and most transportation was by boat.

Staying proved to be a mistake. The southern Egyptians learned to make composite bows and bronze weapons and armor. Most important, they learned to make and use chariots. They drove the Hyksos out of Egypt and ended Egypt's centuries-old isolation. The Egyptians became conquerors and pursued the Hyksos into their homeland.

The Hyksos homeland is believed to be the Arabian Desert, south and east of the cities of Syria. Not much is known about the Hyksos. Some of their rulers had Semitic names like Jacob-her; others had names that cannot be identified ethnically. Their invasion, in about 1750 B.C., was at the southwestern end of a human avalanche that began on the steppes of what is now southern Russia and was sparked by the invention of the light, horse-drawn chariot.

A chariot of sorts had been around for centuries, not in Egypt but in Mesopotamia, in the lands of Sumer and Akkad. The first was a clumsy vehicle with four solid-disk wheels. It was pulled by two donkeys, because no horses had been domesticated. It had high sides and the front of it was almost as high as its occupants' heads. There were two occupants, a driver and a man who threw javelins at enemy troops. There was a supply of javelins in a quiver hung on the side of the chariot. It was obviously heavy, and the four wheels on fixed axles made turning it extremely difficult. Later Sumerian chariots had only two wheels, but they were still heavy and though these donkey-powered war machines must have been slow, nevertheless they proved to be valuable in the many wars between the city-states of Mesopotamia. The high sides protected the warriors in the chariots, and they were faster than infantry, especially infantry formed into a stiff, massive phalanx.

Word of the Sumerian war cart probably worked its way across the Caucasus. There, the steppe peoples had learned to domesticate horses. The horses weren't strong enough to ride, but they could pull carts. The steppe people then developed a specialized war cart. It was light, had two spoked wheels, low wickerwork sides, and a floor made of criss-crossing strips of leather.

The steppe nomads had already developed a composite bow, probably because trees were scarce, and trees providing good bow wood were scarcer. Their bow had a thin strip of wood in the center, but the back was a think layer of animal sinew and the belly was strips of horn. These parts were all glued together and covered with bark or leather and lacquered to keep dampness out. A bow of this type was more elastic than a wooden bow, so it could be much shorter than a wooden bow shooting the same length of arrow. It was so elastic, in fact, that it could be made to curve away from the belly when unstrung. Protecting their herds from predators and their camps from enemies required a lot of long-range shooting, so the nomads developed very powerful bows and excellent archers.

But predators like wolves and leopards were fast-moving beasts. It wasn't until they had their fast, light chariots that the herdsmen hunters could really deal with the hostile fauna effectively. They soon found that what worked on animals worked on human enemies, too. The combination of chariot and composite bow rapidly spread through all the Iranian language speakers of the steppe. The new weapons system led to more far-ranging wars, and tribes began to push each other into new territories. Early in the second millennium B.C., the charioteers from the steppes began to invade the settled lands. They drove east into central Asia and from there into China, where they founded the first historical dynasties. The Aryans, an Iranian people, galloped over the deserts of Iran and through the mountain passes to the Indus Valley, where they wiped out one of the world's three literate civilizations. Other Iranian charioteers, the Mitanni, invaded Anatolia, where they established a kingdom. Some of the Mitanni mixed with the Hittites, who had invaded Anatolia previously, and others moved into Syria, where they made themselves the leaders of the Hurrian people already there.

The Mitanni were acknowledged to be masters of horse training. Among the correspondence of the Hittite kings is a letter to a Mitannian seeking information on the subject. The military success of the Iranian charioteers was so striking that all the peoples of the east Mediterranean shore adopted chariot warfare. Only the Egyptians, happy in their isolation, seemingly protected by their flanking deserts, remained innocent of chariot warfare. That is, until the Hyksos arrived.

After conquering the Hyksos, the Egyptians followed them into what became Palestine and Syria, conquering the cities and nomad tribes of that area. Egypt's charioteers were the Pharaoh's striking force, but he had infantry spearmen and archers to hold the enemy in place. The archers introduced a new tactic: volleying on command. The impact of thousands of arrows striking simultaneously proved to be almost as disconcerting to enemies as a chariot charge. The Egyptian move into Asia brought these African warriors into conflict with another rising power, the Hittite Empire. The clash of the Hittites and Egyptians at Meggido—Armageddon in Hebrew—became legendary in the Near East, a kind of "mother of all battles." Tactically, it was a Hittite victory, although Egyptian inscriptions try to make it otherwise. Strategically, it was a draw, as neither empire advanced any farther.

Chariots were also used in central and western Europe, where the terrain was much less favorable. Forests covered much of the area, and the Balkans, Greece and Italy were mountainous. Farther north, marshes covered wide areas, forests were huge and dense, and wide rivers cut through the land. Chariots seemed to have been used by European nobles to carry them to the scene of a battle, after which they would dismount to fight. Homer's *The Iliad* is full of descriptions of this kind of fighting. In Cyprus, a large and largely deforested island that was a kind of Mycenean backwater in classical times, chariots were still used in the old way during the Greek-Persian Wars. And in Britain, the Romans encountered British chiefs still using chariots long after even the Gauls had abandoned them. The British chariots had sides but no front walls. The Britons would run out on the yoke poles to throw their javelins at the Romans. As a tactic, that wasn't very effective, but the British nobles delighted in showing off their athletic prowess. By that time, the rest of the world had abandoned chariots for everything but triumphal parades and races.

The chariot was gradually abandoned because people had learned to breed horses that were bigger and stronger and capable of carrying men on their backs. When warriors learned to shoot from horseback, they effectively doubled the firepower of their armies. Instead of two horses pulling one chariot containing two men (and only one an archer), cavalry decided that the same number of horses and the same number of men provided twice as many archers. And a few centuries later, a very simple invention gave cavalry even more striking power, as we'll see in Chapter 7.

7

More Horses:
The Stirrup

Ornate Spanish stirrup. This simple device gave the horseman a firmer seat for using the bow, and, especially, the lance.

The Goths had been a pain for the last few years, Valens thought. In 365, Count Procopius had hired an army of Gothic mercenaries and occupied Constantinople. He then declared himself to be emperor. That ended in 366 when the newly crowned Valens defeated Procopius and his Goths, but 10 years later, the Romans allowed the whole Gothic nation to enter the Empire as refugees. The Goths had repaid that generosity by pillaging all through the Balkans. But now, in 378, Valens was going to solve the Gothic problem once and for all.

In the Gothic camp, there were equally hard feelings about the Romans. The Goths had come to the Romans as refugees, fleeing terrible invaders from the east. Goths and Romans had been peaceful neighbors for 100 years, but, when they appeared on the border, the Romans let the Goths in only after they gave up their weapons. Roman officials sexually abused their women and children and reneged on their promises of food. The Goths had no choice but to go to war. In the last century, there were occasional border skirmishes, Romans sometimes intervened in Gothic affairs, and Goths occasionally fought in Roman wars, as in the recent revolt of Procopius against the emperor. But in general, the two peoples had been friendly. All that changed when the Romans took advantage of the Goths' weaknesses.

In spite of the modern stereotype, the Goths were not howling barbarians. They were all Christians, converted by an Arian Christian bishop who had translated the Bible into Gothic. They were about as well educated as the average Roman; many were literate and some were fluent in Latin and Greek as well as Gothic. Jordanes, a Gothic historian, is one of our main sources of information on this era.

The trouble started when a new people, the Huns, began moving west from central Asia. The Huns moved into the pastures of the Alans, an Iranian tribe that was one of the great powers of the western steppes. The Alans were horse archers, of course. But they also wore lamellar armor and used lances. Roman and Goths alike considered the Alans fierce warriors, but they had a major weakness. They were divided into jealous, independent clans that frequently warred with each other. The Huns had that problem in the past, but they had recently become united. The Huns conquered the Alans, probably a bit at a time. Many of the Alans surrendered and were incorporated into the Hunnish horde. Others fled to the Caucasus, where other Alans had settled generations before. Some clans rode north and merged with the Slavs. The rest moved west. Many of those clans joined the kingdom of the Ostrogoths (the East Goths), the second great power of the western steppes. A few continued on into the fringes of the great European forest.

Those who joined the Ostrogoths did not escape the Huns. King Ermenrich of the Ostrogoths lost his life fighting the Huns. Like the Alans before them, many of the Ostrogoths were incorporated into the Hunnish kingdom. The rest elected a new king to replace Ermenrich and moved west. On the western bank of the Dnieper River their way west was blocked by the Antes, a Slavic people ruled by an Alanic nobility. Jordanes says the Antes defeated the Ostrogoths in their first encounter, but the Goths eventually conquered the Antes. Enraged by the Antes' resistance, the Gothic king, Vithimir, crucified the king of the Antes with his sons and 70 Antes chiefs. Those chiefs were related to the Alans now in the Hunnish horde. With the Huns' permission, the Alans attacked the Ostrogoths. Ammianus Marcellinus, a Roman soldier and historian, says, "Vithimir resisted the Halani for a time.... But after many defeats which he sustained, he was overcome by force of arms and died in battle."

What was left of the Ostrogoths elected Vithimir's son king, and two chiefs, Alatheus and Sarfac, became regents. Sarfac had an Alanic name. In this turbulent period, Alans could be found fighting in every war in every side. The Ostrogoths continued west, where they met the Visigoths (West Goths), who for generations had been separated from their eastern cousins by the Antes. The Ostrogoths told the Visigoths about the Huns, and both tribes prepared to resist the Huns on the bank of the Dniester. But although the two Gothic groups spoke the same language and had common traditions, they built two separate fortified camps.

The Huns chose to attack the Visigoths first. They were the stronger foe; the long succession of defeats had greatly reduced Ostrogothic strength. The Huns crossed the river in the dead of night and sneaked up on the Visigothic camp. The Visigoths were surprised and panicked. They dashed in disorder to the banks of the Danube—the frontier of the Roman Empire. The Ostrogoths did not wait for a Hunnish attack. They followed their western kinsmen.

Valens allowed the Visigoths to enter the Empire if they gave up their weapons. The border guards, however, proved easy to bribe with gold or sex, so many Visigoths kept their weapons. There were few boats, so crossing the Danube took some time, and, when they were finally in the Empire, the Visigoths found that the food they had been promised did not exist. Famine was their first experience as refugees in Rome. The Ostrogoths got tired of waiting for the Visigoths to cross the river. They moved to another spot on the river and crossed without asking permission. Once inside the Empire, fear of starvation replaced fear of the Huns. The Goths began pillaging the farms of the Balkans. Two Roman leaders, Lupicinus and Maximus, tried to end the Gothic trouble by inviting King Fridigern and a number of Visigothic nobles to a feast. The plan was to get them drunk and assassinate them, but some over-eager Romans attacked Fridigern's bodyguards in a separate room. The king heard the noise, united his men and they fought their way out of the Roman camp. Eventually, Roman numbers and discipline began to wear down the Goths. Fridigern, from a camp fortified by forming a circle of wagons, offered to negotiate. Valens led his army up to the Gothic camp.

Valens sent an envoy, with a small escort, to the Gothic camp for last-minute negotiations. But as they were walking up to the wagon ring, a Roman thought he saw a threatening movement and he shot an arrow at the Goths. The

Visigoths replied with a storm of arrows. The Roman escort fled, disorganizing the Roman infantry as they ran through the Roman lines. At that moment, a swarm of Ostrogothic and Alanic horsemen emerged from the woods, led by Aletheus and Sarfac, the two regents for the Ostrogoths' boy king. They hit the cavalry of the Roman right wing, drove it from the field and continued on to attack the left wing cavalry, which, well in advance of the Roman infantry, was vainly trying to break into the Visigothic wagon fort. The left wing cavalry, too, was quickly crushed by the armored Gothic and Alanic lancers. The warriors from the steppes seemed glued to their saddles, and their lance thrusts were able to pierce any Roman armor.

The Ostrogothic and Alanic horsemen then attacked the Roman infantry from all sides. Roman infantry seldom worried about enemy cavalry, especially cavalry lancers. Lancers, precariously balanced on a running horse, could not easily thrust hard enough to wound an armored legionary, nor could javelin-armed riders throw as well as a foot soldier standing on firm ground. But these horsemen were different; their feet were firmly planted in metal rings suspended from their saddles. When a stirrup-equipped lancer charged, the strength and momentum of his 1,000-pound horse was concentrated in his lance point. The Ostrogoths and Alans pushed the Romans into a compressed mass, packed so tightly they couldn't use their weapons. Then Fridigen and his Visigoths charged out of their wagon ring. Most of the Romans were killed, including Valens. It was the worst Roman defeat since Hannibal annihilated two combined consular armies at Cannae in 216 B.C.

Adrianople was a decisive battle for two reasons. First, it resulted in the Goths staying in the Roman Empire, living under their own kings and armed with their own weapons—wandering armies completely independent of the emperor—a situation that eventually led to the Visigoths sacking Rome itself. Second, it introduced the stirrup to central and western Europe. The stirrup made possible the heavily armed cavalry lancers—the knights and men-at-arms who were to be the decisive element in most European wars for the next thousand years.

Many histories say the stirrup was not in use in Europe until the 8th century. About the only justification for that statement is that cavalry was not used much in western Europe before that time. The "barbarian" tribes that destroyed the western Roman Empire—the Goths, Alans, Vandals, Heruls, and Huns—were horsemen, but the bulk of the European population, whether Celts, Germans, or Slavs, fought as infantry. It was the many attacks by the highly mobile Moors and Vikings that forced the Franks to organize cavalry.

R. Ewart Oakeshott, in his *The Archaeology of Weapons*, cites literary and pictorial evidence that stirrups were used in the East as early as the 4th century B.C. Engravings on a Scythian vase from that time show a saddle equipped with stirrups, evidence that some Scythians were using stirrups. Most Scythians, being primarily horse archers, didn't feel the need for this equipment, but that was later to lead to their defeat by the Sarmatians. Sculptures in a Buddhist stupa in India dating from the 2nd century B.C. show riders using stirrups. The Sarmatians, whose tribes included the Alans, moved west about the beginning of the Christian era. They wore heavy armor and used lances as well as bows, and all of them had stirrups. They replaced the Scythians as masters of the western steppes. The Goths, Visi and Ostro, learned to use stirrups from them, as did the Vandals, Gepids, Heruls, and all the other "East German" tribes that had trickled down into eastern Europe from Scandinavia. Of course, the Huns, who drove all those other nations into the Roman Empire, also used stirrups. The Huns stayed in Hungary long after the end of Attila's empire and became the eastern Roman Empire's best cavalry.

8

The Most Secret Weapon: Greek Fire

Siege engine throwing a barrel of flaming liquid into a frotress. The substance is often called Greek fire, but the original Greek fire was squirted through a nozzle on a ship.

A huge Arab fleet was threatening Constantinople, the capital of the Eastern Roman Empire. A little more than a generation prior, Arabs were considered a rather minor nuisance—bandits who rode in from the desert to raid small settlements and who preyed on caravans that were not well-guarded. But about 40 years before this, a crazy man in the Arabian town of Medina, who called himself a prophet, had gathered enough followers to unite all the Saracen tribes of Arabia. Then those wild Arabs swept over Palestine and Syria and in 636 destroyed a Roman army in the gorges of the Yarmuk valley. The next year, they decisively defeated the mighty Persian Empire, which, with the eastern Roman Empire, was one of the two superpowers of the world west of China. By 640, the Persian Empire was extinct—entirely under the thumb of these Arab barbarians who called themselves Muslims.

While one Arab army was gobbling up Persia, others conquered Babylon, invaded Egypt and swept across North Africa as far as Carthage. The Roman forces were unable to even slow them down. The Arabs also conquered the seafaring cities of Syria. By recruiting the sailors of Syria, heirs of the ancient Phoenicians, these desert fighters created a formidable navy. In 653, they took the island of Cyprus and two years later defeated a Roman fleet commanded by the emperor Constans himself.

In 672, they sent a fleet into the Sea of Marmara, right up to the gates of Constantinople. The Arab fleet was enormous, and the Empire had not yet recovered from the long and exhausting war with Persia that had ended 44 years prior. That war was the reason the Muslims had conquered Persia so easily. Would the Romans be the second empire to fall before the Arab fury? The Arabs were certain that God had delivered this citadel of infidels into their hands. Their ships formed a line and swept down on the Roman ships that had filed out of their protected harbor. The Syrian sailors strained at their oars while the Arab warriors fitted arrows to their bowstrings. They noticed that the leading Roman ships were highly decorated. On the prow of each were gilded images of lions, bears, and other animals.

The Arabs were drawing their bows when a stream of liquid gushed from the open mouths of the gold lions and dragons. The liquid covered the Arab ships and almost immediately burst into flame. The terrified Arabs and Syrians sloshed water on the flames, but the fire burned on. What was left of the invasion fleet turned and fled. Few of them made it to the Dardanelles and back to the Mediterranean.

The Sons of the Prophet did not give up easily. Again and again they sent fleets against the city on the Golden Horn. And again and again, their ships were burned to the waterline by the terrible weapon that came to be called *Greek fire*.

No weapon in history has caused more speculation than Greek fire. The formula for it was zealously guarded for centuries, because the eastern Romans considered it a gift from God to the people of the Empire—the eastern bastion of Christianity against Islam and paganism. The Empire alone had Greek fire, but after the introduction of gunpowder the miracle weapon had gradually fallen out of use and was forgotten.

There has been plenty of speculation about the composition of Greek fire, probably because there are widely varying descriptions of the weapon by ancient sources. Not everything that has been called Greek fire is the material that was used to destroy those Arab fleets. That, according to the generally accepted tradition, was the invention of Callinicus, a Syrian architect. In 660, Callinicus, seeing the apparently unstoppable Muslim blitzkrieg, brought his invention to Constantinople in the hopes that it could save Christianity. In describing the destruction of the Muslim fleet, the East Roman chronicler Theophanes wrote: "Then it was that Callinicus, the architect of Heliopolis in Syria, who had invented a marine fire, set light to the vessels of the Arabs and burned them utterly, together with their crews."

Writing some four centuries after the battle, Anna Comnena, the brilliant teenaged daughter of the eastern Roman Emperor Alexius, said, "On the head of each ship he had fixed a lion or other land animal made of brass or iron with the mouth open and gilded over, so that the mere aspect was terrifying. And the fire which was to be directed against the enemy he made to pass through the mouths of the beasts so that it seemed as if the lions...were vomiting the fire." Anna's *Alexiad*, a history of the career of her father, is one of our best sources for the weapons available to the east Romans and their enemies. Anna's writings also show that the east Romans had a variety of incendiary weapons. In another place, she describes an incendiary blowgun: "Readily combustible rosin is collected from the pine and other evergreen trees and mixed with sulfur. Then it is introduced into reed pipes and blown with a strong continuous breath and at the other end fire is applied to it and it bursts into flame and falls like a streak of lightning on the faces of the men opposite."

In 900, Emperor Leo the Wise may or may not have been describing the weapon used in 672 when he spoke of "fire prepared in tubes whence it issues with a noise of thunder and a fiery smoke which burns the ship at which it is directed."

Later, the Crusaders reported that the Muslims attacked them with "Greek fire," which was shot at them by mechanical siege engines. Jean of Joinville wrote that the Greek fire was in a container "as large as a barrel and a tail of fire that issued from it was as large as a large lance." When the container landed, it exploded in a ball of fire that covered everything and everybody nearby. This weapon, which seems to have been a container of naphtha that was ignited just before firing was like a giant Molotov cocktail. It was definitely not the Greek fire Callinicus invented. Neither was the rosin-and-sulfur blowgun Anna Comnena described.

Most authorities today believe that Callinicus's flamethrower projected a mixture containing quicklime and some extremely inflammable liquid such as naphtha or turpentine. Quicklime becomes extremely hot when mixed with water. In Greek fire, it became hot enough to ignite the liquid with which it was packed. It was probably projected through the animal heads by some kind of pump. Being projected from a low-freeboard galley in the open sea, it would probably ignite almost as soon as it left the nozzle, and certainly when it hit the wet sides of the enemy ship. Other authorities believe that the incendiary mixture was released into another metal pipe into which sea water was being pumped. As soon as it hit the air upon leaving the animal head, it would burst into flame. As the burning substance was a liquid and lighter than water, throwing water on the flames did nothing but spread the fire. That led to a belief among hostile sailors that fire once started by Greek fire could not be extinguished. So Greek fire became a powerful psychological as well as physical weapon.

Greek fire changed warfare in the eastern Mediterranean for centuries, and it also changed the history of the world. If Callinicus had not invented Greek fire, Islam might have swept over Europe as it did over the Near East, north Africa, and central Asia.

9

Quiet Cannons: Mechanical Artillery

A type of siege engine the Romans called an "onager."

To King Archidamus of Sparta it seemed that his whole world had turned upside down. This was odd because troops had just arrived from Syracuse in Sicily to help him in one of his campaigns.

A Sicilian officer had demonstrated an invention that the Syracusians had used successfully against Carthage. The weapon was a giant bow mounted on a wooden stock. The stock was in two pieces: The top piece slid in a groove cut in the bottom piece. The Syracusians had attached the bowstring to the slider with a catch, then pulled both slider and bowstring back with a winch (a crank or handle). The bow was obviously far too powerful for a man to draw without the aid of machinery. On the sides of the slider were pawls that clicked into ratchet notches on the bottom stock as the slider was pulled back. When the slider had clicked into the last notch, a Syracusian soldier pulled a cord that released the catch. The heavy arrow flew many times farther than any archer could have sent it. The Sicilians reloaded their weapon and shot another arrow at a shield and a corselet. The missile went entirely through all the armor.

The Syracusian officer smiled proudly at the king, expecting praise for the ingenuity of the scientists of Syracuse and gratitude for bringing this powerful new weapon to his aid. Instead, the king was shocked.

"By Heracles," he said, "this is the end of man's valor!"

To most Greeks at that time, around 370 B.C., war was a slugging match between masses of shield-carrying, armored warriors. Valor in battle was the highest virtue for all Greeks, especially for the Spartans. Each Spartan man devoted his whole life to only one thing: becoming the bravest, strongest, most skillful hand-to-hand fighter he could be. Now it was possible for a puny coward with one of these machines to kill the bravest and strongest soldier who ever lived.

The Spartans were not enthusiastic about the new weapon, and most Greeks agreed with them rather than with the Syracusians. Syracuse, a colony of Corinth, was relatively young for a Greek city and even younger as a major power in the Greek world. Its destruction of the Athenian expedition sent against it during the Peloponnesian War was quite unexpected. The ancient traditions of hoplite warfare had less hold on the people of Syracuse than on those of mainland Greece. Moreover, Dionysius, the tyrant of Syracuse, was a man of imagination. Dionysius aspired to lead all the Greek cities of Sicily against the powerful state of Carthage, which had established colonies on the western end of the island. He recruited designers, mathematicians, and craftsmen from all over the Greek world, offering high wages with prizes for outstanding work on new weapons. For stars, there were places at his table. The leading engineers flocked to Syracuse.

One of their inventions was the *gastraphetes*, a type of crossbow with a kind of half-hoop fixed at the end of the stock. To cock it, a man put the half-hoop against his stomach and the front of the weapon against a wall or tree and pushed against it. The soldier was thus able to use the strength of his legs—far more powerful than his arms—to bend the heavy bow. The gastraphetes had the same sort of slider-and-rachet arrangement as the catapult shown to Archidamus. The next step was to build a much larger bow and cock it with a winch. The bow itself was of the ancient composite type, with a layer of sinew glued to a wooden core on the back, and a layer of horn glued to the core on the belly. When the archer drew a composite bow, the sinew was stretched and then snapped back. At the same time the horn was compressed and then regained its length. The wood—a very thin strip—was flexible but added little to the bow's power.

When the engineers had reached what seemed to be the limits of the composite bow, they began looking for a new type of spring. E.W. Marsden, who has studied all the ancient writings on mechanical artillery and built these machines by following the directions of the ancient engineers, believes they studied the elements of the composite bow—horn, wood, and sinew—and decided that sinew was the springiest element. So, they used the sinew in a new way. They made cords of sinew and twisted them around the ends of two poles that were opposite each other on a wooden frame. The poles pivoted in their bundles of twisted sinew. Between the ends of the poles opposite the pivots was a cord that acted as a bowstring. The action was the same as that of the machine Archidamus saw, but instead of a flexible bow there were two inflexible poles powered by skeins of twisted sinew. Sometimes there wasn't even sinew. Someone discovered that hair—human or animal—has the same kind of springiness as sinew, so many catapults were powered by ropes of hair.

The first *catapults* shot arrows (most of them long, heavy arrows that looked more like javelins) but others were made to shoot stones. These usually had a double bowstring with a pouch between the two cords to hold the stone.

It took the original Greek cities, such as Sparta and Athens, a while to really warm up to mechanical artillery, but the engines were adopted in a big way by King Philip II of Macedon. Like Dionysius, Philip scoured the Greek world for engineers and craftsmen. If the cord-powered torsion catapult was not invented in Macedon, it was first used by Macedon on a large scale. In the middle ages, catapults were mainly siege engines, but Philip and his son, Alexander the Great, used them as field artillery, too. At one point in his march through central Asia, Alexander found himself blocked by the hither-to invincible Scythian horse archers who were on the other side of the Jaxartes River. Alexander lined up all his artillery on his side of the river and, according to the historian Arrian, "the machines kept firing salvos at the Scythians riding along the bank, some of whom were wounded by the missiles and one, stricken right through his shield and breastplate, who fell from his horse. Thereupon, terrified by the range of the missiles and because a noted warrior had fallen, they retired from the bank a little." And Alexander's army crossed the river.

The ancient field artillery obviously had a psychological effect even stronger than the physical effects it was capable of causing. The history of warfare is full of psychological weapons (weapons that induce a disproportionate fear). Among them are the cavalry lance, the bayonet, the submachine gun, and the dive bomber.

Mechanical artillery was always useful in sieges. The arrow-shooting catapults made it possible to shoot defenders off a city wall from well beyond the range of their bows. Stone-throwing machines could knock down inferior stone walls or could shoot over the walls to demolish houses and other buildings inside.

The engineers continued to improve their machines' accuracy and durability. The Romans used small catapults, called *carroballistae*, mounted on wheels with the skeins of cord enclosed in metal cylinders to protect them from moisture. The Romans also invented a new stone-thrower called an *onager*, which had a single upright arm mounted in an enormous skein of cord. The top of the arm was either shaped like a scoop to hold the stone or the stone was placed in a rope sling at the top of the pole. Roman artillery, like that of Philip and Alexander, was used for both sieges and field battles. Every *century* in the army (the smallest unit) of the Roman Empire had an artillery piece.

The dark ages that followed the fall of Rome created a temporary hiatus in the development of mechanical artillery in western Europe. Later, when warfare was dominated by armored knights, the powers that be had no incentive to develop field artillery that could mow down mailed horsemen. Sieges were another matter, though. The catapult and the onager were revived and played a prominent part in attempts to capture castles. During the Crusades, the Muslims used their mechanical artillery to throw barrels of flaming naphtha at the Crusaders. The Christian warrior soon adopted this fiery weapon.

The Middle Ages also saw the adoption of a new siege engine in Western Europe. It was called a *trebuchet*. It was a pivoted beam, heavily weighted on the short end. The long end was tipped with a sling, into which a missile was placed. The long end was hauled down and loaded. When it was released, the weighted short end fell, and the long end swung up and shot the missile at the enemy stronghold. The trebuchet was probably copied from the Chinese huo-pa'o, which had been adopted by the Mongols and carried west by them.

The trebuchet's power was limited only by its size. In the Middle Ages, some trebuchets were used to throw dead horses into a besieged city to spread disease. Modern experimenters have built trebuchets capable of throwing an automobile several hundred yards. Around the turn of the last century, Sir Ralph Payne-Gallwey built smaller versions of some mechanical artillery. He found that an onager equipped with a sling could throw an eight-pound shot almost 500 yards, and that a catapult with two arms powered by twisted cord, he found, would shoot a 5 or 6 pound spear 500 yards. The same catapult, equipped to shoot stones, would shoot a 1-pound shot 350 yards. Payne-Gallwey did not attempt to make a *trebuchet*, but he noted that the French Emperor Napoleon III built one with a 33-foot beam and a counterpoise of 10,000 pounds. Napoleon's trebuchet shot a 50-pound cannon ball 200 yards, but, Payne-Gallwey wrote, that it was "so lightly constructed that its full power could not be safely applied."

In the Hellenistic world, during the heyday of mechanical artillery, the mere existence of these machines was a potent factor in international relations. According to Dr. Serafina Cuomo, a British historian of science quoted in the *New York Times*, "You didn't just have to have catapults to use them. You needed your potential enemy to know that you had them so they would not attack you in the first place."

10

The Big Bang:
Gunpowder

"Corned" gunpowder. The two top grains are pressed into special shapes. When gunpowder burns, the outside surface becomes smaller and gas pressure drops. The grain second from the top has a hole drilled into it so that as the outer surface decreases, the inner surface increases, helping the powder charge to maintain pressure in long-barreled gun.

Kublai Khan "ruled most of the world"—from the Yellow Sea to steppes of Russia. But, a true grandson of Genghis Khan, he wanted more. He had not yet finished the conquest of southern China when, in 1274, he sent an army and a fleet to subdue Japan. The fleet was manned by Korean sailors and carried 40,000 Mongol soldiers. They were greeted by 120,000 Japanese samurai. The Mongols had the powerful central Asian composite bow, but their opponents were no mean archers. The Japanese had their unique longbow, which was a good match for the Mongol weapon. But although the Japanese outnumbered the Mongols three to one, Kublai's men pushed the islanders back. One reason was their discipline and training. The Mongol army was organized on a decimal basis: squads of 10, companies of 100, regiments of a 1,000, and divisions of 10,000. All units responded to orders given by the beating of kettle drums and the waving of standards. And at this time, the Mongol armies were the most experienced in the world.

Fortunately for the Japanese, a typhoon swept up the west coast of Japan and wrecked most of the Mongol fleet. The Mongol commander took what was left of his army and armada and returned to China.

Kublai Khan did not give up easily. In 1281, he sent another expedition to Japan. This time, there were 150,000 soldiers. Again the Mongols pushed the Japanese back, but resistance was stiffer this time. The Japanese had built a high stone wall around the area on Kyushu where the invaders had first landed. That turned out to be where they landed the second time. The Japanese brought up a huge crowd of samurai warriors, but they were barely able to hold the wall. During the night, though, they raided the Mongol camp. They attacked the invasion fleet with small boats and managed to set fire to some of the Mongol ships. The Japanese resistance stalled the Mongols for seven weeks. The Mongol commander decided to move his fleet, and then another typhoon struck. Approximately 4,000 Mongol ships were sunk, and more than 30,000 Mongol troops were drowned.

To be saved from a Mongol invasion twice by typhoons seemed to be more than a coincidence to the Japanese. The decided they had been saved by the gods, who sent the *Kamikazes*, the divine winds, against their enemies.

The Kamikazes also left conclusive proof of one reason for the Mongols' success before the storms arrived. Recent exploration of the sunken wrecks of Kublai Khan's warships disclosed ceramic pots filled with gunpowder. Similar pots with ignited fuses had been shot from mechanical artillery against the Japanese defenders. Japanese tradition also maintains that the Mongols shot rockets at the samurai soldiers, and old Japanese paintings show defenders being attacked by exploding bombs.

At the time of the Mongol expeditions to Japan, gunpowder was known in Europe—Roger Bacon's famous manuscript was written in 1252—but there's no record of it being used. For years, it became something of a cottage industry among some Western scholars to prove that gunpowder was not invented in China, but the evidence was mostly negative—neither Marco Polo nor Giovanni di Plano Carpini mentioned seeing gunpowder in China; therefore it was not there. But the wrecked Mongol ships prove that gunpowder was in use, and a standard weapon, in the mid-13th century. And the medieval Arabs, who probably had gunpowder before the Europeans, referred to potassium nitrate, the key ingredient, as "the snow from China." Further, evidence that gunpowder was known in Europe appears immediately after the Mongol conquerors of northern China galloped into Europe.

Early Chinese writing records the use of what could only be gunpowder. Why was there so much doubt about the Chinese?

Besides an enormous ethnic bias on the part of many Westerners, it seems the Chinese did not consider gunpowder a particularly important weapon. From about 1000 A.D. it had been mostly used for firecrackers. Martin van Creveld, in his *Technology and War*, points out that in the 12th century, the Chinese were using crude hand grenades. These were paper and bamboo tubes filled with gunpowder and pebbles or bits of broken porcelain. After another century, they had bamboo guns (devices like the bamboo grenades, but open at one end). Though, like the rockets and ceramic bombs the Mongols brought to Japan, none of these weapons were considered serious weapons. The gunpowder was weak, and so were the shells in which it was exploded. The bombs and rockets were mostly useful in scaring horses—or troops like the Japanese who had no experience with gunpowder.

Lieutenant Colonel H.W. Hine concluded, after much study, that the Oriental gunpowder used unrefined potassium nitrate, which made it impossible to get a powerful explosion.

The first written directions for refining potassium nitrate are in Roger Bacon's letter to the Bishop of Paris. There was great interest in the process in Europe but little anywhere else. Warriors in medieval China ranked just above thieves in popular esteem. Nobody in power felt any need to develop more potent powder. The Mongols' scientific tradition was non-existent. Besides, they were sure they had the ultimate weapon: the horse archer. And, until after guns had developed for several centuries, the Mongols were right. The Arabs and Turks also had complete faith in the supremacy of the horse archer.

In western Europe, however, the desire for better weapons was keen. The Crusades had demonstrated to the Europeans that they could not compete with horse archers on the open steppes. Nor, in their damp, forested homeland, could they develop effective horse archers of their own. But there was a continuous search for better weapons among warriors who never dreamed of leaving their homeland. Europe was a quarreling mass of dukedoms, principalities, and city-states. It was inhabited by armed nobles, armed townsmen, and armed mercenaries, all of whom were trying to find some weapon that would trump everyone else's. Consequently, Europe developed the first effective guns. The Chinese learned to improve their guns only after they'd examined European models. Japan, voluntarily cut off from the rest of the world, ignored guns completely until the 16th century. Then, for a short time, Japan had more handguns—but little artillery—than anywhere else in the world. Guns, however, let a low-born peasant who couldn't even recognize a good sword kill any samurai master of swordsmanship. Therefore the samurai, who controlled Japan, stopped all development and most manufacturing of guns.

Europeans, on the other hand, not only adopted gunpowder, they continued to improve it. They increased the proportion of potassium nitrate to make a more powerful explosive. Then, because the three components of the mixture tended to separate, they mixed them wet and formed them into "corns," which could not separate. Near the end of the gunpowder era, they molded the "corns" into various sizes depending on the size and mission of the gun. Some were made with a hole through them to produce a powder than gave consistent gas pressure. As the outside of a corn burned, the surface decreased, causing pressure to drop. But as the inside of hole in the corn burned, the surface increased, producing more gas and raising the pressure. All this "burning," of course, happened in about 1/100,000 of the blink of an eye.

Guns were not the only use of gunpowder. One use gave new life to one of the earliest techniques of siege craft.

11

Digging Down and Blowing Up: Mines

Marine Corps photo from National Archives

Blowing up enemy fortifications is still being done. Here marines use a demolition charge to destroy a Japanese cave on Okinawa.

U.S. Grant's Union armies were closing in on Richmond, capital of the Confederacy in 1864. Robert E. Lee's men dug an elaborate system of trenches, bunkers, and strong points north of the city, so Grant tried to attack from the south while he held the Confederates in place north of Richmond. But Lee had begun fortifying the southern approach, around Petersburg, before the Yankee move. The Confederate fortifications were immensely strong around Petersburg. At one point, the troops of General Ambrose Burnside's Ninth Corps were only 150 yards from an enemy salient protected by a mass of trenches and dugouts on a hill top. Confederate fire from the fort was so heavy there was no way to move forward.

"We could blow that damn fort out of existence if we could run a mine shaft under it," said a soldier of the Forty-Eighth Pennsylvania Infantry. The forty-eighth, recruited in the anthracite district of Pennsylvania, was full of coal miners. Colonel Henry Pleasants, the regimental commander, overheard the soldier's comment. Pleasants himself was a mining engineer in civilian life. He asked the army engineers about mining the fort. Mining enemy fortifications is an ancient tactic, one that was practiced long before explosives were discovered. The pre-explosive method was to tunnel under a fort's walls, propping them up with timber as you dug. When the mine was completed, the besieger set fire to the timber, and the wall collapsed. But when Pleasants consulted the army engineers, they said the project was impossible. The tunnel would have to be 500 feet long—too long to allow for ventilation.

Pleasants was not discouraged. He convinced his superiors, right up to General George G. Meade, commander of the Army of the Potomac, that the project was feasible. Meade convinced Grant, the commander-in-chief. Grant gave Burnside's Ninth Corps the job of blowing up the fort and opening the way to Petersburg. Burnside was delighted. Breaching the rebel line would make up for his bloody failure in the attack on Fredericksburg in 1862. He began training his only fresh troops, the eight African American regiments of the Fourth Division. When the mine went off, he expected that it would kill most of the enemy soldiers in the fort and stupify the survivors in the nearby trenches. The assault force was to run around the crater caused by the explosion and continue straight on into Petersburg. The troops following them would widen the breach, prevent the Confederates from closing it by blocking reserves, and follow the Fourth Division into the rebel city.

Meanwhile, Pleasants's miners were tunneling toward the Confederate fort. They got no help from the official engineers, so they improvised their own tools and scrounged up lumber to reinforce the shaft. Pleasants, using a borrowed the odolite (an instrument for measuring vertical and usually also horizontal angles), plotted the shaft and designed a ventilation system using a fire to create a draft and suck fresh air through the 511-foot tunnel. When they reached a point they calculated was under the Confederate position, the miners dug lateral shafts and filled them with 8,000 pounds of gunpowder.

The stage was set for an explosion that would be heard around the world. Then at almost the last minute, Meade changed the plan. He decided that Burnside's black troops were not up to leading the assault. Instead of the black division, the assault would be spearheaded by the division led by James H. Ledlie, a general with a mediocre combat record and serious drinking problem. Ledlie's troops had not been trained this unusual type of assault. The black Fourth Division would be the last of Burnside's men to enter the breach.

The mine exploded with a deafening blast. The Confederate strongpoint was replaced by a hole 170 feet long, 60 feet wide and 30 feet deep. A battery of Confederate artillery and a whole infantry regiment were either blown into the air or buried under tons of dirt. Ledlie's untrained riflemen dashed towards the crater while their commander stayed in his headquarters swilling rum. When the Union soldiers got to the crater, they stopped and stared, dumbfounded by the destruction. Some even ran down into the hole; Climbing out of it was not easy, they found. The other divisions, equally untrained, joined Ledlie's in milling around—and inside—the crater. The black division, the only one trained to exploit the explosion, had trouble getting through the mob of white colleagues. By that time, the Confederates had had time to gather their reserves and counterattack. The Union attack was a failure, and the Federal troops were driven back with heavy casualties.

Mining, which had been so devastating against ancient, medieval, and early modern stone forts, has not had nearly as much success against modern earthworks. It was tried again in World War I, opening the Battle of the Somme (see Chapter 27). In preparation for the attack on the German lines, British engineers had mined a German strongpoint called the Hawthorn Redoubt and placed 18 tons of high explosive under it. At 7:20 a.m., 10 minutes before the attack, they touched off the explosives. The blast practically leveled the hill and killed all the Germans manning the redoubt. It did not, however, affect the machine guns in the adjoining German positions. The infantry assault was a total failure. Few of the Tommies even reached the German lines, and the British lost 20,000 dead on that first day of the battle. Mining would have been more successful in the smoothbore era, when the range of small arms was less than 1/10 of that of rifled guns.

The origin of mines is lost in the mists of prehistory. There were two principal defenses against mines in those days. One, known to all fanciers of medieval castles, was the wet moat. At the time primitive mines were being used, there was no way to dig under a body of water while preventing the water from pouring down from the moat through the earth and filling the tunnel, if it didn't collapse the tunnel outright.

The second defense was the countermine. To locate enemy mines, the defenders would listen intently, sometimes using inverted shields placed on the ground to amplify the noise. When the Turks were besieging Constantinople in 1553, Johann Grant, a German engineer helping to lead the defense, half-buried a line of drums just behind the city walls. He put some dried peas on each drum. Vibrations of the drum made the peas dance and showed Grant where the Turks were digging. Grant then had his own men mine the Turkish mines. Some, he blew up with gunpowder; others, he filled with poisonous sulfur dioxide generated by burning sulfur; still others, he flooded. If nothing else was available, Grant sent infantry through his tunnel to the enemy tunnel, where they killed the Turkish diggers and pulled down the reinforcements of their tunnel, causing the enemy mine to collapse.

During the Turkish siege of Rhodes, the defenders, the Knights of St. John, reached into the past for an anti-mine weapon. They built a trebuchet (see Chapter 9) capable of shooting an enormous stone a short distance. The stone landed above the Turkish tunnel and collapsed it. The Knights also used countermines, as Suleiman the Magnificent recorded in his diary: "The miners meet the enemy, who uses a great quantity of flaming naphtha." Pouring flaming naphtha from a countermine into a tunnel was an utterly devastating counterattack. The flames not only killed the miners, they burned the timber support of the tunnel, causing a cave-in.

Strangely, gunpowder had been in use in cannons for some time before it occurred to soldiers to use it in mines. For years, the approved technique was the age-old one of propping up the foundations of a wall with timber, and then burning the props. Even when gunpowder was first used, in the 15th century, historian Christopher Duffy says contemporary accounts indicate that it was merely used to help the underground fire burn more fiercely. The first use of gunpowder to blast down walls appears to have been in 1500, when Pedro Navarro captured a Turkish fortress on the island of Cephalonia.

The earliest mines were called mines because the same techniques were used that the men who burrowed into the earth in search of metals or other minerals used. When gunpowder was introduced, the military was again using a material that was also important in civilian mining, although the way it was used was quite different. Somehow, though, the military term "mine" came to be used for any quantity of explosives not used in guns, shells, or rockets that was used to harm an enemy, even if no tunneling was required. Explosive charges in the water, originally called "torpedoes," became "mines." Then, when explosives were placed on the surface of the ground or barely covered with earth, they were called "land mines," as opposed to those intended to destroy shipping.

12

The Walls Came Tumbling Down: Siege Guns

Soldiers in the early 19th century operate heavy siege mortars.

The Chinese first made guns of paper and bamboo, but neither substance could contain much pressure. That meant the gun could neither fire a very heavy missile or use a very heavy powder charge without bursting. And that meant that these paper and bamboo guns never became important weapons.

They were probably most useful for tossing light incendiary projectiles at inflammable targets. Even after they had metal cannons, the Japanese used them to shoot paper packages of oil-soaked gunpowder at the wooden superstructures of samurai castles to burn them down.

Europeans, on the other hand, made their cannons of metal from the beginning. By the 13th century, when gunpowder became known in the West, Europe led the world in the technology of bronze casting. European bronze founders had learned the secrets of making large castings by decades of casting bells for Christian churches. Bronze was expensive, so some European gunmakers used iron instead. There were no European blast furnaces at that time, so the first iron cannons could not be cast. Instead, the gunmaker welded a large number of wrought iron rods together around a mandrel, then bound them together with iron hoops, heated red-hot and forced over the cylinder of welded rods. As the hoops cooled, they shrank and bound the rods tightly. The whole process resembled the manufacture of a barrel, which is why we now call the tube of a gun that the projectile passes through a barrel.

The early iron guns, having been welded around a cylindrical mandrel, were straight tubes. The bronze guns, however, were shaped on the outside like a flower vase, but the interior was cylindrical. The founders apparently wanted to put more metal around the part of the gun where the powder exploded. These earliest cannons fired balls of stone, lead, or brass and heavy, arrow-shaped projectiles. The earliest picture of a cannon we have is on a manuscript prepared by Walter de Milemete for his pupil, the future King Edward III of England. It shows one of these vase-shaped cannons being ignited by a man in armor. Emerging from the mouth of the cannon is a large arrow.

When he grew up, Edward III took three primitive cannons with him to France and used them at the battlefield of Crecy. These novel weapons may have helped panic the mercenary Genoese crossbowmen in the French army. On the battlefield, the most potent feature of these early cannons was the flash and noise they made. They could scare horses and troops unfamiliar with gunpowder weapons. But for actual destruction, one of these small, primitive cannons didn't compare with a good bow or crossbow.

That was not true when they were used for sieges. For sieges, medieval kings ordered enormous guns that shot stone balls weighing hundreds of pounds. Some of these guns were so heavy they were cast in two pieces to make them easier to move. The halves were screwed together after they were dragged into position. When Mohammed the Conqueror, sultan of Turkey, laid siege to Constantinople, he told his gun founder, a renegade Hungarian named Urban, that he wanted the biggest guns ever seen. Urban told him it would be easier to cast the guns right in front of Constantinople than to move them from a foundry. So they were cast just out of range of the defenders' weapons.

Once they were in position, these huge cannons, called bombards, were completely immobile. They were enclosed in wooden frames that had been constructed around them. Immobility didn't matter. The task of the gunners to was to shoot one huge cannonball after another at the same spot on a wall. It did not take long for the wall to collapse. That was an effect that could seldom be achieved with mechanical artillery.

The introduction of siege guns had a profound effect on the techniques of warfare, and an even more profound effect on European society in general. Designers of fortresses made the walls lower and thicker. They learned that while stone walls would shatter when hit by cannon balls, earth walls would just soak up the missiles. Earth walls, though, could be eroded by weather. Eventually, military engineers built earthen walls faced by stone and reinforced internally so that, if a breach was made in the stone, the dirt wouldn't pour through the break, making a convenient ramp for attackers. The engineers surrounded their forts with deep, wide ditches. Outside these ditches were sloping embankments that hid all but the tops of the walls. This sort of embankment, called a glacis, was kept free of any vegetation but grass, so attacking infantry would have no cover. Just behind the top of the glacis, was a path called a *covered way* from which infantry could fire on attackers making their way up the glacis. There were wide spots on the covered way where the defenders of a fort could assemble for counterattacks. At the corners of the forts, the engineers built arrowhead-shaped projections called bastions, where cannons could be placed to subject attackers to crossfire while the guns on the wall fired on them directly. On the flanks of the bastions, protected from fire from the front, were other cannons that could fire down the length of the ditch. In front of the fort proper, but within the ditch, were detached forts connected to the main fortress with draw bridges or tunnels. This type of cannon-fort took years or even centuries to develop. Most of the early development took place in Italy, where such "renaissance men" as Michelangelo added innovations that made European fortresses by far the strongest in the world.

These modern forts were much larger than the old-fashioned castles, and they were far more expensive. The forts and the cannons needed to defend them were so expensive that only kings, free cities, and very great lords could afford them. Cannons played a big part in ending the Middle Ages—not because they could knock down any fortification, but because they made practical fortification too expensive for the many minor nobles who had previously cut Europe up into thousands of tiny, almost autonomous, fiefdoms.

13

Seizing the Seas: The Sailing Man of War

National Archives from U.S. Bureau of ships

U.S. frigate *Constellation* battles the French frigate *L'Insurgente* in 1799.

The time had come to put an end to the Frankish meddling in the trade with the East. The two great powers of western Islam, Turkey and Egypt, had put aside their rivalries to send a combined fleet of 200 galleys to the Indian Ocean. Each of the galleys had three cannons positioned to fire over its bow, and the fleet carried 15,000 soldiers for boarding the ships of the infidels. The admiral, Emir Husain Kurdi, had spent two years looking for the main Frankish fleet, but at last the warriors of Islam were about to meet the interlopers.

The "Franks" (actually Portuguese, but in 1509, all European Christians were Franks to the Muslims) had sent their ships around Africa and were trading with India. Trade with the East had long been a Muslim monopoly. Overland trade consisted of caravans of Turkish Muslims passing through the Muslim lands of central Asia. Goods that got to Europe this way were extremely expensive, because each local ruler levied a tax on the caravans. Transportation by sea was less expensive. The Arabs of Arabia and the east coast of Africa had pioneered the sea routes centuries before the birth of Mohammed. Europeans had lost the Crusades, but had gained a thirst for the goods of the East. Merchandise from India, Persia, the Indies, and China traveled in Muslim bottoms and brought enormous wealth to the rulers of *Dar es Islam* (the Land of Islam), especially the Sultan of Egypt. The Egyptians shipped these Eastern luxuries to Europe through Venice, and that Italian city-state became a mighty power in the Mediterranean. That's one of the reasons why Venice's ally, the Sultan of Egypt, and its enemy, the Sultan of Turkey, seldom saw eye-to-eye.

This project was an exception. Portuguese capture of the trade with the East would hurt not only Egypt and Venice, but Turkey. The Ottoman Empire controlled much of the land traversed by the caravans. If the spices, gold, silk, and other goods from the East were available from Christian merchants and much lower prices, the Europeans could be expected to ignore the caravan-carried goods entirely.

That day, the Muslim fleet, stationed in the Indian port of Diu, heard that the Portuguese fleet was approaching. The Christians had only 17 ships, so the Muslim sailors rowed confidently out to meet them.

But the Christian ships were all larger than the Muslim galleys. More important, they were a different type of ship entirely, the product of centuries of development, most of which had escaped the notice of the Muslims.

Trade between the countries of western Europe was to a very large extent waterborne. It followed the many navigable rivers; crossed inland seas like the Mediterranean and the Baltic, much rougher seas such as the North Sea and even went into the ferocious Atlantic. Commerce in the Dar es Islam was different. In the arid lands that made up the bulk of Islamic territory, trade mostly happened by caravan. Trade was done by boat in the islands of the East Indies, but most of that was short-range island-hopping. The long distance trade between India, Africa, and Arabia depended on trade winds. For half of the year the winds blew west, for the other half, east. The Arabs had developed a specialized kind of ship, the dhow, to take advantage of that environment. For centuries, warships of the Mediterranean powers, both Muslim and Christian, had been almost identical—versions of the galley. (See Chapter 4.)

Galleys were almost useless for commerce and were totally useless for long-distance trading. Most of a galley was taken up by rowers, and rowers need food and water. So galleys had to make frequent stops to replenish their supplies and had no room for merchandise. For trade, the Europeans developed "round ships," ships much wider in relation to their length than galleys. They had no oars and no rowers, so they could hold more cargo. To move these vessels in the variable winds of the northern seas, the European sailors developed sails that let them proceed against the wind. Weather was a problem for European sailors, especially those in northern waters. The round ships had high sides, unlike galleys, which had to be low to accommodate the oars (a necessity in rough water), and they were heavily built, unlike galleys, which had to be light so the rowers could move them rapidly.

Pirates were another problem. In the late 13th and 14th centuries, new types of ships were developed. They were slimmer than the old round ships and much faster, but they were still strongly built and still capable of carrying a decent amount of cargo. They had high "castles" for and aft, where crossbowmen could be stationed. They also had crows' nests on their masts where more crosssbowmen could stand ready to shoot any pirates. When cannons were invented, ship owners mounted them on their vessels. At first they were placed on the castles, but the weight of the guns made the ships unstable. At the beginning of the 16th century, ship builders began cutting gun ports in the hulls.

With these sturdy, all-weather ships, able to sail against the wind and stay at sea for months without touching land, the Portuguese began working their way around Africa. England and France were immersed in the Hundred Years War, and Spain was still trying to drive the Muslims back to Africa. The Portuguese had already driven the Muslims out of their country, and they were able to look for a new route to the East.

The Turks and Egyptians saw sails and tried to form a line to attack the infidels. Forming a line wasn't easy on the lively Indian Ocean. Galleys were much better adapted to inland seas such as the Mediterranean and the Red Sea. The galleys' guns were loaded and their gunners ready. The musketeers made sure their matches were lighted, and the archers had nocked their arrows.

The Portuguese ships suddenly turned, presenting their sides to the advancing galleys. Then the broadsides began. The Portuguese cannons were heavier and outranged those of the Muslims. And the 17 Portuguese ships had more guns than the 200 Muslim galleys. Cannon balls ploughed through rows of rowers, leaving masses of gore, gory bodies and body parts. They smashed the hulls of the fragile galleys. It was more of a massacre than a battle. Shanbal, a contemporary Arab historian, gave an account of the battle that shows that the tendency to minimize your side's losses and exaggerate the enemy's is, by no means, modern:

Many on the Frankish side were slain, but eventually the Franks prevailed over the Muslims, and there befell a great slaughter of the Emir Husain's soldiers, about 600 men, while the survivors fled to Diu. Nor did he [the Frank] depart until they had paid him much money.

Actually, the Muslim fleet was practically annihilated. The few surviving galleys ran themselves ashore and their crews fled toward Diu. Very few Portuguese were killed. The Muslims tried three more times to drive the Portuguese from the coast of Africa and India. Each time, it was galleys versus sailing ships. And each battle was a replay of Diu.

The introduction of the sailing warship changed warfare and changed the world. The galley suddenly became obsolete. Sailing ships that could travel to the far ends of the world and still outfight galleys replaced all oar-driven warships. There was one more big galley battle in the Mediterranean, at Lepanto, a couple of generations after Diu, but even there, Don Juan of Austria, the Christian admiral, used galleasses—big, heavily gunned ships—to break up the Turkish formation before the galleys clashed. The loss of the trade with the East began to weaken the Muslims, and the first Muslim casualty was Egypt. The Turks conquered the weakened sultanate on the Nile eight years after Diu. Portugal thrived on the trade with the East. One of its India-bound ships made a navigational error and discovered Brazil, but before that a Genoese sailor convinced the king and queen of Spain that he could get to the Far East quicker by sailing west; Columbus made a mistake, but he discovered a whole new world.

14

Guns That Roll:
Mobile Artillery

Moving a field piece into position.

Artillery, as we have seen, revolutionized siege warfare. The early siege guns, though, were far from ideal. They were so heavy that moving one of them was a major engineering project. Barrels were weak, especially those of bombards built of welded iron rods and hoops, so they couldn't contain much pressure. Consequently their projectiles had low velocity. For lobbing one big stone ball after another at the same spot on a wall they were fine, but the rulers of France and Burgundy wanted more. Especially, they wanted more mobility. The French and Burgundians engaged in an arms race beginning during the latter part of the Hundred Years War. The English, although they had introduced guns to that war at Crecy, didn't bother to compete. They were convinced that their longbow was the master weapon. They were to regret that idea.

The new guns were all cast in bronze and could handle much higher pressures than the old bombards. Their barrels were much longer in proportion to the size of their projectiles. This not only increased accuracy, it gave the exploding powder more time to push the projectile, increasing the velocity. The wrought iron cannon balls were smaller than the stones shot from the bombards, but they were heavier in proportion to their size and much harder and tougher. They wouldn't shatter on a stone wall as stone shot often did. The new guns were cast with lugs, called "trunnions," on their barrels near the center of gravity. The guns swivelled on the trunnions so they could be elevated to hit targets at varying ranges. Most important, the guns were mounted on wheeled carriages so they could be easily moved.

The new French cannons brought an end to the Hundred Years War. The French were able to quickly concentrate their cannons against castles the English held, knock their walls down, and move to the next stronghold. But a couple of small engagements demonstrated that the French had a most potent field weapon as well as a wall-batterer.

At Formigny in 1450, French and English forces of equal size met. The English reaction was almost reflexive. Most of the knights dismounted and formed a wall of lance points. The infantry archers stepped forward, planted sharpened stakes to stop a cavalry charge, and strung their bows. All waited for the traditional French cavalry charge.

The French didn't charge. They just hauled up their cannons and blasted the English away. At Castillon, three years later, an English army attacked a French force that was besieging an English stronghold. This time, the English were the attackers. The French had no longbows, but they had cannons. And they proved that cannons were as effective on the defensive as they were on the offensive. The English commander, John Talbot, was killed, and the Hundred Years War effectively ended soon afterwards. Later, mobile artillery was to prove its worth in another theater.

In 1494, Charles VIII of France took his artillery into Italy to enforce his claim to Naples. The result was a sort of 15th century Blitzkrieg. Cities and fortresses surrendered to the French as soon as they saw the French artillery. There was some resistance in Naples. The fortress of Monte San Giovanni, which had previously withstood a siege of seven years, was taken in eight hours, after which the French troops massacred the garrison. Charles took Naples and then returned to France.

His success, however, inspired an alliance of Spain, Venice, the Papal States, and Milan. The Italian Wars, what some historians consider Europe's first "world war," had begun. Before they were over, all the major European powers except England, Sweden, and the Ottoman Empire would be sucked into the Italian battlefield. The principal combatants were the strangely named Holy Roman Empire of the German People—which, under Emperor Charles V, included the rich and powerful kingdom of Spain—and the kingdom of France. The perpetually quarreling Italian mini-states allied themselves with one or another of the great powers. The Swiss cantons supplied troops to both the French and the Imperialists. Infantrymen were, in fact, the main cash crop of Switzerland. Because they had defeated the armies of both Burgundy and the Empire, the Swiss infantry had become the terror of Central Europe. The Swiss cantons rented out their soldiers to the princes of Europe. The Swiss fought in a dense phalanx—mostly pikemen supported by halberdiers, crossbow archers, and men swinging six-foot-long two-handed swords. The Swiss phalanx was quickly copied by the infantry of all the continental powers. The Swiss soldiers considered fighting in these many wars their patriotic duty. They brought money to their home cantons. Their motives were not pure patriotism, however. The loot from enemy camps and cities was a powerful inducement, as was their hatred for the Holy Roman Empire (the Swiss heroes, Arnold von Winkler and William Tell, had resisted the Empire).

Usually, the Swiss fought on the side of the French. In 1513, however, the Imperialists outbid the French, and the *Schweizer* footmen marched with the forces of the Empire to break the siege of Novaro, where a Swiss garrison was holding out against the French. French artillery broke down the walls of Novaro, but the Swiss erected barricades behind the breaches. Then the relieving army swept down on the French, captured 22 French guns and killed all the gunners. They lost only 400 men in their attack. Two years later, at Maringano, the Swiss didn't do so well. This time, they did not attack the rear of a besieging army, but charged directly at the front of a heavily fortified French army equipped with 72 field guns. The Swiss did capture part of the French works but had to dig in under heavy fire. The next day, they were forced back by fire from the artillery and the French harquebusiers. Then the French cavalry turned their retreat into a rout. The attack at Marignano was the last time the Swiss fought French troops and their artillery before the Swiss Guard was wiped out in the French Revolution.

In 1522, the Swiss were again on the side of the French. Prospero Colonna, a condottiere in the service of the Empire, was besieging Milan. The Swiss were eager to attack. As at Novaro, they would come in behind a besieging army, and their enemy was the hated Imperialists. The French commander, Lautrec, was not so optimistic. It looked as if Colonna had fortified the rear of his army as well as the part facing the city. But the Swiss were so insistent, Lautrec was afraid they'd mutiny if he didn't let them attack. So on April 27, 1522, he ordered the attack.

Colonna had placed cannons and Spanish arquebusiers and musketeers behind a breastwork that overlooked a sunken road. The Imperial cannons blasted bloody lanes through the Swiss phalanx. A single shot striking that dense mass of humanity could kill up to 30 men. A thousand Swiss were killed before they even reached the sunken road. When the Swiss reached the ditch and leaped into it, four lines of Spanish handgunners firing successive volleys shot them down. A few Swiss climbed over the bodies of their comrades to reach the top of the breastwork, but Imperial pikemen pushed them back. More than 3,000 Swiss were killed. The survivors fled, and, as historian Christopher Duffy puts it, "The bellicose and independent spirit of the Swiss was broken forever."

Field artillery was improved continuously, well into the 19th century. It became one of the three key elements of warfare and was the key to Napoleon's victories. For a time, its supremacy was challenged by the high-velocity rifle, but then cannons were given rifling and recoil-absorbing mechanisms, and in World War II, it was still the most lethal of military weapons.

15

Power in the Hands: The Matchlock

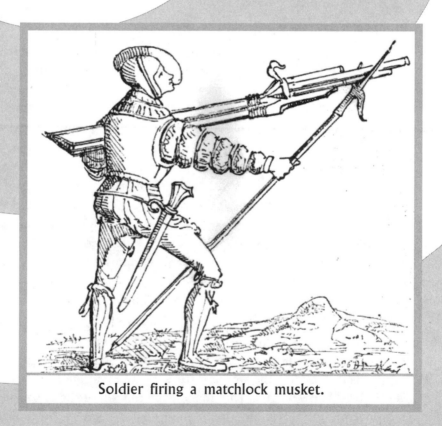

Soldier firing a matchlock musket.

The first gun small enough to be carried by infantry was far from a decisive weapon. A typical "hand cannon" was a short metal tube fitted to the end of a wooden pole. From a distance, it looked like a short spear. The hand gunner loaded his weapon with gunpowder and a lead ball. He then held the wooden pole with one hand, and with the other he poked a red-hot iron wire into a hole, called a "touch-hole" in the top of the gun. Guiding the wire to the touch-hole meant that he was not able to aim. The gun made a bright flash, a terrifying noise, and a lot of smoke. Other than that, it seldom did any damage. There was a good reason why the Arabs and Turks were not interested in guns.

Jump ahead about three centuries: Samuel de Champlain, the French explorer, is asked by some Indians he is visiting (members of the Huron tribe), for help against their enemies, members of the formidable Iroquois confederacy. Champlain loads his gun, a long heavy device that bears no resemblance to the early hand cannons, with a charge of powder and three bullets. He joins the army of his new friends, and they confront the Iroquois army. Both armies consist of naked warriors armed with bows and arrows. Two of the Iroquois chiefs advance to challenge the Hurons. One of the chiefs lifts his bow. Champlain fires.

Both chiefs fall to the ground. The Iroquois flee.

Champlain's shot, hitting two enemies at once, was probably the best the explorer ever made. It was also one of the most historic in North American history. It started the centuries-long hostility between the Iroquois and the French, a development that had the most profound effect on colonial North America.

A lot of development went into Champlain's exceptionally lethal weapon. One of the first was getting rid of the hot wire as a means of ignition. Using wires to fire guns meant that soldiers had to have a fire nearby to keep their wires hot. That was not very convenient in the midst of a battle. Somebody substituted a piece of cord that had been steeped in potassium nitrate and brandy to make it burn slowly and steadily. Its effect was something like the punk used to ignite Fourth of July fireworks. Some fires were still needed in case a match went out, but usually a soldier could reignite his match from another soldier's. A burning match could not be easily poked into a touch-hole, so gunmakers built guns with a small pan above the touch-hole. When gunpowder in this "priming pan" ignited, the fire would flash into the main charge.

The gun, though, was still no easier to aim. Then some genius built a gun with a pivoted arm that would swing the burning end of the match right into the pan. The arm was fastened to the wooden stock, so the pan and the touch-hole were moved to the side of the gun. That made construction of the swivel simpler, but, more important, it made aiming the gun easier—the swivel didn't interfere with the line of sight.

While these improvements had been going on, guns got longer and heavier. Their long barrels could propel a bullet with enough force to be deadly at a distance. Fitting a trigger to let the gunner move the swiveled arm with one finger made aiming still easier. Gunsmiths used a variety of trigger arrangements. The simplest was extending the swiveling arm below the pivot so the gunner could lower the match by pulling the bottom of the arm. That made an awkward reach for the trigger finger, and it required the touch-hole to be too far forward for efficiency. More efficient was the system that put the trigger at the center of the bottom of the stock and had it move the match-holder with an arrangement of levers. A spring returned the match-holder, or "serpentine," to its original position when the gunner released the trigger. It finally became easy to aim and fire a gun—as easy as aiming and shooting a crossbow. To further aid the process, gunsmiths began fitting sights to their products.

The Portuguese brought this more efficient gun to India, and Indian gunmakers were still building this type of weapon well into the 19th century. Another, somewhat later development of the matchlock caught on in Japan, where, again, the Portuguese introduced it. This was the "snapping matchlock." The gunner cocked the serpentine as if he were firing a single-action revolver. When he squeezed the trigger, the serpentine brought the match into the pan with a snap, propelled by a spring. That made it possible for a gunner to fire the instant he lined up his gun on the target. The Japanese were still using this type of gun when Commodore Perry arrived. The snapping matchlock later went out of fashion in Europe because the serpentine sometimes snapped the match into the priming pan hard enough to put the match out.

European gunsmiths continued to improve what had now become the most important weapon on the battlefield. Barrels with spiral rifling appeared. Spinning the bullet gave it far more accuracy: A shot was effective at much longer ranges. These early rifles were difficult to load, however. The bullet had to be bigger than the bore so the rifling would cut into it and make it spin when fired. That meant the bullet had to be pounded down the barrel. And the rather crude gunpowder of the time clogged up the rifling after a few shots making the gun impossible to load until the bore was cleaned. Some wealthy hunters bought rifles, but soldiers continued to use smoothbores. Loading a matchlock was slow enough, even without the need to pound a bullet down the barrel and clean it after every three or four shots. For safety, a soldier had to take the match off his gun before loading, hold it at a safe distance while he poured loose powder down the barrel, rammd a bullet and wad on top of that, and put more powder in the priming pan. He then put the match back on the serpentine, blew on it to expose the burning coal, and aimed it at the target. Prince Maurice of Nassau, a 17th-century Dutch general, prescribed 43 separate movements for his musketeers' drill.

Musketeers used muskets—the latest development of the matchlock. A musket was exactly the same as the earlier and lighter arquebus, but it was bigger. It was so heavy the musketeer had to fire it from a rest—a long forked stick or metal rod. The advantage of the musket was that its heavy bullet would penetrate armor at 200 yards. One marksman wasn't likely to hit an individual enemy at 200 yards with a smoothbore musket, but infantry and cavalry in those days fought in dense masses that made large targets. A volley of musket balls would have a devastating effect on charging heavy cavalry or armored pikemen.

The matchlock quickly replaced the crossbow in continental armies, largely because it penetrated armor better. It didn't make armor disappear, but it required soldiers to wear ever-heavier armor. By the time the musket appeared, most soldiers had stopped wearing most armor. Eventually, infantry wore little more than a helmet and the heaviest cavalry wore only metal cuirasses. Although for centuries, the English had an almost religious belief in the supremacy of the longbow over all other hand weapons, in the early 16th century, the gun replaced the longbow in England. As guns got better and better, armies included higher and higher proportions of arquebusiers and musketeers to other troops.

The use of muskets on a large scale required more complicated and rigorous training for infantry. Just to use their slow-loading weapons efficiently, soldiers had to be drilled until they could perform processes like Prince Maurice's 43 motions almost subconsciously. Masses of musketeers had to be drilled so they could perform the loading and firing motions simultaneously, because generals had found that volleys had a greater shock effect on enemies than individual fire. The drilling of musketeers and arquebusiers had to be done with pikemen because they had to be protected from cavalry by pikemen while they were reloading. The musketeers had to learn how to move into or behind pike formations while loading and how to suddenly reappear and fire volleys when their pieces were loaded.

Warfare had become a lot more complicated. No longer could a country such as England field a highly effective militia whose main training was shooting arrows every Sunday afternoon. Even guard duty had become complex. Here's what Virginia had to say about sentinels:

> ...he shall shoulder his piece, both ends of his match being alight, and his piece charged, and primed, and bullets in his mouth, there to stand with a careful and waking eye, untill such time as his Corporall shall relieve him.

To speed reloading, soldiers literally spit bullets into the gun. The idea was to enable the sentry to fire quickly if a number of enemies suddenly appeared. But holding two or three bullets in his mouth probably also helped him keep "a careful and waking eye."

16

The Spark of Genius: Flint and Steel

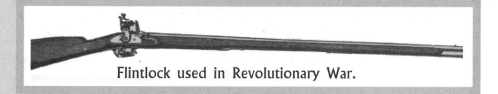

Flintlock used in Revolutionary War.

Captain John Smith, the friend of Pocahontas, had a long career as a mercenary soldier before he came to America. Once, commanding a few soldiers, he learned that a much larger force of Turks was about to make a night attack. He had his troops spread out and carry a long piece of rope. At regular intervals along the rope, he fastened a length of lighted match. Then his troops advanced. The Turks, seeing all those matches glowing in the dark, thought a huge force was about to attack them. They retreated.

Thus, Smith managed to take advantage of one of the matchlock's characteristics. Years later, in Virginia, he demonstrated one of its disadvantages. In 1609, he was carrying a lighted match and seemed to have forgotten that he also had a pocketful of loose gunpowder. He put his hand, with the lighted match, into his pocket. It's hard to believe an experienced soldier like Smith could be so careless, but he was. Fortunately, the powder wasn't confined, so it didn't explode, but Smith was severely burned. While he was laid up, his enemies seized him and sent him off to England to stand trial for alleged misconduct.

Gunpowder does not always have to be confined to explode. A large quantity of gunpowder—nowadays usually called "black powder"—will explode when ignited even when unconfined. Because it can be ignited by the merest spark or even by friction, black powder is a very dangerous substance. Using the matchlock meant manipulating black powder in close proximity to fire. The matchlock priming pan had a cover to minimize exposure, but even so, accidents were frequent.

The matchlock was also dangerous when the match was not lighted. A party of Spanish soldiers learned that the hard way when they approached an Indian village in what is now South Carolina. The soldiers planned to force the Indians to give them corn. Outside the village, some Indians met the soldiers and said they'd be glad to give them food, but the glowing matches made the women of the village nervous. Not wishing to alarm the villagers, the soldiers extinguished their matches and went into village. The villagers then massacred them. Only one man escaped.

Rain was an ever-present danger for troops armed with matchlocks. A downpour could extinguish their matches and leave them defenseless. The matchlock also made a surprise attack at night impossible, as John Smith proved in his mock attack on the Turks. For all of these reasons, in central and western Europe (the area the Muslim Turks called "the Land of War"), there was a fervent search for some way to fire a gun without carrying fire along with it.

There was one attempt even before the matchlock was fully developed. An inventor in Dresden developed something called a Monchbuchse. It was a simple tube with a metal handle underneath it. Along the side was a leaf spring terminating in jaws that held a piece of flint. The spring pressed the flint down on a steel rasp equipped with a handle at one end. The gunner held the handle of the gun in one hand and pulled back the rasp with the other. That produced sparks that ignited the primer and fired the gun. Striking a piece of flint on steel to make sparks fall on dry tinder had long been used to start fires in Europe, but the Dresden invention was the first to use the principle to fire a gun. The Monchbuchse, however, was even clumsier than the hand cannon, so it never caught on.

Somewhere in northern Italy or southern Germany, somebody in the late 15th or early 16th century came up with a more practical gun. This was the wheel lock. It had a jaw that pressed a piece of iron pirates (the "fool's gold" of gold prospectors) on a roughened steel wheel. The wheel revolved in the priming pan. The wheel was connected to a crank, attached to a short chain that was connected to a strong leaf spring. The gunner loaded his weapon, put powder in the pan, and wound up the wheel with a wrench. When he pressed the trigger, a shower of sparks fell in the pan. Ignition, unlike that for the slightly later flintlock, was almost instantaneous. Pyrites were used instead of flints, because pyrites are softer. Continued use of flint would wear out the roughened steel wheel quickly.

The wheel lock had two disadvantages because the mechanism was more complicated than that of any weapon ever seen before. It was expensive, and it was liable to break down. It was expensive because precision machining was unknown in the 16th and 17th centuries. Wheel locks were all handmade by the most skilled of craftsmen, and they were more prone to failure than the simple matchlock.

Expense was the biggest drawback. Even so, wheel lock pistols were welcomed by the cavalry. Although matchlock pistols were made in Japan, such weapons were not popular in Europe. Matchlock muskets and arquebuses were dangerous enough when used by slowly walking infantry. A matchlock on a galloping horse was something few European warriors wanted. Loading a wheel lock pistol on a trotting or galloping horse would be a nightmare. European cavalry, largely descendants of Europe's knightly class, could afford wheel locks. They adopted the new weapon and developed a new tactic. It was called the *caracole*: a column of cavalry, each man carrying two to six pistols, would ride up to a formation of pikemen and, just out of pike range, fire their pistols, and ride to the rear of the column, reloading as they rode.

At its introduction, the caracole was devastating. Then the infantry learned to move musketeers up in front of the pikemen and fire musket volleys before the cavalry got within pistol range.

Meanwhile, the infantry were still using the cheap and vulnerable matchlock. The idea of producing sparks with a single sharp blow instead of a spinning wheel seemed to occur in many parts of Europe soon after the introduction of the wheel lock.

From Scandinavia came the Baltic or Swedish snap lock. The flint in this gun fitted on a long curved device that corresponds to the *cock* of the better-known *flintlock*. A leaf spring pushing up on the heel of the cock drove it into the pivoted steel and struck sparks. Sometimes the steel was attached to the pan cover, so that it opened just as sparks appeared. More often, it had to be opened separately.

From the Netherlands came the snaphaunce, its name derived from the Dutch words for snapping hen. This looked much like the standard flintlock. It had a mainspring inside the lock plate and flint-holding cock that looked like the flintlock's. The priming pan cover, however, was not attached to the steel. In crude specimens, it was opened manually before firing; in most, levers connected to the cock pushed it open as the flint fell.

Spain contributed the miquelet. This had a huge cock powered by an external mainspring. It drove the flint against a short, straight steel that was connected to the pan cover, like the fully developed flintlock. The miquelet looked clumsy, but it was extremely reliable—the most reliable of any of the flintlock variations.

The individualistic Scots developed their own version of a flint-fired gun. It had a lateral-moving sear like the snaphaunce, and in early versions the steel is not connected to the pan cover. Later guns had the steel and pan cover in one piece like the flintlock but retained the lateral sear. One peculiarity of the Scottish weapon was its lack of a trigger guard.

The weapon that Americans think of when they hear flintlock was developed in France, probably by Marin le Bourgeoys, a gunsmith of Lisieux, sometime between 1610 and 1615. It combined the best features of the snaphaunce and the miquelet and rapidly spread all over Europe and the Americas. Instead of the lateral seal of all the other "firelocks" (including the wheel lock), le Bourgeoys invented a vertical sear. This made a half-cock position—a great safety feature—possible and made the action more durable. After le Bourgeoys, improvements on the flintlock were mostly details, such as making the pan cover fit the pan so closely the gun could fire in a driving rain. The flintlock was used on smoothbore muskets, rifles, pistols, and shotguns, practically unchanged from le Bourgeoys's invention for two centuries. Its simplicity, durability, and utility in all kinds of environments made possible, among other things, the settlement of America and the independence of the American colonies.

17

A Knife Doubles Firepower: The Bayonet

An assortment of bayonets. From top, left to right, bayonets fit U.S. M 1 rifle; U.S. M 1917 rifle, U.S. M 1 or M 2 carbine; U.S. Springfield rifle, model 1873; British bayonet for rifle number 4; German dress bayonet for Mauser 1898 carbine. Directly below the bayonet for the British rifle number 4 is another bayonet, the so-called spike bayonet for the same rifle. At bottom is a Russian bayonet that can be fitted to its scabbard to make a wire cutter.

T he flintlock, which eliminated the need to worry about a burning match, greatly speeded up the infantry's rate of fire, but the musketeer was still practically defenseless for too long a time between shots. Musketeers carried swords, but having a sword is not much comfort when faced with a phalanx of pikes or a swarm of charging horsemen. At times, musketeers arranged themselves in successive lines. The first line would fire and move to the rear, reloading as they went, while the second line would fire and do the same. This system allowed quickly repeated volleys, and, at times, it was quite successful.

At the battle of Bunker Hill, John Stark's New Hampshire militiamen were holding the flank of the American position that terminated at the Mystic River. Stark hid his men behind a stone-and-rail fence and arranged them in three lines. British General William Howe had planned to make a demonstration in front of the American lines while the elite light infantry companies of his force would run along the river bank, hidden from the sight of both those in the American fort and the members of the main British force. They would sweep around the apparently unguarded left flank of the Americans and hit them from the rear as the main body advanced on the rebel front.

The light companies double-timed along the river in columns of four, one company behind the other. When the lead company, the light company of the Welch Fusiliers, got to about 80 feet of the fence, there was an ear-splitting blast, and the company ceased to exist. The light troops of the King's Own Regiment dashed forward, knowing that, however fast the rebels could reload, they couldn't resist a bayonet charge now. There was another blast and another cloud of smoke and another company annihilated. The third light company hesitated, then they leveled their muskets and charged. For the third time, a British light infantry company was blown away. It would not happen again. The rest of the light infantrymen turned around and dashed to the rear. If they had continued on, the Battle of Bunker Hill would have been all over. Stark's first line had not had time to reload.

The trouble with firing in successive lines was that it was only practical on a narrow front. In open country, the musketeers could easily be flanked, especially by cavalry. In most battles, the musketeers relied on pikemen to protect them while reloading. Infantry practiced various formations and drills that allowed musketeers to hide behind the pikes while reloading and to take up firing positions as soon as their weapons were ready to use. This system worked pretty well, but it obviously cut down the army's firepower—sometimes by more than half.

The solution to the problem was to turn the musket into a spear. According to some sources, this was the idea of Sebastien le Prestre de Vauban, the great French military engineer in the armies of Louis XIV. It was a solution at least for soldiers. Hunters in France and Spain had for some time been jamming knives into the muzzles of their muskets for protection against dangerous game. It seems that Bayonne, a French city noted for its cutlery, made a type of hunting knife that was favored for this use. When the French army adopted this weapon, it was called a "bayonet." The earliest reference to the use of the bayonet is in the memoirs of a French officer who wrote that on one campaign, his men did not carry swords, but knives with handles one foot long and blades of the same length. When needed, the knives could be placed in the muzzles of the guns to turn them into spears. The bayonet proved to be a much more effective defense against cavalry than the sword.

There were some drawbacks to these "plug bayonets." If someone put a plug bayonet in the muzzle of a loaded musket and then fired it, the gun might blow up. This sort of accident seems to have been much more prevalent among civilians who, unlike soldiers, did not load and fire on command. It was so prevalent that in 1660, Louis XIV had to issue a proclamation forbidding the placing of daggers in the muzzles of hunting guns. The trouble with plug bayonets in military guns was that, when the bayonet was in place, the gun could not be loaded or fired, although there were situations when it would be most helpful to be able to do either with the bayonet in place.

The first attempt to remedy this condition was to fit the handle of the bayonet with a pair of rings that could be slipped over the barrel of the musket. The blade hung below the barrel so there was nothing to stop bullet from either entering or leaving the muzzle. The person who first invented the ring bayonet is uncertain. Hugh Mackay, a Scot in the service of William of Orange who campaigned for the Netherlands-born English king in Scotland in the late 1680s and early 1690s, wrote that his men had no time to place or remove their plug bayonets when the Highland clansmen charged them firing their pistols and brandishing their swords. He had rings put on the bayonets so his men could fire while their bayonets were in place.

The ring bayonet was a major improvement, but it could easily fall off a musket barrel—or be pulled off by an enemy. That led to the invention of the socket bayonet, a type that was universally used from the mid-18th to the mid-19th century and was revived in the late 20th century by the British Army. Basically, the socket bayonet is a blade set at an angle to a tube that fits over the barrel of a gun. Its advantage over the ring bayonet is that the socket includes a way to lock it on to the gun.

The socket bayonet was an extremely efficient weapon when mounted on a musket or rifle. It was much less satisfactory when used without the gun, as the socket was awkward to hold. As time went on, the bayonet became increasingly less important as a weapon. The universal use of rifles in the late 19th century, as in the American Civil War, made it unlikely that enemy soldiers would get close enough to use bayonets. In World War I, repeating rifles and machine guns made bayonets almost useless. American authorities in that war estimated that no more than .024 percent of their casualties were caused by bayonets.

But although the rifle was seldom used as a spear, bayonets were far from useless. Every infantryman has a need for a good knife. The old socket bayonet was not a very good knife, but it began to be replaced by the bayonet that was. This type was a knife or a short sword that typically had a catch in the pommel that attached to a stud on the gunstock and had a ring in the guard that slipped over the muzzle of the rifle. The German bayonet of the two world wars did away with the muzzle ring and attached the handle of the bayonet to a long bar below the rifle barrel. At first, most of these bayonets were quite long, one early British type had a blade more than 30 inches long. The idea was to make a bayonet long enough to keep cavalry at a safe distance when attached to a rifle. When it dawned on military authorities that cavalry was no longer a major combat arm, the bayonet started to shrink. Still, the M1917 bayonet the United States used in World War I had a blade 17 inches long. That made a handy short sword, but swords were even less likely to be used as serious weapons than bayonets. What the soldier needed was a knife—something that could open cans and other types of packaging, cut rope, carve wood or meat, cut the throat of an enemy sentry, or be used in very close quarters combat. In World War II, the bayonet for the M1 Garand rifle at first had a blade 10 inches long. In a later version, the blade was only 6.7 inches long, the same length as the bayonet for the M1 carbine.

When armies dropped the socket bayonet, they began issuing bayonets that could double for other types of tools. Both the British and the Germans once issued bayonets with saw teeth on the back. This was not, as some charged, to make a more frightful wound, but so that the bayonet could also be used as a saw. The United States issued a number of these specialized bayonets. One was *trowel bayonet*, which was designed to be either a weapon or an entrenching tool but was good for neither use. Another was a *Bowie bayonet*, a very peculiar device that bore little but superficial resemblance to the traditional Bowie knife. There was also the bolo bayonet, an excellent bush knife for use in the Philippine jungles but that, when mounted on a rifle, seriously unbalanced the weapon. Today, most bayonets are short knives with a special scabbard that allows them to be used as wire cutters.

In the 17th century, the bayonet changed warfare by making the pike obsolete and making all infantry gunners—in effect, doubling the firepower of the infantry. Since then, its importance as a serious weapon has greatly diminished, although it is still useful for crowd control. And in the Korean War, a bayonet charge by Company E of the Twenty-seventh Infantry Regiment routed the entrenched North Koreans opposed to them.

It should be noted, though, that this charge by a single infantry company was later hailed as "the greatest American bayonet charge since the battle of Cold Harbor" in the Civil War.

18

Little Bombs With Big Results:
Hand Grenades

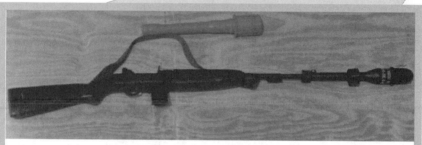

Two grenades. At top is a German "potato masher" hand grenade used in both World Wars. Below it is a rifle grenade fitted to a U.S. M 1 carbine.

The crowd lining the streets of Sarajevo was in a festive mood. Archduke Franz Ferdinand (the heir to the throne), was visiting, and the weather was perfect on July 28, 1914. The mayor of Sarajevo, proud as a peacock, rode by in the first car. The next car was the archduke's. He sat in the back seat, next to his beloved Sophie, the woman he married against the wishes of the emperor himself. As the royal car approached, a young man named Nedjelko Cabrinovic took what looked like a whiskey flask from a pocket, unscrewed the top, and struck it against a lamp post. Spectators heard a pop, then they saw Cabrinovic hurl the flask at the Archduke. Franz Ferdinand saw out of the corner of his eye what looked like a rock flying toward Sophie. He threw up his arm and blocked the missile. It fell on the street and exploded with a loud bang. People screamed. Several bystanders were wounded. Franz Ferdinand ordered the car to stop. He got out to make sure the injured spectators would get medical treatment, then got back in the car and proceeded to the city hall.

In a sense, the first shot of World War I had been fired. It was fired with a hand grenade.

Later, after a reception at the city hall, the archduke insisted on going to the hospital to visit people wounded in the attack. On the way to the hospital the chauffeur suddenly learned that he was going the wrong way. He stopped so he could turn around. He stopped right in front of another young man named Gavrilo Princip, who was, as Cabrinovic was, a member of the assassination conspiracy. Princip pulled out a pistol and shot and killed the archduke and his wife.

Princip used a Browning automatic pistol, a weapon so popular that "browning" became a synonym for automatic pistol in several European languages. But Cabrinovic's weapon was a Serbian army hand grenade. A description of the Serbian grenade shows how these little bombs had declined from being a major weapon of war from the 15th through 18th centuries to being mainly an assassination weapon in 1914. The Serbian grenade was flat, not as convenient a shape for throwing as later grenades, but a shape that let it fit in a pocket without causing suspicious bulges. Under the screw top of the "flask" was a percussion cap. Striking that on a hard surface ignited a short fuse. In short, the Serbian grenade was a weapon for clandestine use, not the battlefield.

The hand grenade had seen some battlefield use in the Russo-Japanese War and somewhat less by defenders of forts in the America Civil War and the American Revolution, but most military authorities saw little use for it before World War I. That's somewhat surprising, because the hand grenade was probably the earliest of all gunpowder weapons. The Chinese were using bamboo joints filled with gunpowder before anybody had guns. European records mention the use of grenades in the 15th century, when the principal missile weapons were the *longbow* and the *crossbow*. The grenade at that time was an iron sphere filled with gunpowder with a fuse projecting from a hole. A picture in *La Pyrotechnie*, a book published in 1620, shows a grenade filled with gunpowder and pistol balls. The bullets were packed like seeds in a pomegranate, and is why it was called a "grenade," which is Middle French for pomegranate.

Those early grenades weighed about 3 pounds. Both garrisons of fortresses and besiegers tossed grenades over walls at their enemies. Because few men could throw a 3-pound ball far enough to be out of range of those lead "seeds," grenade throwers liked to have a wall between themselves and their target. In the 17th century, when all European war revolved around capturing enemy strong points and supply depots, the grenade became a most important weapon. To use it, European armies picked tall, strong men. They had to have strong throwing arms, and they had to be able to lug sacks of grenades, which weighed between a 1 1/2-3 punds each. These "grenadiers" were most impressive-looking on parade, which some rulers such as Frederick William of Prussia seemed to think was an army's most important function. Grenadiers wore high, brimless hats so the brims wouldn't interfere with their throwing arms and to make them look even taller. The big, strong grenadiers were essential to the rapid storm tactics the Duke of Marlborough devised. They threw grenades to demoralize the enemy, then finished him off with musket and bayonet. Occasionally, though, they couldn't use their grenades. In 1710, Marlborough sent his grenadiers through neck-deep water to attack a position outside Bouchain. After that immersion, the grenade in the grenadiers' bags were as useful as so many sacks of stone. The water not only soaked the powder in the grenades, it extinguished the slow match every grenadier carried in a perforated metal case.

That slow match was one of the reasons the grenade was almost abandoned shortly before the Revolution. It made the grenadiers' job as dangerous as that of the matchlock musketeer. If a spark fell on a grenade fuse, the grenadier would become a human bomb, wiping out himself and anybody near him. Sometimes a sharp jar would set off a grenade. In addition to that, the weight of a sack of grenades detracted from mobility. So the grenade was largely abandoned. But the grenadiers were not. They looked too good. They became an elite corps, just as paratroopers have in modern times (even though the parachute is obsolescent and mass parachute jumps like those on D-Day in World War II will probably never happen again). Even countries with hardly any airplanes have parachute troops.

What brought the hand grenade back was trench warfare. The Western Front in World War I was a massive siege—the longest siege line in the history of the world with the most besiegers and defenders (each side had both). In the kind of close-quarters fighting that characterized struggles in the zigzag trenches and dugouts of the Western Front, the hand grenade was sometimes the *only* weapon that would work. The front-line infantrymen adopted the grenade before the military authorities. They filled old cans with TNT or gun cotton, sometimes with nails taped to them, sometimes with scraps of metal in the can with the explosive. To get more range when throwing the explosive, some soldiers taped their home-made bombs to wooden handles. Later, the German government issued its famous "potato masher" grenade with a wooden handle. Through World War I and later World War II, all nations continued to develop types of grenades.

There were incendiary grenades and gas grenades, smoke grenades and anti-tank grenades, offensive grenades and defensive grenades. *Defensive grenades* were designed to be used from cover: They sprayed the area with metal fragments, covering distance farther than most men could throw. *Offensive grenades* relied on concussion: they would kill only at a short distance, although at a somewhat longer distance they might temporarily disable an enemy. An attacker in the open could safely throw them. *Antitank grenades* had some sort of tail—fabric fins, bundles of hemp, or cloth streamers to make them fly point-first. They had to strike point-first because they had armor-piercing shaped charges in the nose. One Soviet antitank hand grenade was the RPG 43. "RPG," obviously, did not stand for "rocket propelled grenade" on this arm-propelled bomb any more than it does on the well-known RPG 7, a Soviet antitank weapon, which uses a recoilless gun to launch a rocket-assisted shell and has become every guerrilla's favorite hardware. Some incendiary grenades used thermite to create an intensely hot fire. Thermite could burn anything and could not be extinguished by water. Pushed down the barrel of a cannon, the thermite fire would weld the breechblock to the barrel and render the gun useless. Another type of incendiary grenade used white phosphorous, known to World War II and Korean War veterans as Willy Peter. White phosphorous ignites when exposed to air. When the grenade bursts, fragments of burning phosphorous filled the air. Willy Peter could inflict horrible burns on anyone it touched, but its primary purpose was to create a smoke screen.

The hand grenade was a favorite weapon of Orde Wingate, the maverick British general who invented new tactics in Palestine, Ethiopia, and Burma. Wingate favored the grenade for night fighting, when a rifle could not be aimed, because there was no way an enemy could tell from where the weapon had come. In World War II, Korea, and Vietnam, grenades were widely used as the basis for booby traps, as well as for attacking pill boxes and bunkers.

Some "military experts" have expressed doubt that hand grenades are worth their weight in modern warfare (such as Ray Bonds, author of *Advanced Technology Warfare*). One wonders if such experts have ever studied war from the vantage point of a front-line infantryman.

In World War I and later wars, there were frequently situations in which soldiers wished they could throw the grenade a little farther. That led to the rifle grenade. There were several ways of throwing a grenade with a rifle. One way was to place the grenade in a cup on the muzzle of the rifle and fire a blank cartridge. The gas blast armed the grenade and threw it toward the enemy. Another way used a long rod attached to the grenade. This was pushed down the barrel of the rifle, then propelled with a blank cartridge. Grenades especially designed to be fire from rifles were then issued. These usually had a hollow tail with fins that fitted over a device called a "grenade launcher," which was attached to the muzzle of the rifle. Again, a blank cartridge was the propelling force. After World War II, some grenades were made that could be launched with a regular cartridge. These had a steel block in the base of the grenade that stopped the bullet.

Presently, the United States and other forces use "grenade launchers" that are really separate guns. These use a 40 mm cartridge that has a small grenade instead of a bullet. The earliest models of this type of gun looked like a short, fat single-barrel shotgun, but now the U.S. grenade launchers are minimal guns that fit below the barrel of the standard rifle. NATO and Warsaw Pact countries also had automatic grenade launchers that looked like machine guns on steroids and fired a more powerful 40 mm grenade cartridge.

19

"Bombs Bursting in Air": Explosive Shells

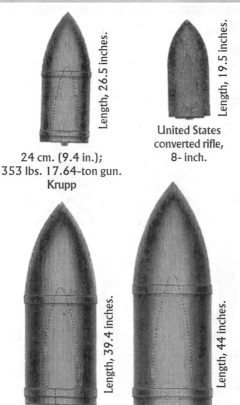

Length, 26.5 inches.

24 cm. (9.4 in.);
353 lbs. 17.64-ton gun.
Krupp

Length, 19.5 inches.

United States
converted rifle,
8- inch.

United States
smooth-bore,
15- inch

Length, 39.4 inches.

35.5 cm. (14 in.);
1155 lbs. 51-ton gun.
Krupp

Length, 44 inches.

40 cm. (15.7 in.);
1711 lbs. 71-ton gun.
Krupp

Length, 49.25 inches.

45 cm. (17.72 in.);
2005 lbs. 100-ton gun.
Krupp

One cannonball and a variety of explosive shells.

When Francis Scott Key located the flag by "the rockets' red glare and the bombs bursting in air," he was watching the effects of two weapons which had been developing for centuries and would turn into devices no one in the early 19th century could have imagined. Of the two—the rocket and the artillery shell—the rocket was far older. The Chinese had been using rockets in war before anybody had guns. And as we know, rockets would not only put men on the moon, they would develop into intercontinental engines of destruction.

The artillery shell, in contrast, was not quite three centuries old. The first recorded use was by the Turks at the siege of Rhodes in 1522. The Turkish bombards hurled huge shells over the walls of the fortress. The shells made a tremendous flash and noise when they exploded, but they weren't much good for knocking down walls. They could knock down flimsy houses and they could kill by concussion anyone unlucky enough to be near them when they went off. But mostly, they were useful only to terrify the defenders. In the case of Rhodes, though, the defenders were the Order of the Knights of the Hospital of St. John the Baptist of Jerusalem (the Crusading Knight Hospitalers), a military unit that was among the least susceptible to terror in all history. The Turks eventually took Rhodes after expending rivers of blood, but the explosive shells weren't much help. There was no indication in those days that the explosive shell would someday be the most deadly device in land warfare and the supreme weapon at sea.

The explosive shell developed from the hand grenade. The first shells were hollow metal spheres filled with gunpowder. There was a hole in the ball, and it was covered with a fireproof sack filled with a flammable compound. A hole in the sack, on the other side of the sphere, faced the gun's powder charge. When the gun went off, it ignited the compound in the sack, which burned around to the hole in the shell, and the shell exploded. Later, artillerymen used wooden or metal tubes filled with a priming compound. They hammered these into the hole in the shell. At first, they loaded the shell with the tube facing the gun's powder charge. Too often, though, the propelling charge did not merely ignite the shell's fuse. It drove the fuse into the shell, which then went off inside the gun, destroying the gun and gunners.

That led to double-firing—the gunner placed the shell in the gun with fuse facing the muzzle. He then lit the fuse and, immediately after, applied fire to the gun's touch-hole. This could only be done with short-barreled guns. There was no way a gunner could reach deep into a cannon's bore to ignite the shell. The early bombards had short barrels for the size of their shells. Later shell-firing guns were the mortar, a very short barreled gun that shot shells only at a high trajectory, and the howitzer, a gun with a slightly longer barrel that could fire shells at a higher velocity and on a flatter trajectory. With any gun, double-firing called for good reflexes and may be one of the reasons artillerymen, unlike most soldiers, were reputed to abstain from drunkenness, lechery, and the use of naughty words. If the gun misfired, the gunner would be standing right next to a bomb that would explode an instant later. Finally, someone discovered that the flash of the propelling charge would ignite the shell's fuse even if the fuse was facing the muzzle.

Early shells, then, were pretty dangerous gadgets to use. They were not much more dangerous, though, to the enemy. Because shells were hollow, they were useless for battering walls. The shell would either flatten or shatter on striking a stone wall, and an unconfined explosion would have little effect. Used against personnel, a shell would break up into a few large pieces. Gunpowder did not have the shattering effect of high explosive, so the carnage caused by shell fragments was unknown until the very late 19th or early 20th centuries. That's another reason first shells were used in mortars: those short-barreled cannons were used to threw their projectiles at a high angle to clear the walls of forts. The timing of shell bursts was none too precise in those early days. Shells frequently did not explode for some time after landing. At other times, they exploded before reaching the target—Keys's "bombs bursting in air."

A British artillery officer, Lieutenant Henry Shrapnel, saw a way to improve the shell's performance against personnel. He invented a shell that was much like the early hand grenades—an iron ball filled with lead bullets and enough gunpowder to burst it open.

Before the *shrapnel shell*, artillerymen had only three missiles to use against infantry. For long range use against infantry, they used *cannonballs*—"solid shot," in gunners' lingo. They fired directly at the lines of marching men. The shot skipped along the ground, ricocheting at flat angles and destroying whatever it hit. Against masses of infantry, like the Swiss or Spanish phalanxes, cannonballs were deadly, indeed. Fired against the flanks of the later "thin line" formation, they could also kill a number of men with one shot. That, however, took either extremely good marksmanship or a great deal of luck. Infantry could often evade destruction all together by falling flat, so the cannonballs flew over them. When the infantry got close, the artillery became extremely deadly. *Grape shot*—a number of iron or lead balls packed in a wood-reinforced canvass bag—, spread out like shot from a giant shotgun and took out bunches of infantrymen or cavalrymen before they got to musket range. When the attackers came closer, the gunners switched to *case* or *cannister shot*—smaller and more numerous balls packed in tin cans, which was even more deadly. Shrapnel's invention made it possible to produce the effects of grape or cannister shot at ranges impossible with small shot fired directly from the cannons Shrapnel shells accelerated the development of *howitzer*, shell guns that could fire directly at infantry. The knowledge that a cannon's muzzle blast would ignite a fuse even when facing away from the powder charge made shrapnel a popular choice for use against infantry or cavalry.

When rifled artillery capable of firing elongated projectiles was introduced, shrapnel shells were adapted to the new guns. These new shrapnel shells have been called "guns fired by guns." The bursting charge of gunpowder was in the rear of the shell. When ignited by the time fuse, it shot the load of lead balls out of the front of the shell. The shell was a kind of flying shotgun. Shrapnel was used extensively in the late 19th and early 20th centuries. It was the reason all armies adopted the steel helmet in World War I. Experience in that war, however, showed that shrapnel was no more effective against personnel than ordinary high explosive shells. High explosives shattered shells into thousands of jagged fragments, which killed exposed enemy soldiers quite efficiently, and high explosive could also destroy fortifications, something shrapnel could not do. Although the term is common today, shrapnel has not been used since the Spanish Civil War of 1936-1939. When newspaper accounts mention "shrapnel" they mean shell or bomb fragments.

High explosives have been around since the late 19th century, but at first they were far too sensitive to use as filling for shells. Around the turn of the 19th and 20th centuries, a peculiar weapon called a "dynamite gun" appeared. It had a long barrel and fired a comparatively small-caliber brass shell filled with dynamite. It did not use a normal propelling charge: The shock of the explosion might well detonate the shell before it left the gun. Instead, a small charge of black powder was fired in a tube beneath the gun barrel. This forced gas through a hole the barrel, giving the dynamite shell a gentle shove. The dynamite gun was used to some extent in the Cuban rebellion and the Spanish-American War that followed. When the shell landed, the blast was most impressive, but the thin-walled shell did not provide much fragmentation, and it exploded as soon as it hit anything more solid than air, which prevented penetration. And it was so dangerous, the gunners who used it were terrified of their weapon. As a result of these problems, the dynamite gun's career was short, and dynamite has not been used as a shell filling since. Artilleryists switched to more stable explosives like picric acid and TNT.

Shells and *cannons* have developed steadily. In World War II, a new, high tech fuse was developed to replace the ancient timed fuse based on a burning train of gunpowder and the more modern clockwork fuse. Timing was never precise with the gunpowder fuse, and even the clockwork type left much to be desired. The new "proximity fuse" used a miniature radar to explode the shell when it was a fixed distance from the target. No longer would air bursts be too high to be effective or delayed so long the shell buried itself in the ground before exploding. The new fuse made artillery an even more potent antiaircraft and anti-personnel weapon. In World War II about two thirds of the casualties among soldiers were caused by artillery.

20

The Spinning Ball: The Minie Rifle

Four Minie rifles, all with percussion locks, and a smoothbore flintlock.

General Lee's troops had been fighting here for three days. At around 3 p.m., July 3, 1863, the final stroke was about to begin. The three Confederate brigades of Pickett's division, joined by six more from Hill's corps—15,000 to 17,500 men—dressed ranks in a line 1,000 yards long and marched, rifles on their shoulders, toward the Union positions on Cemetery Ridge about a half-mile away.

Regimental battle flags fluttered in the breeze, as the troops marched in time with their drums. Robert E. Lee watched the steady lines admiringly, confident that his "invincible" troops would pierce the Union center and end this dreadful war.

A few minutes later, the steady lines, most of the regimental colors and all of the drums were gone. In their place was a panicked mob of about 7,000 men. Pickett's division, which had led the charge, had lost two thirds of its men.

Histories give much of the credit to the destruction of Pickett's Charge to the Union artillery, which had held its fire to save ammunition during the artillery duel that preceded the charge. But a much more potent force was the weapon in the hands of the common infantry soldier: the *minie rifle*. Because of the invention of Captain Charles Claude Etienne Minié of the French Army, rifles could at last be loaded as fast as smoothbores. In all modern armies, the infantry was equipped with rifles, called *rifle muskets* to show that they were basic military weapons, able to take bayonets, not the specialized rifles of the past, which were basically hunting weapons.

Rifles had been around since the 16th century, but they were so slow to load that the military had ignored them. The lead bullet had to be large enough to force the "lands," the raised portion of the spiral rifling, to cut into the bullet. That was necessary to impart a spin to the projectile as it traveled down the barrel. And that meant the slug had to be literally hammered down the barrel. Later, sportsmen discovered that, if the bullet was wrapped in a greased piece of cloth or leather, the rifling would spin it if the twist were not too rapid. But even using a greased patch, loading was still far slower than loading a smoothbore. Besides, black powder, the only propellant available at the time, left a lot of solid residue in the barrel. After a few shots, this black gunk filled the rifling grooves and made loading practically impossible.

What Captain Minié did was invent a bullet that was considerably smaller than the bore, so there was no trouble loading it, but that when the charge was fired, expanded into the rifling grooves and spun as it left the muzzle. Minié's first bullet had an iron cup inserted into the hollow base of the conical lead bullet. When the powder charge exploded, it drove the cup into the bullet, which forced the sides of the bullet into the grooves. Later ordnance experts discovered that the iron cup was not necessary: the explosion alone was enough to expand the base of the bullet. Because the Minié bullet was longer than a round ball, it was also heavier. That meant it had greater "sectional density," which resisted retardation by the atmosphere and gave it greater penetration. The close fit of bullet to the bore greatly increased accuracy. The bullet of a smoothbore, being smaller than the bore, literally bounced around inside the barrel as it traveled through the gun. And, of course, the spin imparted gyroscopic stability and prevented unequal air resistance on the front of the bullet.

A British officer in the Revolutionary War, Major George Hanger, said, "A soldier must be very unfortunate indeed who shall be wounded by a common musket at 150 yards, provided his antagonist aims at him." Hanger also said that only if a musket were perfectly bored, as few of them were, would a soldier be likely to be hit at 80 yards.

The rifled musket would hit man-sized targets at *800 yards*.

The American Civil War was a good—and gory—example of how generals fight the previous war and what happens when they do. Lee's tactics at Gettysburg would have seemed quite familiar to his fellow Virginian, George Washington. Pickett's troops lined up, dressed ranks, shouldered their rifles, and marched up to the enemy. But where soldiers in the 18th century might wait to see the whites of the enemies' eyes, the Yankees began picking off Pickett's men almost as soon as they began to march.

In the 1860 census, the population of the United States was 31,443,321. In the Civil War, there were 364,512 Union deaths and 133,821 Confederate deaths—although Confederate figures are almost certainly incomplete. Even with the grossly inadequate Confederate figures, that 498,333 death toll amounts to 1.6 percent of the entire population. In World War II, U.S. forces suffered 407, 316 deaths; the U.S. population was 132,164,569 in the 1940 census. The American Civil War remains in both proportionate and absolute term the bloodiest war in our history.

That was the result of the universal use of rifled weapons and smoothbore tactics.

Besides the slaughter of infantry, the Minié bullet—"minnie ball" to the troops—also meant the end of the traditional cavalry charge. A man on horseback makes a big target, and he can seldom lie down or take advantage of cover provided by the terrain. After a few bloody lessons, the generals adapted cavalry tactics to the new conditions more quickly than they changed infantry tactics. Most of the cavalry fighting in the Civil War was done by dismounted troopers. Cavalry were used mostly as mounted infantry and some mounted infantry outfits, like Wilder's "Lightning Brigade," were used as cavalry.

Towards the end of the Civil War, American infantry occasionally modified the traditional charge by increasing the use of skirmishers and advancing by rushes. On the defensive, they used trenches and other field fortifications to an extent unseen until World War I. It took a long time for the lessons to really sink in, though, especially in Europe. In South Africa, the British had to relearn the lessons in 1881 and in 1899 when faced with improved rifles (see Chapter 24). And in World War I, there were still cavalry units on the Western Front preparing to exploit the breakthroughs that never came.

21

Sailing Into the Wind: The Steam Powered Warships

U.S. steam frigate *Pensacola* in 1861.

For thousands of years, most mariners had dreamed of being able to take a large cargo anywhere they wanted without worrying about wind and currents. High-ranking British naval officers in the 19th century were the exception. We'll come to that in a moment.

Ships propelled by oars could, of course, proceed into the wind (although progress was a lot slower than if there were no wind), but the large number of rowers precluded carrying much cargo and ensured that such ships as the Greek triremes (a galley with three banks of rowers) could not go far from land. Primitive sails like those of the classical galleys or the Arab dhows could take a vessel a long distance if the wind were favorable, but not if it were in the wrong direction. That's why a dhow plying the Indian Ocean trade took a year to make a round trip. Half of the year the winds blew to the West; the other half, to the East. Scandinavian seamen learned to manipulate a square sail to allow some progress against the wind, as did Arab sailors using the lateen sail. But even after Europeans developed the full-rigged ship, progress could be slow unless the weather cooperated. If there was no wind, progress was nil.

The steam engine changed sailing radically, and that transformed warfare at sea. But the steam engine would not have been possible without a previous advance in the art of war. In the 18th century, a Swiss gunfounder named Jean Maritz, improved the rough, sometimes-crooked bores of cannons by inventing a machine for boring out the barrel after the gun was cast solid, instead of incorporating the bore in the casting. A few years later, in 1774, a British engineer named John Wilkinson improved the machine. Wilkinson's device created an extremely smooth and precise hole. With a machine like that, the pioneers of steam power were able to build cylinders with tight-fitting, efficient pistons. Such cylinder and piston arrangements are essential to early steam engines as well as modern internal combustion engines.

The first *steam engines* worked by filling a cylinder with steam, then condensing it to water. The vacuum created drew the piston *into* the cylinder. These "atmospheric" engines were useful for pumping out mines and other tasks where their weight was not important. They were far too heavy and bulky to use aboard ships, however. James Watts's improved steam engine drove the piston in the opposite direction—expanding steam, rather than atmospheric pressure on a vacuum was the driving force. Such engines could be made small enough to power a ship. Their earliest use was to turn a pair of huge side wheels.

Steam gave navies a great strategic advantage. Steam warships no longer depended on weather and could cross the oceans much faster than sailing ships. "Seizing the weather gauge" (maneuvering into the best location to take advantage of the wind) had long been a favorite tactic of British seamen. It no longer gave any advantage. For that reason, Britain, although it was the home of the first steam engines and it utterly depended on its navy for its primacy in world affairs, tried to retard the development of steam-powered ships. British naval personnel were the most skilled in the world; British shipyards devoted to building sailing men-of-war were the biggest in the world; British technology in preserving food for long journeys, manufacturing the heavy, short-range cannons, called *carronades*, and everything else needed for wooden, sail-driven warships, led the world. If the world's navies went to steam, all of that would be worthless.

In 1828, the British admiralty expressed their views on steam-powered warships:

> Their lordships feel it is their bounden duty to discourage to the utmost of their ability the employment of steam vessels, as they consider that the introduction of steam is calculated to strike a fatal blow at the naval supremacy of the Empire.

In spite of the size of the British Navy, this policy bore more than a little resemblance to the actions of an earlier British authority figure: King Canute, who tried to tell the tide to reverse itself. The American, Robert Fulton, had built a working steam ship as early as 1807. In 1837, the paddle wheel steamer *Sirius* crossed the Atlantic in 18 days—breathtaking speed in an era when *Atlantic* crossings were measured in months.

Although the new method of propulsion had manifest advantages, the world's navies did not immediately board the steamship. The French started building steam warships in the 1840s, but they did so on a small scale. There were a number of reasons for this slow progress. There was the natural conservatism of sailors and military men, and that the British, owners of the world's most powerful navy, professed to see little value in the new technology. And, most important, there was the fact that the early steamships could not survive a battle with sailing warships of comparable size. The huge paddle wheels on each side of the vessel were vulnerable to gunfire, and they made it impossible for the ship to carry enough cannons along the side to match the broadsides of a sailing ship. Another drawback was that steamships could not stay at sea nearly indefinitely, as the sailing ships could. They had to be near a supply of coal.

The paddle wheel was the first drawback eliminated. In its place, ship builders used the screw propeller. The new device had to rotate much faster than a paddle wheel, which meant both major changes in gearing and much more efficient engines. John Ericsson, a Swedish engineer, invented both a screw propeller that worked and an engine to drive it. He sold the designs to the U.S. Navy, and in 1842 the U.S.S. *Princeton* became the world's first screw-propelled steamship. *Princeton*'s engine and drive shaft were located below the waterline for protection, and the ship was able to carry enough guns for a broadside. In 1843, the British steamer *Great Britain* became the first screw-equipped ship to cross the Atlantic.

The age of steam had arrived. Ship builders were still hedging their bets by equipping their vessels with masts and rigging that could be used if the engine failed, but it was hard to navigate a paddle wheeler using sails alone. Screw propellers made sailing easier, but even the propeller caused interference.

The next major improvement in warships was adding armor (something we'll look at in the next chapter). Another huge advance in steam engines after the introduction of armor was the steam turbine engine, which used a spinning wheel turned by rapidly expanding steam to propel the vessel. These engines made possible the high-speed torpedo boats that threatened the supremacy of the battleship at the turn of the 19th and 20th centuries. At the British Jubilee Naval Review in 1897, the steam launch *Turbinia* stole the show as it dashed in and out of the line of battleships at the unheard-of speed of 34 1/2 knots. We'll have another look at these torpedo boats in Chapter 26 on the "locomotive torpedo."

22

Iron Floats...and Sinks:
Armored Ships

Monitor and *Virginia* slug it out in 1862.

I n 1592, Toyotomi Hideoshi, the only peasant in Japanese history to make himself supreme ruler of that ancient empire, invaded the neighboring land of Korea. Hideoshi, called "Old Monkey Face," but not to his face, was a man of immense ambition and the energy to match it, although his esthetic tastes ran more to gold chamber pots than to his country's exquisite poetry. After Korea, he planned to conquer China and then the Philippines.

He never quite made his first goal (Korea). The biggest reason was a Korean secret weapon and an admiral named Yi Sun Shin.

While the Japanese fleet was unloading at Pusan, several strange-looking objects moved into the harbor. They had no sails. They may have been towed or rowed—accounts differ. All agree, however, that they looked like immense metal turtles. Below their curved iron shells, Yi's *turtle boats* had rows of cannons. That day the turtle boats, designed by Yi himself, sank 60 Japanese ships and stalled Hideoshi's invasion at its opening.

The Japanese eventually began moving up the peninsula. At that time, the Japanese army had more guns per capita than any other in the world—including anywhere in Europe. Almost all of their guns were matchlock harquebuses; they had few cannons. The Koreans had few handheld guns, but quite a few cannons. And they had allies. Chinese troops flooded into the peninsula. The Japanese were better armed, better trained, and more experienced soldiers, but they couldn't match the Chinese numbers. Then Yi Sun Shin returned with his turtle boats. In 1598, at Chinhae Bay, Yi and his ironclads sank 200 of the 400 Japanese ships. Yi lost his life in the battle, but he saved his country. The rest of the Japanese fleet fled back to Japan, where they brought news of the disaster to the ailing Hideoshi, who promptly died. The Japanese invasion died with him. Korea was to be free of Japanese troops until 1910.

Fast forward 270 years. Yi Sun Shin and his works have been forgotten everywhere but Korea. In the United States, no one is interested in old tales from exotic places. The country has split into two parts, North versus South, and brothers are fighting brothers. Ships from the North, what is left of the United States, or the "Union," are blockading ports in the South, or the "Confederacy."

Confederate troops captured the navy yard at Gosport, Virginia. The Union made an attempt to destroy everything of value before they evacuated the yard, but the Confederates managed to raise the sunken U.S.S. *Merrimack*, a 40-gun steam frigate. Confederate naval architects changed the former Union warship into something entirely new. They gave the frigate a sloping superstructure composed of two 2-inch-thick layers of wrought iron. The weight of all that iron pushed the ship low in the water, but the Confederates added still more iron—a 1-inch belt of iron around the hull that extended 3 feet below the waterline. The completed vessel, rechristened the C.S.S. *Virginia,* had a draft of 22 feet. There was no way it could take the weight of the old *Merrimack's* 40 guns. It had four smoothbore cannons on each side and one 7-inch rifled gun at the bow and another at the stern. Even with the reduced armament, *Virginia's* draft was too deep to allow movement in shallow water, and its deck was so close to the waterline that steaming on the open ocean would be extremely hazardous.

The prime Confederate objective, though, was not to create an ocean-going warship. It was to get rid of the Yankee ships blockading Virginia. For that, this new class of ship, called a *ram* (because its bow carried that ancient weapon of the classical galleys), seemed ideal. On March 8, 1862, the C.S.S. *Virginia*, chugged into Hampton Roads and confronted five Union warships, the United States Ships *Minnesota, Roanoke, St. Lawrence, Cumberland,* and *Congress*. The clumsy, underpowered ram chugged toward *Cumberland*, firing as she advanced. *Cumberland* fired back at what one witness said looked like "a barn roof floating on the water." The Union ship's iron cannonballs merely bounced off the monster, and its shells exploded harmlessly on the armor. The *Virginia* drove its ram into *Cumberland*'s hull. When it backed away, the ram was wrenched off, but there was a 7-foot hole in the Union ship. *Cumberland* went to the bottom, some of its guns still firing as the water closed over them.

Virginia next engaged the U.S.S. *Congress*. Its guns proved as potent as its ram. One shot hit *Congress's* powder magazine and blew the blockader up. News of the Confederate ironclad's victories caused a near panic in Washington. Ironclads were not unknown to the U.S. Navy. They had already been tried in Europe.

Until the mid-19th century, all warships were protected by enormously thick hulls of seasoned oak. To make any impression at all on these masses of hardwood, ships closed to pistol range before firing their cannons. The missiles fired were exclusively solid shot—cast iron cannonballs, sometimes two cannonballs connected with a chain ("chain shot") or an iron bar ("bar shot") to take down masts and rip up rigging. In 1822, Colonel Henri Joseph Paixhans, a French army officer, proposed firing shells in naval warfare. Shells, being much lighter for their size than cannonballs, had no chance of penetrating those massive oak hulls, so they had never been used. But Paixhans, being a soldier, was not inhibited by naval tradition. He pointed out that even if a shell did not penetrate one of those wooden walls (if it lodged in a hull and exploded), it would do a lot of damage. It would also throw hot metal fragments and bits of blazing wood far and wide. Sails, tarred rope, and wood all burn readily.

In 1853, the Russian Navy tested Paixhans' theory. At the Battle of Sinope, a Russian squadron firing shells burned a 12-ship Turkish squadron. France and Britain, fearing the Russian capture of Constantinople and the entrance to the Black Sea, went to war with Russia. To counter the scary new "shell gun," they turned to iron. In the ensuing Crimean War, the French used three armored floating batteries to demolish Russian forts. They followed that by launching, in 1859, *La Gloire*, the first armored, steam-powered battleship.

Word that the Confederates were building an ironclad woke up authorities in Washington. Congress appropriated money for three armored ships, *Galena*,

New Ironsides, and *Monitor.* The first two looked like conventional ships, but *Monitor,* the smallest, was revolutionary. Its deck was barely above the water. It had a 4-inch-thick belt of homogeneous armor and a revolving turret—the word's first—made of 4-inch-thick iron. The two ironclads slugged it out for two hours. At one point, *Virginia* ran aground, but she backed into deeper water before *Monitor* could make a kill. Later, a shell from *Virginia* exploded on *Monitor's* pilot house—a tiny, boxlike structure on her deck—wounding the captain. *Monitor* temporarily stopped firing, and *Virginia* took advantage of the pause to steam back to Norfolk and the protection of the Confederate forts. Because *Monitor* stopped firing, the Confederates claimed a victory, and, because *Virginia* ran away, the Yankees claimed a victory. Actually, it was a draw, tactically. Strategically, the Confederates had been defeated. *Virginia* never again threatened a Union ship and the Confederates scuttled her when they had to abandon Norfolk.

The affair at Hampton Roads was the first battle between ironclads, but it was hardly the only use of iron ships during the Civil War. The Union built a number of sea-going ironclads, including *New Ironsides*, which mounted the heaviest gun yet put on a ship and which won renown as a fort-destroyer, a whole fleet of monitors with one or two revolving turrets, and a swarm of iron-clad river boats, which were instrumental in the Union's victorious campaigns in the West. The Confederacy, too, built a number of ironclads, although its industrial capacity was limited. The biggest was the C.S.S. *Tennessee,* which was defeated and captured at the Battle of Mobile Bay. *Tennessee*, like *Virginia*, was a ram, a class of warship invented by the Confederates and used only in the Confederate Navy. The U.S.S. *Monitor* was also the original of a class of ships called monitors—small, low-lying ships with extremely heavy guns in revolving turrets. Monitors were used in many navies: the British and Austrians were using them in World War I. Neither the rams nor the monitors were good for ocean travel because their decks were so low, so neither type was the wave of the future.

Armored ships with high freeboards were, however. Unlike the original ironclads—wooden ships covered with iron armor—the new warships were built entirely of iron and, later, steel. All steel construction made it possible to build them bigger and drive them with more powerful engines.

The victories of Yi Sun Shin in the 16th century were spectacular, but they led to no permanent change in naval warfare. The indecisive fight between *Virginia* and *Monitor*, however, changed warfare permanently.

23

"Damn the Torpedoes!": Naval Mines

From the Connecticut River Museum, Essex, Connecticut

Reproduction of David Bushnell's submarine, *American Turtle*, which failed to place a mine beneath a British frigate in 1776. This model, in the Connecticut River Museum in Essex, Connecticut, was actually tested and found to work as a navigable submarine.

Drawing showing how Bushnell's *Turtle* was operated.

It was 1864, and only one port in the Confederate States—Mobile, Alabama—remained open. Now David Glasgow Farragut, commanding a fleet of four ironclad monitors and fourteen wooden ships, was attempting to close it. Mobile was heavily fortified, and in its harbor was the C.S.S. *Tennessee*, a huge armored ram, a larger version of the famed C.S.S. *Virginia* (*nee Merrimack*).

Farragut was on the wooden frigate *Hartford*. When the battle began, Farragut wanted to be able to see what was happening, and he could get a better view from the tall *Hartford* than from one of the low-lying monitors. The old sea dog climbed a mast so his view wouldn't be obscured by the smoke of *Hartford's* guns. Farragut was not a young man: he was a veteran of the War of 1812. So a quartermaster tied him to the mast for safety. His age and long service in the navy had not made Farragut a tactical conservative. He sensibly positioned the monitors between the Confederate Fort Morgan and the more vulnerable wooden ships.

Suddenly, the water under the lead monitor seemed to explode. The armored ship lurched, tipped up, and sank like a piece of iron. The Union fleet stopped.

"There are torpedoes ahead," someone told the commodore.

"Damn the torpedoes! Full speed ahead!" the old man yelled.

Crewmen on *Hartford* later said they could hear the "triggers of the torpedoes snapping" as the flagship steamed past them. Fortunately, none exploded. Then *Tennessee* tried to ram the Union flagship, but Farragut's frigate was too agile for the armored monster. The monitor U.S.S. *Chickasaw* got behind *Tennessee* and pounded one spot with 11-inch cannonballs until it made a breach in the big ram's armor. *Chickasaw* continued firing and the Confederate flagship filled with smoke. One shot cut the ram's tiller chain, and another injured Confederate Admiral Franklin Buchanan. The Confederate ship surrendered. Farragut had closed the last Southern port in spite of the torpedoes.

The *torpedo* (what we call a *mine* today) was a relatively new weapon in 1864. A few years before then, in 1829, a 14-year-old Yankee inventor named Sam Colt had demonstrated how an underwater powder charge could be set off by electricity. The demonstration did not increase young Colt's popularity: Onlookers were showered with muddy water, but Colt showed how devastating a small charge of explosive could be when exploded against a boat under water. The water tamped the explosive, so that the greatest force of the explosion was directed against the boat.

The Russians used mines during the Crimean War of 1855-56, but no ships were sunk. The first ship sunk by a mine was the gunboat U.S.S. *Cairo* at the Battle of Yazoo River in 1862.

In 1866, a Scotsman and an Austrian invented a new kind of torpedo—one that went after an enemy ship instead of waiting to be hit. At first (as we'll see in Chapter 26) the new weapon was called a "locomotive torpedo." Later, it became simply the torpedo. That meant there had to be a new term for the stationary weapon. For centuries, stationary explosive charges had been placed in tunnels under enemy positions—in a mine (one that was dug to put something in rather than take something out). So the explosive charge buried in water instead of land became the naval mine or simply the mine.

Although the new torpedo could chase enemy ships, the old mine did not become obsolete. Far from it. Mines have become a key part of just about all wars that involve ships. Weak naval powers depend on them heavily. Mines cost less than ships, but few ships can hit a mine and avoid a trip to Davy Jones's Locker. Strong naval powers also used mines extensively. Both sides used mines in the Russo-Japanese War. The Russians lost a battleship, a cruiser, two destroyers, and a couple of smaller ships to Japanese mines. The Japanese Navy suffered more losses from mines than from any other weapon—two battleships, four cruisers, two destroyers, a torpedo boat, and a minelayer. In World War I, the British laid a "mine barrage" between Britain and Norway and between Britain and France to cut off Germany's access to the Atlantic. Later, the British Navy, the world's largest, was joined by the U.S. Navy, the world's second largest at the time, and the two allies made the mine barrage practically leakproof. Germany began to starve.

Mines in the mine barrage were all moored mines. Belligerents sometimes used drifting mines, but a loose mine is worse than a loose cannon. One can seldom accurately predict where winds and currents will take a drifting mine, so it is a danger to neutral and friendly shipping. A moored (or anchored) mine, like a drifting mine, has enough air in it to float, but it is attached to a sinker. As the sinker sinks, it pays out a previously determine length of cable. When the predetermined length is reached, the sinker's cable drum locks, and the sinker pulls the mine down to a predetermined depth below the surface.

There are a variety of ways to detonate a mine. In World War I, the British used the Elia mine, which had a long lever attached to its side. If a ship struck the mine, it would probably move the lever, which would release a firing pin to strike the detonator. A more common mine, used by all belligerents in both world wars, relied on Hertz horns. The Hertz horn, a German invention, contained a glass vial with a bichromate solution. When the horn was crushed, the solution poured out of the broken vial and completed an electrical circuit that exploded the mine. A typical mine had Hertz horns protruding from all sides.

Some mines planted close to the shore have been detonated by electricity shot through a cable from the shore. This type, however, requires an observer to decide when an enemy ship is close enough to the mine, so it's much less popular than mines that set themselves off. Magnetic mines were widely used in World War II. The ship's magnetic field triggered the mine's firing mechanism. Because of magnetic mines, all steel naval ships in World War II were equipped with *degaussing cables*. These were cables run around the gunwales of the ship. An electrical charge ran through the cables, neutralizing the ship's magnetic field. "Limpet mines" used magnetism to attach themselves to the bottoms of ships. A United States model, intended to be attached by divers, had a plastic case and weighed only 10 pounds. It was attached by six magnets and had a timing mechanism that allowed divers to get away.

An Italian mine of this type looked like something devised for the Japanese Imperial Navy, the home of the kamikazes. It was a long torpedo, straddled by two divers. The divers would steer their subsurface craft up to an enemy ship, detach the large warhead below the enemy ship, set the timing mechanism, and get away as fast as they could.

The Italian "human torpedo" was designed to be launched by a submarine mother ship. Subs frequently laid mines, usually through their torpedo tubes. Other mines were parachuted into the water from airplanes. Some of them had sinker mechanisms for mooring them. Others, especially magnetic mines or those set off by the noise of a ship's engines, merely lay on the bottom of the sea. These were, of course, most useful in relatively shallow waters.

The mines Farragut encountered were defensive weapons. Almost all mines were defensive until World War II. In that war, though, the airplane and the submarine, particularly the former, allowed one country to mine an enemy's harbors. Because the enemy had probably mined its own harbors, distinguishing friendly from enemy mines complicated the minesweepers' task.

Mines, unseen and almost undetectable, have added a spooky element to naval warfare that would have been utterly foreign to John Paul Jones.

24

Hidden Gunmen: The Breech-Loading Rifle

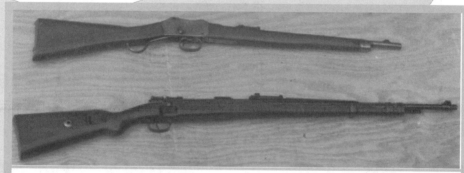

Two breech-loading rifles: top, Martini-Henry single shot carbine, used by both sides in the Boer War; bottom, German Mauser 1898 k, from World War II.

It was December 20, 1881, and the Boers were making trouble again. To keep the "dumb Dutchmen" in line, the British authorities in Capetown sent a column of Connaught Rangers under a colonel named Ansthruther into what the British called the Transvaal and the Afrikaners called the South African Republic. Ansthruther and his men had no particular worries. British troops had soundly defeated the Afrikaners in 1842 and again in 1848. The British considered the Afrikaners, whom they called "Boers" (Dutch for farmers), a feeble foe—not to be compared with such native warriors as the Zulus.

Colonel Sir Owen Lanyon, the British proconsul in the "Transvaal," said that the "Boers" were incapable of united action and, moreover, they were "mortal cowards."

Actually, united action did not come easy to these descendants of the Dutch settlers who came to South Africa about the same time their countrymen were landing in New York. The government of the South African Republic could be described as anarchy tempered by bankruptcy. That was the reason the British gave for taking over the country in 1877. The fiercely independent Afrikaners had no regular army. When danger threatened, all the men in a district would form a military unit called a commando and elect officers. Each man brought his own weapon and his own horses. The system had been reasonably effective against native warriors who had no guns, no wagons, and no horses, but it had not been able to cope with highly trained troops like the British regulars.

As Ansthruther's column approached a stream called Bronkhorst Spruit, a mounted Afrikaner galloped up and told the colonel that any further advance would be considered an act of war by the South African Republic. He gave Ansthruther two minutes to decide what to do.

Ansthruther didn't need two minutes. He told the messenger he had orders to march to Pretoria and he intended to follow his orders. The messenger galloped away. Ansthruther halted the column and waited for a reply. He took no security measures. His soldiers saw a few men in civilian clothes flitting through the scrub. They began to unsling their rifles.

A long, ripping volley exploded from the bushes. In a few minutes, Anstruther was dead and 120 of the Irish troops were dead or wounded. Afrikaner losses totaled two killed and five wounded.

That British defeat was followed by a series of disasters. General Sir George Pomeroy Colley, high commissioner for South Africa, gathered 1,200 troops, six cannons, and a rocket battery to attack Afrikaner trenches in the Drakensburg Mountains. The British were repulsed with heavy losses. Of the 480 men who made the charge, 150 never returned. The losses were heavier than the statistics indicate. A newspaper account reported that "Sublieutenant Jopp now commands the Fifty-eighth Regiment." Sharpshooting Afrikaners had taken out all the regiment's senior officers. Colley led a 300-man reconnaissance patrol that ran into an equal number of Afrikaner mounted infantry. The South Africans dismounted and crept through the bushes, sheltering behind rocks and in low places in the ground, firing all the time. They surrounded Colley's force and would have annihilated it if a cloudburst hadn't given the British an opportunity to sneak out of the trap.

Finally, the Afrikaners attacked Colley and his men, who were holding a mountain called Majuba Hill. Hidden riflemen at the base of the mountain fired at every redcoat who tried to look over the crest of the hill, keeping the British force blind. At the same time, the attacking commando made its way up the slopes, taking advantage of all available cover. They reached the crest, stood up, and fired at the front-line troops, killing most of them. Then, mostly hidden by brush and earth, they fired into the mass of the British. They killed Colley and killed or wounded most of his men. The rest fled precipitously, some falling to their deaths from cliffs on the mountainside. The Afrikaners suffered one killed and five wounded.

The Afrikaner militia were rank amateurs in war; the British were long-service troops, some of whom had recently been in combat in Afghanistan. How could this have happened?

Afrikaner success was entirely dependent on a single item:the *breech-loading rifle*. The breech-loader let the South African farmers take advantage of their natural strengths, but it did nothing for regular troops like the British who clung to the techniques of fighting with the *muzzle-loader*.

It was not impossible to load a muzzle-loader without standing up, but it was extremely difficult. The muzzle had to be higher than the breech of the rifle, and that meant that the rifleman could not load his piece from the prone position. Consequently, all armies for most of the 19th century trained their troops to stand up when loading. And, after loading, it was easier and quicker to fire from the standing position. In the British and other regular armies this was done by firing volleys on command. And, in spite of the slaughter that resulted from their use in the American Civil War, most armies continued to use the charges Frederick the Great had perfected for troops armed with smooth-bore muskets.

In 1881, the Afrikaners were blessed by having no regular military tradition. They knew nothing of close-order drill, volley firing on command, saluting, or any other regular military practices. Every man was a hunter, though. They depended on hunting for most of their meat. Hunters learned early to stalk game, to stay hidden from the animals' suspicious eyes while they closed in on their targets. The breech-loading rifle was a great boon to hunters. They could lie prone and hidden from the game while they loaded and fired their rifles. Hunters knew, too, that if they missed, the game would probably be long gone. Most of the Afrikaners had single-shot breech-loaders such as the Westley Richards, the Martin-Henry, or the Remington Rolling Block. Only a few had repeaters like the Winchester or the Swiss Vetterli. They learned to make the first shot count. Target shooting was a major sport for Afrikaner farmers. They usually shot at hens' eggs perched on posts 100 yards away.

The British, on the other hand, were not marksmen in 1881. They got little rifle practice, and what shooting they did was volley firing in a way that would have warmed the heart of General Edward Braddock in 1755.

The "Boer" farmers in 1881 were at least a generation ahead of their time. Although only a few of them had repeating rifles, the tactics they used proved to be just right for hand-operated repeaters like the bolt actions almost universally used in the early 20th century, and even for semiautomatics such as the U.S. M 1 (Garand) rifle used in World War II and Korea. Most regular armies, however, did not seem to appreciate that modern rifles allowed a soldier to produce lethal fire while remaining hidden from his foe until the time of the Spanish-American War of 1898 or the Second Boer War of 1899.

The development of automatic weapons opened a new chapter of infantry tactics, as we'll see in the sections on machine guns, submachine guns, and assault rifles, but, in the development of infantry tactics, the introduction of the breech-loading rifle was the most revolutionary advance since the introduction of the rifle itself.

25

The Ultimate Horse Pistol: The Revolver

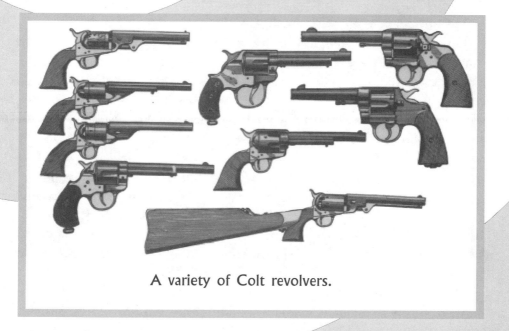

A variety of Colt revolvers.

For a while, the westward expansion of the United States stopped at the edge of the forest, a line that ran roughly south from central Minnesota to eastern Texas. Would-be settlers faced a new and daunting environment: the Great Plains. There were almost no trees, making it difficult to build log cabins. Streams and rivers were also rarer—a hardship for people who did much of their travel by canoe. And the Indians were different; they rode horses. The Plains Indians were the biggest obstacle to settling that sea of grass. The weapons pioneers had evolved for life in the forested wilderness, the long knife, the tomahawk, and the long rifle were less effective against the riders of the plains. Plains Indians seldom closed for hand-to-hand fighting unless their foes were exhausted, greatly outnumbered, or otherwise severely handicapped, so the knife and the tomahawk were almost useless. The long rifle was still lethal, but it was slow to load and hard to manage on a horse. To cope with the Indians, the pioneers needed horses. The Native Americans specialized in hit-and-run raids, disappearing into the vast grasslands whenever they encountered serious resistance. They fought on horseback, riding around their enemies while they shot dozens of arrows from their short, powerful bows.

Horses were no problem to the newcomers to the West, but the earliest ones had no weapon to match the rapid fire of the Indians' bows. Their rifles were slow and clumsy; their single-shot pistols were not clumsy, but they were painfully slow if rifled and horribly inaccurate if smoothbores. A new weapon was needed.

At the right time the revolver appeared.

Among the earliest users of revolvers were the Rangers of the Republic of Texas. The Texas Rangers of the 1830s and 40s were not a mere state police force. They were a military organization primarily charged with protecting settlers on the frontier (which included most of Texas). They found that the revolver was just the weapon they needed. In one instance, a group of 15 rangers under Captain Jack Hays drove off a war party of 75 Comanches, reportedly killing 35 of them.

The revolver was not really a new weapon. Since the 16th century, inventors had been making pistols with either revolving barrels or revolving chambers that lined up with a single barrel. There were *matchlock revolvers*, in which the barrels or cylinder were rotated by hand to a place where the match could reach the priming pan. There were *snaphaunce* and *flintlock* revolvers, some that rotated automatically when the cock was pulled back and others that had to be rotated by hand. Inventors had been trying for centuries to build a pistol that could fire several shots without reloading. But until the 19th century, nobody had come up with a practical gun. The multi-barrel pistols were inevitably heavy and clumsy, and all of the early revolvers had trouble keeping powder in the priming pan over each chamber. In addition, in that pre-machine tool era, it was difficult to make the cylinder and barrel of a single-barrel revolver fit closely enough to prevent excessive amounts of gas escaping at the juncture of the cylinder and the barrel.

In 1818, three Massachusetts men—Artemas Wheeler, Elisha Collier, and Cornelius Coolidge—patented a flintlock revolver with a number of improvements. There was no need to keep powder in each priming pan: It automatically primed a chamber when cocked. Further, when the cylinder was aligned with the barrel and the shooter pulled the trigger, a spring forced the cylinder forward so it fitted over the end of the barrel, eliminating gas escape. In 1895, Russia adopted the *Nagant revolver*, which was widely hailed as revolutionary, because it had a similar system of closing the cylinder-barrel gap. In spite of its improvements, only about 300 of these so-called Collier revolvers were made. They were probably too complicated for reliability.

The introduction of percussion caps gave a boost to revolver manufacture. At first, the only revolvers were multi-barrel "pepperbox" pistols. They were too heavy and most of them had heavy, double-action trigger pulls, which, as they had no sights, made them inaccurate. Then Samuel Colt brought out his *single-barrel, percussion-primed revolver*. Colt's revolvers, made at a plant in Paterson, New Jersey, had a cylinder that could be easily detached. Soldiers found that they could carry separate loaded cylinders to give them a quick reload after emptying their guns. The Texas Rangers snapped up Colt's revolvers and put them to good use. That brought the new weapon considerable publicity, and the U.S. Army ordered more for its mounted dragoons in the Seminole War. When the war with Mexico broke out, there was a big demand for Colt's revolvers. Unfortunately, the Colt revolver business had gone out of business, and Colt could not even find one of his guns to use as a model for resuming production.

General Zachary Taylor on the Mexican border requested a thousand Colt revolvers and sent one of his officers, Captain Samuel Walker—a former Texas Ranger—to Whitneyville, Connecticut, where Colt had borrowed factory space to make new guns. Colt worked from memory in designing a new gun, incorporating many suggestions from Captain Walker, who had used the older model in combat. The huge, powerful "Walker Colt" was received enthusiastically, and the Colt business, which moved to a new factory in Hartford, Connecticut, was assured permanent prosperity. Improved revolvers were churned out by Colt and its competitors. Metallic cartridges made loading easier and greatly increased reliability. Double-action trigger mechanisms increased the speed of fire and improved metallurgy made guns stronger and more reliable.

The American Civil War not only established the revolver as a standard military weapon, it changed cavalry tactics. The traditional cavalryman was armed with a saber and a smoothbore carbine or a pair of smoothbore pistols. And the traditional cavalryman disdained his firearms.

"The fire of cavalry is at best innocent," said "Light Horse Harry" Lee, the Revolutionary father of Robert E. Lee. For Lee, the saber was the only effective weapon for the horseman. Epaphras Hoyt, another Revolutionary cavalryman, wrote, "It is generally agreed by experienced officers that fire arms are seldom of any great utility in a cavalry engagement."

The revolver was rifled—making it far more accurate than the smoothbore horse pistol—and it could get off six shots before the older gun could fire two. Moreover, the revolver could be quickly reloaded with spare cylinders. Still, most regular cavalry officers had much the same view of cavalry pistols as "Light Horse Harry." In 1870, the U.S. Army's Small Arms and Accoutrements Board declared that the single-shot Remington pistol was "an excellent weapon." The British lancers did not replace their single-shot muzzle-loading pistol until 1872. And in the 20th century, right before World War I, Erskine Childers, an Irish veteran of the Second Boer War, gained a reputation as a revolutionary military thinker by writing two books deploring the British cavalry's dependence on the saber and the lance.

In the American Civil War, many of the senior officers were catapulted to high command from civilian life or from the ranks of very junior officers. One of the latter was Philip H. Sheridan, a captain at the beginning of the war, who rose to command all of the cavalry of the army of the Potomac. Sheridan, no physical giant, recruited cavalrymen who weighed 125 pounds or less, so they wouldn't tire the horses. They were light but heavily armed. In addition to their sabers (de rigueur in the Union Army), they had repeating carbines and two revolvers each. They relied on their carbines when they fought dismounted (which was frequently) and their revolvers when they fought on horseback. John Singleton Mosby, a lawyer in civilian life, went from being a private in the Confederate Army to a guerrilla leader who controlled a wide expanse of northern Virginia, including much of what is now suburban Washington, D.C. Mosby's men always fought mounted, and, for them, the revolver was almost the only weapon. Many carried as many as four or six revolvers.

On April 1, 1863, Mosby and 69 of his troopers were surprised by 150 Union cavalrymen led by Captain Henry C. Flint of the First Vermont Cavalry. Mosby's men barely had time to get on their horses.

"As Capt. Flint dashed forward at the head of his squadron, their sabers flashing in the rays of the morning sun, I felt like my final hour had come," Mosby later recalled. He and his men met the sabers with their revolvers. Flint was killed and his men routed. Mosby was promoted to major. Two weeks before that promotion, he had been promoted to captain.

The revolver had changed cavalry tactics, but the day of the horseman was rapidly fading, thanks to the rifle and the machine gun. And, as Childers pointed out in his two books, *War and the Arme Blanche* and *The German Influence on British Cavalry*, European cavalry officers had still not learned to take advantage of the revolver.

The revolver had a profound, but very short-lived effect on warfare. It and its successor, the *semiautomatic pistol,* are still important weapons. In the United States, until well into the 20th century, the prime criterion for selection of a handgun was its stopping power on horses. One American officer, evaluating the .38 caliber service revolver in 1900, complained of its lack of power: "Time after time I have seen it necessary to fire several shots in a horse's head in order to bring him down, when the man was very close. The Cavalry Pistol should be of such caliber and power, that either horse or man hit will be out of the fight."

In 1911, the United States adopted the .45 caliber Colt semiautomtic as the M1911 pistol, because the military authorities believed it had enough power to stop man or horse. The cavalry pistol was still to see some action, as in the mounted pistol charge at the Ojos Azules Ranch during the army's pursuit of Pancho Villa, but, after that, the pistol's main purpose was as a last-ditch self-defense weapon for officers and NCOs. One notable instance of that was in World War I when Corporal Alvin York used his M1911 to kill six Germans who charged him with bayonets during his celebrated skirmish in the Argonne Forest when he captured 132 Germans almost single-handed.

26

David as a Tin Fish:
The Modern Torpedo

National Archives from War Department

Torpedo being loaded aboard a U.S. submarine in 1918.

Not all torpedoes in the American Civil War were like those Farragut had damned (see Chapter 23). They didn't all lie in wait for a ship to hit them. There were two kinds that went after their prey. One was the *spar torpedo*, an explosive charge on the end of a long pole. The pole was attached to the bow of a small, fast surface vessel or a submarine. The attacker either rammed the torpedo into its prey, setting off the explosive, or it poked the torpedo under the enemy hull, then detonated it by pulling a string that released a firing pin. The second type was the *towed torpedo*. This was dragged through the water by a small fast boat that cut across the path of an enemy ship. The enemy ship hit the tow rope and dragged the torpedo against itself.

Some pirates in the South China Sea use a similar method. Two pirate boats connected by a cable straddle the path of a freighter during the night when most of the ship's crew can be expected to be asleep. The ship hits the cable and drags the two pirate boats against itself. The pirates then climb aboard and take over the ship.

This scenario indicates one of the problems in the use of the towed torpedo: What happens to the boat that was towing the torpedo? If the enemy did not hit the rope at the right spot, the tow boat would be slammed against the side of the enemy ship before the torpedo. The problem with both types of torpedo was that ideally they should be used by crews with suicidal tendencies. When the C.S.S. *Hunley*, a Confederate submarine, sank the U.S.S. *Housatonic* in the Civil War (the first time a submarine ever sank another ship) with a spar torpedo, *Hunley* sank herself.

In 1866, in what is now Trieste, Italy, but was then part of Austria, an Austrian naval captain named Luppis considered these problems. How could he make a torpedo that did not require a crew of Kamakazes? He consulted a Scottish engineer named Robert Whitehead, who was living in that part of Austria. Together, they devised a miniature unmanned submarine that carried an explosive charge, or "warhead," in its nose. Whitehead later made further improvements to the weapon and set up a company to manufacture "locomotive torpedoes," as they were called. He finally sold the company to Vickers, the British armaments giant.

Whitehead and Vickers managed to sell quite a few torpedoes although the early Whitehead torpedoes were not all that impressive. They carried a mere 18 pounds of explosive, traveled at a speed of six knots and had a maximum range of 370 yards. Furthermore, they lacked reliable control of direction and depth-keeping. Progress was rapid, however. By 1876, Whitehead torpedoes had a range of 600 yards; by 1905, they had a range of 2,190 yards. The next year, 1906, the range had jumped to 6,560 yards. By 1913, the year before World War II, the torpedo could travel 18,590 yards. Speed and control improved at the same rate as range. By World War II, the Japanese "Long Lance" torpedo—by far the best torpedo in the war—had a range of 11 miles at a speed of 49 knots while carrying a 1,000 pound warhead.

Even the primitive torpedoes gave the world's battleship admirals a fright. Battleships in the late 19th and early 20th centuries were the most expensive of all war machines. Compared to them, the cost of a torpedo was negligible, but one torpedo could sink the most expensive battleship. The battleship was *Goliath*—huge, powerful, and fearsome—but the torpedo was David. The short range and inaccuracy of the early torpedoes was no consolation to the naval powers-that-be. Small fast steam launches, whose cost was also negligible compared to battleships, could race up to battleships and release their torpedoes at ranges so short they couldn't miss. The guns of most battleships, particularly those of Britain, the world's premiere naval power, probably wouldn't be able to stop the little boats. France, Britain's ancient rival, decided to concentrate on building torpedo boats and commerce raiders to neutralize British control of the seas.

An ambitious and imaginative British naval officer, Captain John Arbuthnot "Jacky" Fisher, began a campaign that radically changed the armaments of the Royal Navy and, consequently, that of all the world's navies.

British battleships in 1880 were comparatively heavily armored and slow. Their ponderous wrought-iron guns were muzzle-loaders—a few accidents with early breech-loaders having convinced the Royal Navy that muzzle-loading was safer. Muzzle-loading the huge guns now needed on battleships required a complicated arrangement of cranes and was slower than breech-loading.

The first attempt to cope with the torpedo boat threat was to add very heavy machine guns to the ships' armament. *Gatling* and *Nordenfelt mechanical machine guns* in calibers of an inch or more appeared on ships. The *Hotchkiss revolver cannon*—a multi-barrel gun that threw a 37 mm explosive shell—became popular with the world's navies. Then Maxim introduced its *one-pounder automatic cannon*, the famous "pom-pom," but, as the range and speed of torpedoes increased, these light cannons were no longer adequate. The British began purchasing steel breech-loaders capable of firing a 6-pound shell 12 times a minute with a three-man crew. Steel artillery and breech-loading had been pioneered by continental firms like Krupp in Germany and Hotchkiss in France. Breech-loading mechanisms were far safer than the early ones, and steel was far stronger than wrought iron. The new guns let more powerful ammunition be fired more quickly. Torpedoes, though, were improving at least as fast as guns. Something more was needed.

In 1886, Jacky Fisher, now director of naval ordnance, was authorized to get guns from private corporations instead of the royal arsenal. Armstrong, with Vickers, the second British armaments giant, had just what he was looking for—steel breech-loaders that took a 6-inch shell and had a new, French-developed recoil mechanism that absorbed the recoil and returned the gun to its point of aim. (See Chapter 28 on quick-firing artillery.) About the only limitation on its speed of fire was the strength of the gun crew. The breech-loading and recoil systems could be applied to big guns, too, making possible smaller turrets and quicker, more accurate fire. The modern battleship was born, and all navies that didn't have such ships began to copy the British.

Fisher, an early torpedo enthusiast, still wasn't satisfied that battleships were adequately protected from torpedo boats. As a rear admiral and third sea lord in the British admiralty, he got the navy to change to a new type of steam boiler that greatly improved the power of its engines. Then he introduced a new fast ship, smaller than a cruiser but bigger, faster, and more heavily armed than a torpedo boat. It was called a "torpedo boat destroyer," and that was its mission. Today, its name shortened to destroyer and with different missions, it is still a staple of all navies. Fisher also pushed for more and better submarines, but, although he eventually became first sea lord (the top officer in the Royal Navy), he could not totally overcome the opposition of other naval brass who hated the thought of submarines, which they saw as the greatest threat to the surface fleet. The British did adopt the submarine, but built only a few.

In both world wars, the submarine, whose main weapon was the torpedo, proved to be the most efficient user of those miniature submarines sailors call "tin fish." (See Chapter 29.) Airplanes were a close second.

Surprisingly, in World War II, the United States, the country with the largest, and in most ways, most modern, navy, had the worst torpedoes. Admiral Samuel Morison, the official navy historian of World War II, attributed the deficiency to a combination of poor design, obsolescence, false economy and inefficiency at the navy-owned torpedo factory in Newport, Rhode Island. Most of the torpedoes were left over from World War I. The detonators sometimes failed to work even if the target was hit squarely, and too often the target was not hit because the depth regulator was faulty. Submarine commanders returned from patrol reporting they had heard as many as nine torpedoes strike a Japanese ship without exploding.

The U.S. Navy was convinced that the next war's naval battles would be fought at long range with big guns, so it took the torpedo tubes off its cruisers. The torpedo, in spite of the phenomenal Japanese "Long Lance," was essentially a short-range weapon. And to much of the naval brass, and an even higher proportion of Congress, battleships and aircraft carriers were glamor weapons—not destroyers and submarines.

By mid-1943, however, American torpedo troubles had been cured, and U.S. submarines proceeded to sink most of Japan's cargo fleet and a high proportion of its navy with torpedoes. (See Chapter 29.)

Torpedoes appeared in a wide variety of forms during the two world wars. Most, as with the original Whitehead torpedo, were powered by a miniature steam engine using compressed air or oxygen to allow combustion. The steam engine provide great speed and long range, but it left a visible wake, giving target ships a chance to evade the missile. The Germans introduced a torpedo with an electric engine that left no wake, but it was slow and short-ranged. Later the Americans captured one and improved it, producing a faster, longer-ranged torpedo that still left no wake. The Japanese, not satisfied with their Long Lance, developed a special torpedo for use at Pearl Harbor, a location considered unsuitable for aerial torpedoes because of the constricted space and shallow water. The new torpedo traveled fairly close to the surface and armed itself almost immediately after it was dropped. Another German innovation was an acoustic torpedo that homed in on the noise of a ship's engines and propellers. The Allies foiled this with the "Foxer," a device towed by a ship that produced noises that made the acoustic torpedo hit the decoy. The United States also produced a homing torpedo and used it as an anti-submarine weapon. "Fido," it was called, because it "smelled" its prey in deep water. When it saw a U.S. plane approaching, an enemy submarine invariably dived. When that happened, the plane dropped Fido, which pursued the now invisible sub and sank it.

A post-war torpedo guidance system uses active acoustic homing. The torpedo sends out sounds, like a sonar system does, to locate a submarine lying motionless on the sea bottom, then homes in on the target. Another type of torpedo is steered by signals reaching it over a long, thin wire. Wire guidance is not really new. The Brennan torpedo, a 19th-century rival of the Whitehead, used wire guidance. Wire technology at that time was primitive, however, and the wire was thick. The Brennan torpedo required a mass of wire so large it was inconvenient and even dangerous aboard a ship. The wire-guided torpedo had to wait another half-century.

With all its forms and ways of delivery—surface vessel, submarine, or aircraft—the torpedo has thoroughly changed naval warfare, and it may bring more changes in the future.

27

10 Shots a Second:
The Machine Gun

National Archives from Marine Corps

Marines with Browning machine gun (center), Thompson submachine gun (front), and M1 carbine (rear) repulse Japanese counterattack in 1944.

It was July 1, 1916. Nineteen British divisions, the majority of them part of Kitchner's "New Army," volunteers so far untested in battle, were poised to effect the breakthrough their commander, Sir Douglas Haig, expected to end the war. The Somme had been a quiet area for the last two years. For the last week, though, it had been anything *but* quiet. A thousand field pieces, 180 heavy guns, and 245 heavy howitzers had dropped 3,000,000 shells on the German trenches and artillery positions. The no-man's-land and the German positions were a churned-up mass of shell holes. It looked as if nothing could have survived. To make sure that nothing did, the infantry would be preceded by a "creeping barrage": the artillery would pound the first German trenches, then as the infantry drew close, it would shift to positions farther away. The attack was expected to consist of a stroll across a field, through the ripped up ruins of what had been a formidable German barbed wire entanglement and into the area that once held German trenches.

The Boer War had taught the British infantry "fire and movement." Some of the men would rush forward for a short distance then take cover, while the rest, firing from prone or behind cover, would cover their advance with rifle fire. The advanced troops then would fire on the enemy while their comrades rushed forward. This greatly reduced casualties, but it was harder to control the troops. Because his soldiers were so green, and because much German resistance was unlikely, Haig decided to have the troops stay in line and walk to the enemy trenches. Also, if there were enemy fire, the high command was afraid some of the untried troops would flop into shell holes and refuse to advance. Orders stated that "The assaulting troops must push forward at a steady pace in successive lines, each line adding fresh impetus to the preceding line."

Nothing turned out as expected. The enormous artillery barrage did not cut the barbed wire. It just tossed the wire up and tangled it more. It was harder to get through than it was originally. Few of the Tommies even got to the wire. The Germans had dugouts 30 feet below the surface in the chalky soil. They dragged their Maxim machine guns out and cut loose.

A German soldier recalled that attack:

> When the English started advancing we were very worried; they looked as if they must overrun our trenches. We were very surprised to see them walking.... When we started firing we just had to load and reload. They went down in the hundreds. You didn't have to aim, we just fired into them.

Two British battalions were practically wiped out by a single machine gun. Many of the troops never got farther from their own trenches than a few feet. Long-range machine gun fire killed many others from reserve trenches before they even reached the *British* frontline trenches. On that first day of the Battle of the Somme, 20,000 of the 100,000 attackers were killed; 40,000 were wounded; and many of the wounded later died.

In spite of that, Haig kept the offensive going for more than four months. It was always the same: No matter how heavily the artillery pounded the enemy trenches, a few German machine guns survived and cut down thousands of attacking infantrymen. The British gained a little ground, but never achieved a breakthrough. For the first two weeks, they didn't gain an inch. In the middle of September, the British introduced a new weapon: the *tank*. The tanks gained 3,500 yards, the biggest one-day advance, but by the end of the day, all 36 tanks had broken down. By November 19, when the offensive was called off, the deepest British penetration was 7 miles from their starting point on July 1. They lost 419,654 men. For comparison, that's more deaths than all United States forces suffered in *all of World War II*. The overwhelming majority of the dead fell to the machine gun.

The Battle of the Somme was not, of course, the first use of the machine gun in World War I. And World War I was by no means the first war to see machine guns. A practical machine gun, the *Gatling gun*, had been around since 1862. It had seen a little use in the American Civil War. Although the U.S. government refused to adopt it during the war because its inventor, Dr. Richard Gatling, had been born in South Carolina, General Benjamin Butler bought 12 of them with his own money and used them at the siege of Petersburg. In the Spanish-American War, Captain Charles H. Parker organized a Gatling battery and showed how massed machine gun fire could facilitate an attack. The British had used Gatlings and other mechanical machine guns in their colonial wars to mow down uncounted hordes of native warriors. Somehow, the British didn't think machine guns would work in "civilized" warfare.

The Gatling was a mechanical machine gun. It was powered by human muscle—a gunner turning a crank. Hiram Maxim, a mechanical genius from Maine, had a better idea. He once fired a caliber .45-70 army rifle, was impressed by the kick, and thought that energy might be used to reload and fire the gun. What he eventually built was the first automatic machine gun. The recoil of the shot forced back the barrel and breech block. After moving about 3/4 of an inch, the breechblock was separated from the barrel. The barrel stopped moving while the breechblock continued to the rear and ejected the empty shell. The breechblock's movement also moved an arrangement of levers that pulled an ammunition belt into the gun a short distance and placed a cartridge from the belt in line with the barrel. A spring pushed the breechblock back towards the barrel breech and chambered it. The striker then struck the cartridge and fired it. It would continue firing until the gunner released the trigger. The Maxim gun could fire up to 600 rounds a minute—10 shots a second. It had a water jacket around the barrel to keep the gun from overheating. In fact, if you kept the water jacket filled and had an unlimited supply of ammunition belts, you could practically fire the gun indefinitely. In practice, this type of machine gun usually fired about 250 rounds a minute. In combat, some guns have actually fired 15,000 shots an hour.

When the target was small or hidden in bushes, the machine gun functioned like a long-range shotgun, a somewhat dispersed burst of bullets acting like a charge of buckshot. At shorter ranges, it was easier for a partially trained soldier to use than a rifle. By using tracer bullets or noticing where his bullets kicked up dust, the gunner could see where he was hitting and instantly correct his aim. It was like the difference between throwing a rock at an object or hitting it with a garden hose. And against masses of foot soldiers, it was the most lethal gun ever invented.

Masses of foot soldiers were what the British encountered at Omdurman in Kitchener's campaign against the Sudanese dervishes. The British had six Maxim guns. The followers of the Mahdi, a self-appointed Muslim messiah, had thousands upon thousands of spear- and sword-armed warriors. They jogged up to the square of British infantry in a huge mob. The Maxim guns opened fire. Hardly any of the dervishes got within a quarter mile of the British lines.

"It was not a battle, but an execution," an eye-witness wrote. "The bodies were not in heaps, bodies hardly ever are; but they spread evenly over acres and acres."

Eleven thousand Sudanese were killed, almost all of them by the machine guns. British losses came to 48: 28 British and 20 Egyptians. Officially, Kitchener was leading an Egyptian army. Almost all of the British losses were the result of an extremely foolish cavalry charge in which the young Winston Churchill participated, before the big show.

The British Maxims spread bodies all over Africa. So did German Maxims. As a matter of fact, the Maxim machine gun, used by the British (called the Vickers), the Germans (the Spandau), and the Russians in World War I, is supposed to have killed more human beings than any other gun in history. The French also had a pretty horrendous body count, but they used the Hotchkiss machine gun, one of the first automatic guns after the Maxim. In the Russo-Japanese war, the Russians used the Maxim and the Japanese the Hotchkiss. European military attaches noted the destruction these guns achieved, but that didn't impress their general staffs. Ferdinand Foch believed French *elan* and the bayonet was the key to victory. Lord Kitchener, who had seen the slaughter at Omdurman, thought that more than four machine guns to a battalion would be a luxury. The British had even used a few Maxim guns in the Boer War, but the Boers were not soldiers—just an irregular rabble. The trouble was that all the European officers had the romantic notion that wars are won by human valor. The machine gun made valor useless.

When war came in 1914, the European military expected a short war of movement and maneuver with heroic charges with the lance and bayonet deciding the outcome. Instead, the machine guns drove armies underground for four years of siege warfare broken only by the tank.

28

Block that Kick!:
Quick-Firing Field Pieces

National Archives from Army

Howitzer shelling Germans in
1944 recoils after firing a shot.

It really wasn't like the movies. In films about the American Revolution or the American Civil War, for example, the muzzle-loading cannons fire, throwing out some smoke, and the gunners, who have been standing beside them and behind them, immediately reload and fire again. Actually, the guns of those days threw out a lot more smoke, because the film-makers don't use full charges of black powder. And the real gunners didn't stand behind the cannons and reload as soon as they fired. The recoil of the shot blew the gun back quite a few feet, and standing behind a heavy cannon when it fired was a good way to keep from growing old. The movie cannons don't recoil, because they really don't fire shot or shell. Property-owners in the vicinity would take a dim view of cannonballs holing their roofs or shells exploding in their gardens.

Before the cannon could be fired again, it had to be swabbed out with a wet "sponge" (actually a wad of wool on the end of a ramrod) to kill any sparks that might be in the gun. Otherwise, the powder charge might ignite and drive the ramrod through the gunner before he had a chance to load the shell or cannonball. Swabbing took some time. Even more time-consuming was the need to realign the gun. The gun crew had to manhandle the cannon back to its original position and aim it again. Even a comparatively light gun such as the 12-pounder "Napoleon" of the Civil War weighed more than a ton, and aiming the gun usually involved lifting the trail of the heavy carriage to swing the gun around.

By the Civil War, another problem had appeared. Rifles had become so accurate at long range that using artillery at traditional ranges had become almost suicidal. Artillery could no longer be used in the front line with the infantry. The gunners stood in the open, and there was nothing to give them protection from enemy rifle fire. Recoil made it impossible to hide behind the gun.

The latter part of the 19th century was a period of tremendous progress in artillery design. One prime objective was to increase the effective range of cannons. Another was to increase their speed of fire. Achieving both of these objectives meant overcoming recoil.

One way to increase the range was to fire guns at a higher elevation. Most of the cannons until this time were what artillerymen technically call guns—comparatively heavy, long-barreled weapons that have a higher muzzle velocity than the shorter barreled howitzers and mortars and fire their projectiles on a flatter trajectory. If a gun could be elevated to fire on a higher trajectory, its projectiles would go farther. But more of the recoil would be directed down at the carriage. That proved to be too much strain on the old wooden carriages. Gun makers switched to metal carriages, particularly steel carriages. Steel, much stronger than bronze, cast iron, or wrought iron was just starting to become available in large quantities at reasonable prices. Krupp pioneered making gun barrels from steel. Steel barrels could handle heavier powder charges, which also increased range.

Rifling a cannon barrel also increased its effective range. The main problem was getting a hard iron or steel shell or solid shot to "take" the rifling. Various methods were tried, including casting lugs on the shell that would fit in the grooves of the rifling. The method finally adopted was surrounding the projectile with a band of softer metal, usually a copper alloy, that the "lands," the raised portions of the rifling, could bite into. That, and another soft metal band that rode above the lands, sealed the bore so that none of the expanding gas from the explosion of the propelling powder charge leaked around the projectile. Before that, muzzle-loading cannons had to allow for "windage." The projectile had to be smaller than the bore. On the 12-pounder Napoleon that difference came to .01 inches. The absence of windage increased both the range and accuracy of the cannon. So did the fact that rifling made a projectile travel nose-first. Rifled guns could use an elongated projectile, one much heavier for its diameter than a round ball. This increase in "sectional density" meant that an elongated projectile had far more range than a round one with the same muzzle velocity.

It's much easier to load a rifled cannon from the breech than from the muzzle. The use of steel and improved breech blocks made breech-loading so attractive that muzzle loading practically disappeared except for small trench mortars. Two types of breech block were used. One was a sliding block of steel; the other resembled a small, extremely thick bank vault door that was locked by an interrupted screw surrounding it.

There were three types of ammunition for breech-loading cannons—fixed, semi-fixed and bagged. *Fixed ammunition* resembled a rifle cartridge, with the shell fitted into a brass cartridge case containing the propelling charge. *Semi-fixed* also had a brass cartridge case, but the powder charge, packed in bags, could be varied to vary the range. With *bagged ammunition*, the shell was loaded first then the powder charge in one or more bags. Fixed ammunition and semi-fixed ammunition depend on the brass cartridge case expanding when the propelling charge is ignited. That seals the breech against escaping gas. To use bagged ammunition, the interrupted screw breech block has a "obturation pad" on its inner face that expands when the propelling charge explodes. To use the sliding breech block with a bagged charge, a gunner inserts a separate copper sealing ring behind the bagged propelling charge.

Steel, breech-loading, rifled guns were a huge step forward. They had more range and far more accuracy than their predecessors. But when makers like Hotchkiss and Krupp advertised their quick-firing field pieces they were using a bit of hyperbole. They still hadn't dealt with that old devil, recoil. After a gun fired, the gunners had to push it back into position and aim it once more. Only if someone found a way to keep the gun in position and on-target during firing, could the cannon be truly said to be quick-firing.

Inventors came up with a variety of systems to hold the gun in place. On sailing ships, guns were allowed to roll back a certain distance, then the motion was stopped by a thick rope attached to the gun. Gun crews then used other ropes and pulleys to haul the cannon back to its gunport. If the restraining rope broke, however, you would have the proverbial "loose cannon on the deck"—a most undesirable situation. In some fortresses, guns were allowed to roll up a steep ramp. Gravity then repositioned them. One ingenious device, also used in fixed fortifications, was the *disappearing gun*. The gun was in a concrete-lined pit below the surface of the earth. Machinery raised it to firing position with the aid of counterweights. When the gun fired, the recoil returned it to its pit. An enemy would have only a brief glimpse of the gun before it fired and disappeared. Airplanes made the disappearing guns obsolete, but they were still used in U.S. coastal defenses in World War II.

Recoil was easier to treat in forts than in the field. Some designs attempted to absorb recoil with rubber buffers, but rubber wore out quickly, froze in cold weather, and wasn't all that effective at any time. The 15-pounder field piece the British used in the Second Boer War had a "recoil spade" attached to the carriage axis. The spade was attached to a steel spring fixed to the carriage trail. Gunners dug the spade into the ground. When the gun fired, the whole gun and carriage rolled back, but the spring drew it back to position—more or less. It sounds better than it worked. The spade itself did not stay immobile. The recoil pulled back the arm to which the spade was attached, changing its angle to the ground, so the gun never returned to exactly the same spot.

The first field gun to solve the recoil problem was the French 75 mm Model 1897. A retired officer, Commandant de Port, modified a German invention to produce the system upon which all modern recoil systems are based. The "French 75," as American World War I veterans called it, had a barrel that could slide back but that was attached to a piston in an oil-filled cylinder. When the gun barrel recoiled, the piston pushed the oil through a small orifice and into a second cylinder. That oil pushed back a floating piston in a second cylinder, compressing the air in that cylinder. Squeezing the oil out of the first cylinder absorbed much of the energy of the recoil; compressing the air in the second cylinder took care of the rest. Air is an extremely elastic material. When the gun's motion stopped, the compressed air reasserted itself, bringing the gun back into firing position. The trail of the gun carriage had a spade that was planted in the ground to keep the gun carriage from moving. The gun was ready to fire another shot immediately. Because the gun carriage didn't move at all, it was possible to hang a bullet-proof shield on the gun. That was a great boon to gunners. It also made possible the U.S. World War II experiment of attaching "cannon companies" to the infantry. The cannoneers worked right up with the riflemen, providing close-in support with their 105 mm howitzers. That was dangerous work, to be sure. But without the shield, it would have been suicide. The recoil mechanism also made it much easier to dig in artillery pieces, a practice that was common in both world wars, Korea, and Vietnam. Without something to absorb their recoil, guns of the power of those used in modern wars would have to roll back a long way, so digging them in would require an enormous pit.

The French 75 used fixed ammunition. When a gunner opened the breech, the brass cartridge case was automatically ejected, and another round could be loaded. A trained crew could fire 30 shots a minute from the 75—faster than most infantrymen could fire a bolt-action rifle. The M1897 75 mm was the standard French and American light artillery piece all through World War I and for many years afterwards. The French were still using it in World War II.

Every field gun in the world and most of the naval guns and the big siege guns copied the recoil system introduced on the French 75. As a result of the speed of fire it made possible, artillery was far and away the greatest killer of all guns used in World War II. Artillery and mortars killed two thirds of all the soldiers who died in that war. Speed of fire was especially important to antiaircraft guns. German antiaircraft fire during World War II probably shot down more Allied planes than German fighter planes, and in Vietnam antiaircraft guns destroyed 91 percent of all American planes lost in combat.

29

The 1st Stealth Weapon:
The Submarine

National Archives from Nav.

Torpedoed Japanese destroyer sinks while being photographed through the periscope of a U.S. submarine.

On the night of September 6, 1776, a small group of men on the shore of New York harbor silently lowered a most peculiar-looking object into the dark water. The strange contraption was made of two solid curved pieces of wood closely fitted together to form a waterproof joint. It had a hand-cranked propeller, a rudder at the rear, and another propeller on its upper surface. One man, Ezra Lee of Old Lyme, Connecticut, had entered through a hatch at the top. Lee planned to propel his strange craft to the British 64 gun frigate H.M.S *Eagle*, dive below the surface when the got near the British flagship, attach an explosive charge to the ship, and leave as fast as he could.

The peculiar craft, named the *American Turtle* because it looked like a turtle tipped over on one side, was the brainchild of Captain David Bushnell, an engineering officer in the Continental Army. When he was 29, Bushnell had sold the farm he inherited and attended Yale, where he studied science for four years. When the Revolution broke out, he joined the Continental Army. With the help of another Yale scientist, he designed an underwater bomb with a time-delay mechanism. When the preset time was up, the mechanism activated a flintlock that set off the charge. That led Bushnell to consider some means of getting the bomb to the enemy. The British ships had lookouts watching the water at all times. Even at night, it was unlikely that a rowboat or canoe could get close enough to one of their ships to attach a bomb. And it was almost certain that the inevitable noise of the attaching work would attract attention. The only sure way would be to approach under water.

So Bushnell designed *Turtle*. The boat would travel most of the way to its target with its hatch open and just above the surface of the water. Driven by a hand-cranked propeller it would be too slow to make a noticeable wake. When it got near the British ship, *Turtle's* pilot would use the upper propeller to force his craft below the surface. The bomb was attached to a screw on the front of the submarine that could manipulated from inside the craft.

Bushnell's brother, Ezra, volunteered to bomb H.M.S. *Eagle*. He had piloted the submarine for weeks in waters where no British were to be found. But at the last minute, Ezra Bushnell fell ill. Ezra Lee volunteered to take his place although he had much less experience with Bushnell's invention. With the hatch open and barely above the surface, Lee slowly made his way to the British ship. In a modern reproduction of *Turtle*, built for a television documentary, the pilot found it was easier to move the boat by sculling with the rudder than cranking the propeller. An earlier reproduction, built for the U.S. bicentennial celebration reportedly worked as intended. Whatever method he used, Lee got near *Eagle* and dived. In addition to the difficulty in handling a brand-new weapon of war and the danger that the British would learn what he was doing, Lee was working under a serious deadline. The timing mechanism of the bomb had already been activated. He tried to drive the screw into the hull of the ship, but *Eagle* was sheathed in copper below the waterline to foil barnacles. The screw wouldn't penetrate the metal. Lee tried again and failed. Time was running out. Lee jettisoned his bomb and moved away. The floating bomb exploded with a shocking flash and bang. The British ships hauled in their anchors and hoisted their sails.

On shore, David Bushnell roundly cursed the unfortunate Lee. Then he and his party loaded *Turtle* into a sloop to take it back to New England. A British warship chased the sloop and sank it.

After the Revolution, Bushnell petitioned the Continental Congress for some form of recognition or compensation. But, although General George Washington said in 1784, "Bushnell is a man of great mechanical powers, fertile in invention and a master of execution," Congress ignored him. Bushnell moved to France and tried to interest the French in his submarine. He failed, although he apparently interested another American, Robert Fulton, inventor of the steamboat. Fulton launched another submarine, called *Nautilus*, in France in 1800. Fulton, who had received a commission in the French Navy, almost succeeded, but at the last minute Napoleon decided that underwater warfare was also underhanded and cancelled the sale.

Bushnell had returned to the United States in 1795 but, disillusioned, he had changed his name and moved out of New England. It was only after his death in 1824, that residents of Warrentown, Georgia, learned that "Dr. Bush," who taught science and religion at the local academy, was really David Bushnell, the Revolutionary inventor.

Bushnell's submarine was not the first one, but it was the first to be used in war. The first sub was built in England in 1620—the year before the Pilgrims landed—by a Dutchman named Cornelius van Drebbel and tested in the Thames.

After Bushnell and Fulton's boats only Americans seemed to have any interest in submarines. Both the Union and Confederacy used submarines in the Civil War. In 1862, the U.S. Navy purchased its first sub, the U.S.S. *Alligator*, to plant mines ("torpedoes" in those days) in Confederate harbors. *Alligator* sank in April, but it was followed by several other submarines. *Alligator* carried two air purifiers, a chemical means of producing oxygen, and a bellows-driven ventilation system. The Confederacy also had a fleet of submarines. One of them, the C.S.S. *Hunley,* sank the U.S.S. *Housatonic*, the first time a submarine ever sank an enemy ship. But the blast also sank *Hunley*.

After the war, John Holland, an Irish immigrant, and Simon Lake, a New Jersey foundry owner's son, continued to work on submarines. Holland at first was financed by the Feinians, an Irish secret society dedicated to winning Irish independence from Britain. In 1881, he launched a submarine called *Feinian Ram*, intended to end Britain's command of the sea. It needed further work, but Holland and the Feinians quarreled and the society cut off its financial aid. Holland continued working and built a boat named *Holland IV*, which won a U.S. Navy award for submarine design. The Navy was not yet ready to buy a submarine, though. Holland designed more boats and sold *Holland VI* to the navy, which renamed it U.S.S *Holland* in 1900. *Holland* was powered on the surface by an internal combustion engine, which also charged storage batteries. When submerged, it ran on an electric motor. That system was used by all modern submarines until the advent of nuclear power. In the meantime, Lake had been designing other subs. In 1898, he launched *Argonaut*, which sailed from Norfolk to New York, becoming the first submarine to travel a significant distance on the open sea. *Argonaut*, which had wheels beneath her hull, was also equipped to roll along the ocean floor. Lake also invented even-keel hydroplanes, ballast tanks, divers compartments, periscopes, and twin hull design—all of them essential to modern submarines.

In World War I, the submarine, like the airplane, came into its own as a serious weapon. Armed with torpedoes, German submarines seriously interfered with Allied supplies. Britain, an island that had to import much of its food, was especially hard hit. It was hit even harder in World War II. "The only thing that really frightened me during the war was the U-boat peril," Winston Churchill said. At the beginning of the war, submarines had improved far more than antisubmarine tactics. Later, such innovations as airborne radar and the cracking of German naval codes more than evened the odds, but it was a close thing. It was a different story on the other side of the world. By 1943, U.S. submarines finally had efficient torpedoes. That year they sank 22 Japanese warships and 296 merchant ships. The next year, the submarine U.S.S. *Archerfish* sank the huge, 59,000 ton Japanese aircraft carrier, *Sinano*. A month later, another sub, U.S.S. *Redfish*, knocked out two more Japanese carriers, *Junyo* and *Unryu.* By the end of the war, U.S. submarines sank 2,117 Japanese merchant ships—60 percent of all those destroyed—and 201 of the 686 Japanese warships sunk.

For most of its existence up through World War II, the submarine's biggest handicap was speed. On the surface, it was the slowest of all naval vessels. Submerged , it might have trouble outrunning a row boat. That changed after the war, when the U.S. Navy launched the U.S.S. *Skipjack*. Almost all previous subs had been compromises—designed for surface travel but usable under the water. The somewhat tubular hull interfered with surface speed, while the surface-type bow and deck, not to mention the complicated conning tower, impeded subsurface travel. *Skipjack*, which resembled a whale with a smooth dorsal fin, was designed for subsurface travel alone. Submerged, she was faster than most surface craft. When the navy combined the *Skipjack* hull with a nuclear engine, in the U.S.S. *Nautilus*—the name taken from both Fulton's submarine and the craft of Jules Verne's Captain Nemo—the modern submarine was born.

Today's nuclear subs can stay submerged almost indefinitely and outrun most surface ships. In contrast to the small, fragile submarines of World War I, they are extremely durable and huge. They carry torpedoes with a variety of guidance systems and three times the range of the best torpedoes of World War II. They also carry a variety of rockets, including intercontinental missiles, and they can fire them while submerged. During the Cold War, U.S. submarines were able to intercept Soviet messages by tapping undersea cables. During the Iraq War, American submarines fired Tomahawk cruise missiles at Iraqi targets—some from tubes designed for that purpose, some from ordinary torpedo tubes.

In the two centuries or so since David Bushnell created *American Turtle*, the submarine is now bidding to take the place of the aircraft carrier as the new capital ship.

30

Bigger (and Cleaner) Bangs for the Buck: Smokeless Powder and High Explosives

Eight-inch dynamite gun being tested. This weapon's military service was short because it was so dangerous to use. Dynamite is too sensitive to be a shell filling.

President Theodore Roosevelt is famous for advising his countrymen to "Speak softly and carry a big stick." But prior to this day, July 1, 1898, he and his fellow war hawks had been roaring at the top of their voices while carrying a toothpick—at least as far as land forces went. The navy was moderately large and more than moderately modern. The army, though, had only 28,183 men, and many of them were needed on the still-not-quite-settled western frontier. Consequently, at least half of the troops here in Cuba were volunteers, not regulars. And that requires a brief explanation of just what "volunteer" means.

Volunteer units were an outgrowth of the country's ancient militia system, which has its roots in the Dark Ages. Militia were originally all men able to bear arms. They could be called upon by the monarch to fight in his wars. Later, there were limitations on who could be called up and for how long and where. Age limits were set. In the United States today, all males are between the ages of 17 and 45 are the militia. In England, in the Middle Ages, militia were required to serve for only 40 days, and they had to be paid by the royal treasury for any duty outside their own counties. In colonial America, militia could not be required to serve outside their own colonies. For troops to be used outside the colonies, colonial authorities relied on "volunteers." These were men who formed their own military units, elected their own officers, provided their own weapons, and served under regular army officers for a limited time or for the duration of the war. Until the 20th century, the United States depended heavily on volunteer units in its wars.

Originally, the volunteers provided their own weapons, but, by the end of the 19th century, the states provided many units with their arms. The *Krag Jorgensen repeating rifle* and *carbine* had just been adopted for the regular army. Krags were not for sale to private owners, however, and none of the states were ready to invest large sums in new rifles for militia units—many of which were not even in existence. Consequently, most of the troops closing in on Santiago de Cuba had single-shot rifles using the old standard cartridge, the .45-70, adopted in 1873. Single-shot rifles could not, of course, fire as fast as repeaters. But the big disadvantage of these single-shots, most of them varieties of the Springfield "trap door" action rifle, was that they used black powder, not smokeless. We'll see in a moment what that meant. Only one unit of volunteers, the Rough Riders, composed of cowboys and Ivy Leaguers recruited by Theodore Roosevelt, had Krags. Political connections are a wonderful thing.

The Spanish regulars had the Model 1893 or 1895 Mauser, 7 mm bolt action repeaters. Mauser's late model rifles were by far the best military rifles of the day. The Spanish also had Krupp quick-firing field pieces. (See Chapter 28.) Of the U.S. troops, neither regulars nor reserves had modern artillery.

What the Americans had, at least in the field, were numbers. The right wing of the American army, under Brigadier General Henry L. Lawton, had 6,653 men and four field pieces. It was moving against the Spanish fortifications around the village of El Caney, where Spanish General Joaquin Vara de Ray had 520 men. Lawton's troops were to take El Caney and swing around the main defenses of Santiago de Cuba. At the same time, the main body was to attack the Spanish line on the crest of the San Juan Heights. The dismounted cavalry division, which included Roosevelt's Rough Riders, the 9th and 10th regiments of African American cavalry ("Buffalo Soldiers") and the 1st, 3rd, and 6th cavalry regiments, formed the right wing of the main body. It faced fortifications on what became known as Kettle Hill—not San Juan Hill, which was a short distance to the south. The Rough Riders were the only volunteers in the force, and like the rest of the division, who were regulars, they had modern rifles.

The day before, Lawton had surveyed his objective and estimated that his men would take it in two hours. Planning for the main assault was based on that estimate. Given the odds Lawton enjoyed, that was a most reasonable estimate.

To understand what kind of advantage 10-to-one odds gives a military unit, let's consider some extremely simplistic propositions. Say one side has 100 men and the other side 1,000, and say that, on each exchange of fire, 10 percent of each side score hits. On the first exchange the larger force will be reduced to 990 men, but the second will be annihilated. Say only 5 percent score hits on each exchange. On the first exchange, the larger force will be left with 995 soldiers; the smaller one with 50. Of course, real life is more complicated than that (at least now). In the days when soldiers stood shoulder to shoulder and fired volleys at each other, that proposition would have been more accurate. But if the defenders are entrenched, as the Spanish were, they are harder to hit, especially if both sides are relying almost exclusively on rifles, as both sides were. When they are hit, though, the wound is likely to be fatal, because it would usually be in the head. Attackers were harder to hit, too. American troops had learned in the Civil War to advance by rushes, dropping down behind shelter and firing to cover other soldiers' advances. Attackers, when hit, are less likely to be hit fatally, because hits would not be confined to the head. All their rifles—repeaters and single-shots—were breech-loaders, so a soldier need not expose himself to reload.

Even with all these qualifications, though, 10-to-one odds gave the larger group a tremendous advantage. As the previous propositions show, the longer the fight goes on, the more heavily the weaker side is outnumbered. An old rule of thumb is that an attacker should have a 3-to-one numerical advantage over the defender. Lawton had better than 10-to-one.

Artillery support for the American attackers was virtually nonexistent. Lawton's artillery fired about one round every five minutes, and they fired from long range without much accuracy. It may be that they were trying to avoid the troubles being suffered by the main force artillery. Those four guns were emplaced on a hilltop, because the Americans had no guns capable of indirect fire. Each time a gun fired, it generated an enormous cloud of thick white smoke that made it impossible to see the target. It also made the guns obvious to the Spanish, who had two Krupp quick-firing pieces using smokeless powder. The Americans couldn't locate the Spanish guns if the air were clear. It wasn't clear. Their gunners were blinded by their own smoke. Finally, they were driven off the hill.

Back at El Caney, the 2nd Massachusetts Infantry, a volunteer outfit, advanced and opened fire on the Spaniards. The Spanish soldiers were hidden in trenches, fox holes, wooden block houses, and a stone fort, so the Yankee volunteers could only fire at the general area. The Spanish, though, knew that behind each puff of smoke was an enemy rifleman. Their return fire was so heavy the volunteers were forced back. The regulars in the division, including the 24th and 25th Regiments, "Buffalo Soldier" (African-American) infantry, had smokeless powder, but there were so many volunteers among them that the Spanish soldiers could easily see where to concentrate their fire.

Troops in the main body were told to march up to the San Juan River and wait for further orders. The "further orders" were presumably to advance when Lawton had taken El Caney and moved south. They waited, some standing in the river. The trouble was compounded when an American observation balloon, which had been observing the area from a half-mile behind the front line, was moved to the front line and then its anchor ropes became entangled in the treetops. Stuck 50 feet above the front line, the balloon showed the Spanish exactly where the American troops were, even though they were hidden in the jungle. The Spanish fired into that area.

Eventually, doing nothing but taking casualties got to be too much for the Americans. They moved up the hills. Teddy Roosevelt's Rough Riders got the credit for taking Kettle Hill, but the black "Buffalo Soldiers" of the 9th Cavalry got to the summit first. San Juan Hill proved to be a tougher proposition. The turning point was provided by a maverick second lieutenant. John H. Parker, six years out of West Point, was considered a machine gun fanatic by his comrades. When he saw that the expedition to Cuba was leaving behind four Gatling guns, he begged his commanding officer to take them. He was refused. Although Gatling guns had been used effectively in the Civil War, the army still didn't believe in machine guns. Parker went through channels until he found a general who let him form a machine gun battery and take the Gatlings with him.

With the American troops pinned down on the slopes of San Juan Hill, Parker's mule-drawn Gatling guns galloped up and his troops unlimbered them. The four guns opened fire, each squirting out bullets at the rate of 900 rounds a minute. Fortunately, Parker's guns used the .30 smokeless Krag cartridges. His men could see what they were shooting at. The American troops saw the dust kicked up by the spray of bullets as they swept across the Spanish trenches. The Spanish began to withdraw. By this time, many of the American officers had been killed or wounded, but their troops spontaneously charged up the hill and took the fort at its summit.

El Caney had still not been taken. The hill that was to have been taken in two hours held out for 10. Finally, the Spanish troops began to run out of ammunition. The Spanish commanding general, Arsenio Linares, kept the bulk of his army in Santiago and sent Vara de Ray neither men nor more ammunition. The American stormed the fort. They took 120 prisoners. Of the 520 men in the garrison, 215, including General Vara de Ray, had been killed and some 300 wounded. American casualties came to 205 killed and almost 1,200 wounded.

Both the Spanish and Americans at El Caney were brave soldiers. And both had been let down by their leaders—the Spanish by their commander's refusal to reinforce or even resupply them; the Americans by their leaders' failure to amend the order to wait at the San Juan River, by their neglect of what proved to be the decisive weapon—the Gatling gun—and by the government's failure to obtain smokeless powder.

Smokeless powder had been invented in 1885 by Paul Vieille, a French chemist, and the French put it into service almost immediately, bringing out a new 8 mm rifle to use the new powder in 1886. That was 12 years before the Spanish-American War. The development of smokeless powder was part of a chemical revolution that began in the mid-19th century and included, among other things, dyes from coal tar, anaesthetics, aspirin, heroin, and dynamite.

Dynamite, patented in 1866, was made in many varieties, some, such as *gelatine dynamite*, extremely powerful, all extremely sensitive. Dynamite is based on an early explosive, nitroglycerin, which is too sensitive for almost any use. Alfred Nobel first mixed nitroglycerin with an absorbent earth to desensitize it. He later mixed it with other explosives, such as ammonium nitrate, potassium chlorate, or nitro cotton to obtain a very powerful explosive that was still safe to handle (with care). Gun-makers tried to use dynamite for a shell filling (Chapter 19) but it proved to be too dangerous. It could never be used as a propellant. It is what is called a high explosive: one that almost instantly decomposes into a huge amount of gas, whether it is confined or unconfined. This reaction is called detonation. Propellants, like black powder or smokeless powder, decompose more slowly. They are said to burn, although smokeless powder, if confined tightly enough, may also detonate.

Nitroglycerin is a compound of nitric acid and glycerin. About the time Nobel was experimenting with nitroglycerin, other chemists were nitrating other organic substances. Nitrating cotton a little produced nitro cotton, a component of gelatine dynamite. Nitrating it a lot produced guncotton, a rather sensitive explosive once used as a filling for torpedoes, but now an ingredient of smokeless powder.

TNT, or *trinitrotoluene*, became extremely popular as a filling for shells, torpedoes, aerial bombs, and hand grenades because it combines great power with a reasonable lack of sensitivity. It was widely used in both world wars.

Many new high explosives have been developed since the war. They are never used as propellants—the many varieties of smokeless powder handle that chore—but they have completely replaced "low explosives," such as black powder as fillings for shells and bombs. When a black powder shell exploded, it burst into a few large pieces, none with enough velocity to carry far. High explosives shatter a shell into thousands of tiny, sharp metal fragments traveling at high velocity. These fragments are so effective against personnel that they have completely replaced shrapnel. Against solid objects—forts, tanks, ships, and so on—high explosives are infinitely more effective than black powder. And they make possible the shaped charge.

31

Big Bertha and Her Cousins:
The Super Siege Guns

National Archives from War Dept.

The French army's largest gun, caliber 320 mm (12.6 inches) fires on German positions in 1914.

Belgium, sandwiched between France and Germany, knew it occupied dangerous real estate. Its territory had been a battleground since Roman times, and now it occupied the space between two large and unfriendly powers—unfriendly to each other, that is, and oblivious to the rights of small neutrals. Of the two, the German Empire, born in 1870 and pursuing an aggressive foreign policy ever since, seemed the greatest danger. The kaiser had been bullying old King Leopold II and his nephew, King Albert I. "You will be either with us or against us," he told old Leopold. A German officer told Albert's military attache in 1913 that war was inevitable and that it was "imperative for the weak to side with the strong."

To discourage an invasion, the Belgians built what some authorities said were the strongest forts in Europe around such vulnerable cities as Liege and Namur. The forts circled each city and were about 2 or 3 miles apart. They were mostly underground, with armor cupolas that could be raised above the surface to fire. Each fort was surrounded by a triangular ditch 30 feet deep. Above each fort was a revolving searchlight that could be lowered beneath the surface. The ring of forts at each city had some 400 guns, not counting the numerous machine guns. And hidden by the turf that covered the forts were thick walls and ceilings of concrete. They were guaranteed to withstand anything that could be hurled from a 210 mm (8.4 inch) gun. The 210 mm was the heaviest in any army, and when the forts were built—between 1888 and 1892—it was believed to be the heaviest gun that could be used. Years of experience had shown soldiers that there was a practical limit to how much weight horses could pull.

Back then, soldiers had not thought much about the limits of internal combustion engines.

At first, the forts at Liege did hold up the Germans. A staff officer named Erich Ludendorff went up to the front to reconnoiter, discovered an undefended gap in the Belgian forces surrounding Liege, and led German troops into the city. Ludendorff captured the city—the first step on a path that would lead to his becoming German commander-in-chief. But the forts were still in Belgian hands.

But Germany had an answer. The Skoda plant of its ally, Austria-Hungary, had developed a 305 mm (12.2 inch) howitzer that could be disassembled into three pieces and towed by gasoline-powered tractors. When they arrived at their destination, they could be reassembled and ready to fire in 40 minutes. The Austrians loaned several of these guns to Germany. Meanwhile, Krupp, Germany's premier gun-maker, had been developing a true monster—420 mm (16.8 inch) howitzer. The gun, nicknamed Big Bertha after the wife of Krupp's proprietor, was hardly as mobile as the Skoda gun. The first version had to be moved by rail, and tracks had to be laid to its firing position. Krupp's people worked frantically to develop a version that could be towed over roads. On August 12, 1914, nine days after German troops confront Liege, the first Big Bertha arrived. The bombardment of the Belgian forts by the 305 mm Skodas and the 420 mm Krupp began. The huge guns pounded the forts to pieces. By August 16, they had all the forts. The Germans then moved their monster guns to Namur and destroyed those forts.

The Skoda mortars enjoyed equal success on the Eastern Front, where they pulverized Russian-held forts and field fortifications. On the Western Front, though, the super guns made no other noteworthy appearance until 1918. At that time, March 23, 1918, a 210 mm shell burst in the middle of Paris. Ludendorff's last offensive, intended to end the war before the United States could land a substantial number of troops, had begun on March 21, but the Germans were far from Paris. That shell burst and the many that followed it were supposedly intended to break the French morale. Actually, it seems more likely that it was a project undertaken by German artillery experts to see if it could be done. Officially dubbed *Wilhelm Geschutz* or William's gun, the "Paris gun," also called "Long Max," was the most complex piece of ordnance ever designed up to that time. It was firing on Paris from 74 miles away—about three times as far as the largest conventional naval gun, a 16 inch rifle, could shoot. To build it, the German engineers took the barrel of a 381 mm (15 inch) naval gun, 55 feet, 10 inches long, reamed it out and inserted a 210 mm tube. That second barrel increased the length of the gun by 36 feet, 11 inches, making the finished barrel almost 93 feet long. To that, they added an unrifled tube to the end of the gun, making the whole assembly 112 feet long. It weighed 138 tons. To take advantage of this enormous length, the German ballisticians devised a special slow-burning smokeless powder. This was packed into a chamber 15 feet, five inches long. The heat generated by this giant powder charge and the tremendous velocity of the shell, would wear out the barrel rapidly. The gun would have to be rebored every 65 rounds. The weight of each shell, from the first to the 65th was altered to make up for the loss in velocity and accuracy. The long, long barrel was braced with a cable truss to keep it from sagging.

To move it, the gun was disassembled as far a possible, loaded on special railroad cars, and hauled to its firing position, a spot in the forest to which track had been laid. There were at least two of these guns, each emplaced on a massive concrete foundation. At 7:15 a.m., the Germans fired the first shell. Three minutes later, the shell landed in Paris. At that range, the guns needed a target as big as a city. The rotation of the earth, air currents, and even air temperatures at various heights up to an altitude of 23 miles had to be considered. "William's Guns" kept firing from March 23rd until August 9th. They fired 367 shells and killed 256 people, 90 of them when a single shell fell into a crowded church on Good Friday. As a weapon, the Paris guns were useless, wasteful, and cruel. They did, however, help develop techniques that would be used on other giant guns in the next world war.

In World War II, the Germans took up where they left off and produced the biggest and most powerful gun in all history. The engineers at Krupp, remembering their success against the Belgian forts, began work on two guns that were to blast through France's Maginot Line. By the time the first was finished, in 1942, the German Army had already flanked the Maginot Line and France had surrendered. The new gun, named Dora, was rushed to the Eastern Front, where the fortress city of Sevastapol was holding out in the Crimea. Marshal Erich von Manstein, the German commander in that sector, called it "a miracle of technical achievement. The barrel must have been 90 feet long and the carriage as high as a two story house."

It had a bore of 800 mm (31.5 inches), almost twice that of Big Bertha's 420 mm. Dora was a gun, not, like Big Bertha, a howitzer. It was capable of long-range, high velocity fire as well as high trajectory bombardment. It could fire five-ton high explosive shells at targets 29 miles away. To penetrate armor and concrete, it used a heavier shell—7.1 tons—that had a range of only 23 miles. To propel each of these projectiles, Dora used 1 3/4 *tons* of powder. Using high-angle fire against the forts of Sevastopol, Dora sent these enormous shells into outer space, from which they fell on the target with enormous velocity. One shot from Dora penetrated 100 feet of earth and rock to blow up a powder magazine. German tests showed that Dora's armor piercing shells could penetrate 5 *feet* of armor plate at 23 miles.

After pulverizing the Russian forts, Dora was disassembled and sent back to Germany. On June 22, 1942, Dora was renamed Gustav to make Allied intelligence believe Germany now had the second super gun in service. Actually, the would-be Gustav was never completed. While Dora/Gustav was waiting for its next assignment, the Krupp engineers were designing new ammunition. One shell was a dart-shaped discarding-sabot, "light weight" shell of only 2,200 pounds. It was to have a range of 90 to 100 miles and allow Dora to bombard England. A second, rocket-assisted shell would have a range of 118 miles. Neither were ever used.

Dora/Gustav's last assignment was to bombard Warsaw, where the Polish underground rose up against the Germans as the Red Army was approaching. The Soviets stopped their advance to let the Germans destroy Warsaw and all the restless elements in it so they wouldn't trouble the Red Army when it occupied Poland. Then the Russians captured the biggest of all big guns.

Dora had been joined at the siege of Sevastopol by two other monster guns. Germany built six 600 mm (23.6 inch) mortars of the Karl class, the largest self-propelled artillery pieces ever made. There were six of these cannons, a class that took its name from the first one built. The two at Sevastopol were Eva and

Thor, presumably named after Hitler's mistress, Eva Braun, and a pagan god. "Self-propelled" is used loosely—they could travel three miles per hour on level ground for a short distance. For traveling longer distances, Karl-class mortars were slung between two custom-built railroad cars. Each gun had a crew of 109 men.

Although Dora/Gustav never bombarded England, another gun did. Krupp built a 210 mm weapon that looked like a slightly modernized version of the Paris gun called *Kanone 12*. Located in northern France, it fired shells into the county of Kent in southern England.

Germany did not have a complete monopoly on outsized artillery. The United States fielded the biggest-bore gun of the war. Called Little David, it was intended to blast through Germany's Westwall. (Westwall was what the Allies called the Siegfried Line. The Siegfried Line was actually the name of a World War I fortification that the Allies called the Hindenburg Line.) But, like Dora, when Little David was ready to go into action, the enemy line had already been breached.

Little David began as a device to test aerial bombs. The U.S. Army ordnance people wanted to drop the bombs on a small target, but no aircraft could reliably hit such a target. So they built a mortar with a 36 inch bore (914 mm) that could lift the bombs high in the air and drop them on the target. Then somebody decided this would be just the thing to destroy German forts.

Little David weighed 60 tons. It sat in a steel base 18 feet long, 9 feet wide, and 10 feet high that had been installed in a pit. Its barrel was 22 feet long and was installed and removed with the aid of six hydraulic jacks. It was loaded from the muzzle. In place of a breech was a solid steel arc with teeth that fitted the cog wheel used for elevation. To load, the gunners lowered the barrel until it was almost horizontal. It took between 136 and 216 pounds of powder to propel its 3,650-pound shell. The shell's driving band was engraved to fit the rifling. Machinery lifted the shell from a truck and inserted in the barrel. It took 25 seconds for the shell to slide down the barrel. Then the barrel was lifted to the proper elevation and a gunner fired the propelling charge with a percussion cap.

Little David would have undoubtedly smashed any fortification unfortunate enough to be its target. But alas, its gunners never fired a shot in anger.

Dora/Gustav was undoubtedly better at pounding fortifications than any other weapon. It could put heavier armor-piercing projectiles on a target more accurately than any bombing plane of the time. Its shells were heavier than almost any aerial bomb in the war, and they arrived with a velocity no free falling bomb could achieve and with far more velocity than a dive bomber could give its missile. But the big gun had to be disassembled with special heavy machinery to move any distance. For limited movement around its firing area, it needed four parallel railroad tracks for its 80 railroad wheels to roll on. To operate, maintain, and protect the gun, 4,120 troops commanded by a major general were needed.

Marshal von Manstein, who praised Dora, also explained why such guns were always a rarity and now, with guided bombs, rocket-assisted bombs, rocket and jet missiles guided by satellite, are obsolete.

"The effectiveness of the cannon bore no real relation to all the effort and expense that had gone into making it," he said.

The super gun, like the submachine gun and the mass paratrooper attack, is one of those military techniques that were born in the first world war, reached a peak in the second and became obsolete before the end of the Cold War. The last person to be interested in super guns was Saddam Hussein, in the 1980s. Any military method espoused by that egotistical military moron was sure to be useless.

32

Winged Victory:
The Airplane

National Archives from Navy.

Navy Sky Raiders from the U.S.S. *Valley Forge* fire
5-inch rockets at Noth Koreans in 1950.

In August, 1914, the First German Army of General Alexander von Kluck
had turned south, trying to envelop the British and French armies facing the
rest of the German forces. The move exposed von Kluck's right flank to attack
by the substantial garrison of Paris. A British reconnaissance pilot, chugging
over the front in flimsy wood-and-canvas aircraft, noticed the change of front
and notified his superiors.

The French attacked the German right flank. Lord Kitchener, the British commander-in chief, ordered Sir John French, the British field commander, to attack, too, but Sir John moved as if he were wearing lead shoes. Kluck's troops, facing the French flank attack, became separated from the other German armies. John French was finally induced to move, and the British marched for the gap in the German lines. A German reconnaissance pilot, flying in another glorified box kite, noticed the enemy columns heading for the gap. He notified his superiors. The German Great General Staff ordered all field armies to withdraw to a defensible position.

The Battle of the Marne, almost a non-battle, but one of the decisive battles of the world, was over. The key people were a couple of airmen in machines that few sane people today would consider getting into.

Only 11 years before this, Orville Wright made the world's first manned, controlled flight. It lasted just 12 seconds. Ninety years later, airplanes had established themselves as the most important of all military weapons. They had replaced the battleship's guns as the main weapon of naval warfare. They took over much of the role of artillery in World War II, making possible the Blitzkrieg. They flattened cities. From Orville Wright's altitude of a few feet and speed of about 7 miles per hour, improvements in planes over the years let the U.S. Air Force's SR-71 "Blackbird" travel 2,189 miles per hour at an altitude of 86,000 feet—more than 16 miles above the earth's surface, high enough to qualify its pilot for an astronaut badge.

Progress after the Wright flight was rapid. The idea of flying was unbearably exciting to adventurous spirits. The range, speed, ceiling, and solidity of airplanes grew like Jack's beanstalk. When the war broke out, pilots no longer had to lie on the wing, like Orville Wright, nor sit out in front of the wing on a totally exposed seat like the 1912 soldiers who made the first trial of a machine gun in an airplane. In 1914, aviators sat in cockpits.

In the first days of the war, all belligerents ordered their pilots not to engage in air-to-air combat. Planes were for observation only. Some pilots and observers took to the air with pistols, however. (There wasn't room in most cockpits for bigger weapons.) Some even used bricks on the end of wires to snag enemy observers' propellers. The authorities gradually relented. They began issuing pistols with oversized magazines and wire cages to catch the ejected cartridge cases so they wouldn't strike the pilot or a sensitive part of the plane. Cockpits got big enough to let observers carry rifles and shotguns. At least one plane was reported to have been downed by a shotgun. German observers took the Mexican-invented Mondragon semiautomatic rifle up, making it the first semiautomatic rifle to see combat.

Finally, machine guns were allowed, usually manned by the observer in two-seater planes. Machine guns could fire in any direction except straight ahead for fear of striking the propeller. An interrupter gear that coordinated the gun with the propeller solved that problem. Specialized fighter planes to escort the observation craft were developed. Fighter pilots were glamorized as "knights of the air," but theirs was a nerve-wracking and often short life, even for some of the greatest aces. They confirmed an old airman's axiom: "There are old pilots and there are bold pilots, but there are few old, bold pilots."

Bombing got off to a slow start in World War I, although Italian planes bombed Turkish forces in Libya during the Italo-Turkish War of 1911 to 1912. The Italian aviators carried the bombs in their cockpits and dropped them over the side by hand. The Germans used zeppelins, the dirigible airships invented by Count Ferdinand von Zeppelin, to bomb Paris and London. Both sides used small bombers, some armored against ground fire, to attack enemy troops, and towards the end of the war, both sides built large bombers to bombard enemy cities.

After the "Great War," most aeronautical progress was made in the civil sector, spurred by air races and adventurous pilots striving to set records. A new school of military theorists sprang up, however, that greatly influenced strategic thinking about airplanes. Giulio Douhet, an Italian general, was the first of these apostles of air power. In Britain, Air Marshal Hugh Trenchard took up the cause, and in the United States, Brigadier General William "Billy" Mitchell. All held that air forces should be as independent of the other armed services as the navy was of the army. Air forces, they said, were not only the equals of the other services; they were far more essential. By bombing enemy countries, they could destroy their infrastructures, break the will of their people, and leave the armies and navies little to do.

Perhaps strangely, Germany, so ruthless otherwise, never subscribed to this doctrine. Hermann Goering, chief of the Luftwaffe, was a former fighter pilot, an ace in von Richthofen's circus. He saw fighter and Stuka pilots as knights, but called bomber pilots mere truck drivers. That's one reason Germany failed so miserably in the Battle of Britain.

When Germany became bogged down in the Soviet Union, the balance of power in the air shifted to Britain and, a bit later, Britain and the United States. The British began daylight raids over Germany, but objectives were out of range of their fighters. The horrendous losses they suffered from enemy fighters made them switch to night raids. But flying over a blacked-out Europe, the flyers frequently missed whole cities. Advanced electronic navigation aids partly remedied that trouble, but precision bombing was impossible at night. The British used "carpet bombing," simply blanketing an area with bombs. The civilian population became as much a military target as an oil refinery or a factory.

The United States was committed to precision bombing. It had the Norden bomb sight, which reportedly would allow a bombardier to hit a pickle barrel from 10,000 feet. It had the B-17, the "flying fortress" with the speed of a fighter plane and ten .50 machine guns. It sent its flying fortresses to knock out the Schweinfurt ball bearing works. The raid was a disaster. Fighters had gotten much faster since the B-17 was adopted, and the 20 mm cannons on the Messerschmitts outranged the .50 machine guns. So did the Germans' rockets. As for the Norden bombsight, it turned out to be the most overrated military secret since the Montigny Mitrailleuse (a multi-barrel breech-loading gun that was France's secret weapon at the beginning of the Franco-Prussian War). The U.S. Army Air Forces joined the RAF on night raids and carpet bombing. Long range fighters—the P-47 and the P-51—arrived to drastically cut bomber losses in both day and night raids.

There was no doubt that the bombing plane created almost unprecedented devastation. There had been nothing like it since the armies of Genghis Khan and Tamerlane. The air raids on Germany killed 600,000 people and seriously wounded 800,000 more. A single raid on Tokyo and Yokohama killed 97,000 people, seriously injured 125,000, and burned most of both cities to the ground. Altogether, 668,000 Japanese were killed by American bombers. But in spite of Douhet, Trenchard, Mitchell, and their followers, no civilian populations panicked—not the British in the "Blitz," not the Germans in the carpet bombing, not the Japanese in the horrendous napalm raids. Two nuclear bombs gave the Japanese Emperor a face-saving excuse to ask for peace. But that might have happened earlier if the allies had dropped their politically correct but essentially meaningless demand for "unconditional surrender."

As for effects on the war effort, consider this: In 1942, the British dropped 48,000 tons of bombs on Germany, and the Germans produced 36,804 heavy weapons (tanks, planes, and artillery). In 1943, the British and American dropped 207,600 tons of bombs, and the Germans produced 71,693 heavy weapons. In 1944, the Allies dropped 915,000 tons of bombs and the Germans produced 105,258 weapons. Although the airplane in World War II proved itself the master weapon in both land and sea fighting, much of the strategic bombing looks like wasted effort.

Technical progress in air forces continued after the war. All combat planes now have jet engines. They drop smart bombs and smart rockets that home in on their targets with uncanny accuracy. It is now possible to avoid the mass slaughter caused by World War II's carpet bombing. Some planes have no pilots (a cruise missile is a form of jet plane, so is a drone). The space shuttle is both a plane and a rocket. (The Germans had a rocket plane in World War II, the Me 163 Komet. Its range was extremely short, it could not land, and its engine was liable to explode.)

Some have suggested that missiles might replace planes altogether. This is not likely for quite a while. At present, missiles are programmed to fly one route. It is possible to program them to take an alternate route if so signaled. But a missile cannot sense danger in flight, as a human pilot could, nor can it make a split-second decision about choosing alternative actions. Airplanes apparently will be the master weapon of warfare for the foreseeable future.

33

Sticky Situations:
Barbed Wire

Barbed wire. Designed for fencing cattle, it became an indispensable military tool.

In the long, confused, and bloody affair called the Mexican Revolution, Venustiano Carranza had seized the presidency over the objections of two other rebel leaders, Emiliano Zapata and Pancho Villa. Carranza, a wealthy planter, was no military man, while his two rivals were experienced commanders. Carranza's army was commanded by Álvaro Obregón, a keen student of the war raging in Europe at this time (1915), who also picked up some German military advisors. From what he knew of the Western Front, Obregon calculated that launching an offensive would be the wrong move. Instead, he fortified the village of Celaya and defied Villa to do anything about it.

Pancho Villa, known as "the Centaur of the North," was a bandit turned revolutionist. He had charisma. In 1913, he returned from exile in the United States with eight friends. They rode through towns and ranches shouting "Viva Villa!" and every man with a horse and rifle joined the legendary bandit and guerrilla. Within 30 days, Villa was leading an army of 3,000 cavalrymen. Villa was shrewd, too. He once sneaked an army into Ciudad Juarez in a train that federal troops thought contained part of their own army. And he was colorful. Villa's army attracted scores of reporters, and newspapers were filled with stories about his brilliance, his daring, and his humanity. By 1915, he had come to believe the stories. He thought he was invincible.

So when Obregón, a middle-class pipsqueak from the state of Sonora, fortified Celayo, Villa decided to put him in his place. He got 25,000 of his best cavalrymen, *Los Dorados* (the Golden Ones) and launched them at Orbregón's fortifications. Singing *La Cucuracha*, the Dorados galloped at the Carrancista trenches. They never got there. The horses were caught in the miles of barbed wire, which formed entanglements in front of Celaya's trenches, while Obregón's machine guns and quick-firing field pieces mowed them down. The Dorados fell back, then charged again. And again…and again. At the end of the day, when the remnants of the Golden Ones and their horses could barely stand, Obregón brought his own cavalry out from behind the wire and swept them from the field.

Barbed wire, an American invention of the late 19th century, was intended for nothing more warlike than keeping cattle on their own pastures. It was quickly adopted by armies all over the world for non-peaceful purposes. In Cuba, during the Spanish-American War, the Spanish surrounded their forts with barbed wire fences. In South Africa, during the Boer War, the British had criss-crossed the veldt with barbed wire to limit the movements of mounted Afrikaner guerrillas. The wire was strung between bulletproof block houses, each block house within a long rifle shot of others. In the Russo-Japanese War, both sides used great tangles of barbed wire, which, as we saw in Chapter 27, could not be cleared by artillery fire.

Barbed wire, trenches, masses of artillery, and machine guns were what created the Western Front of World War I, the longest and bloodiest siege in history. It is still being used, although sometimes in a modified form, razor wire. Razor wire was invented by the Germans in World War I, because it could be produced more cheaply than standard barbed wire. Razor wire isn't wire at all but long, thin strips of metal with sharp, jagged edges. It is cut from sheet metal, is harder to sever with standard wire cutters and deters as effectively as the original barbed wire. One recent improvement to razor wire is adding a fiber-optic core to the wire. Anyone tampering with the wire would break the core, thus indicating exactly where he was and providing a target for defenders' fire.

Barbed wire can be used in several ways besides as a simple fence or fence top. One is in an ankle-high entanglement, which may be hidden in high grass. It can be laid as "concertina wire," in which troops place it in coils resembling the body of a concertina. Several rolls of concertina, some of the coils overlapping, may be used to make a particularly difficult barrier. Perhaps the most common way in carefully prepared field fortifications is in a wide entanglement with wire running in all directions and securely staked to the ground. In World War II, movies of troop training often showed soldiers falling on the wire while other soldiers crossed the wire on their backs. In real life, that seldom happened, if ever. The attackers' object is to cross the wire without getting shot. Anyone prancing over the top of an entanglement on the bodies of his comrades makes an excellent target. The prescribed method of crossing wire is to go under it, if possible on your back so you can see what to avoid or what to cut. Of course, there is always the possibility that the enemy has planted land mines under the wire to make your crawl more interesting.

It is a testimony to the importance and prevalence of barbed wire that most modern bayonets are designed so that they can be used as wire cutters.

34

Trouble in the Air:
Poison Gas

National Archives from War Dept.

French troops launch a gas attack during World War I.

April 22, 1915 had been a delightful day, warm and sunny—not all that common a spring day in Flanders. The war-ravaged village of Neuve-Chapelle was being held by French Algerian and Canadian troops. About 5 p.m. a grayish-green fog seemed to rise from the German trenches across no-man's-land from the Allied line and drift toward the Algerians. The fog covered the Algerian trenches and flowed into them like water. Then the Canadians saw the North African riflemen running to the rear, coughing and choking. Their departure left a gap in the line 8,000 yards wide. A few minutes later, a bit of the fog drifted into the Canadian lines. The Canadians got a small taste of what the Algerians had been through, but fortunately, it was only a taste. They were able to hold their line and beat back the German infantry, who pushed forward as the green fog began dissipating.

This was the first use in modern times of deadly gas in war. A few months earlier, on January 3, 1915, the Germans had used tear gas on the Russian front, but it had had no effect on the Russians. The weather was so cold that the chemical in the gas shells had frozen instead of vaporizing. This may have been the reason the Germans made their second gas attack by opening cylinders when the wind was right: they could see whether the gas was vaporizing.

The gas this time was chlorine, a common chemical used in scores of compounds. Second-year high school students produce small quantities of chlorine gas in school labs. Engineers at I.G. Farben, the German chemical giant, worked out a way to produce vast amounts of chlorine gas, pack the liquid gas in cylinders, and release it from the trenches. It was the second scientific triumph for Farben and Germany's leading industrial chemist, Fritz Haber of the Kaiser Wilhelm Institute. Earlier, Farben and Haber had invented a way to draw nitrogen from the air, a development essential for Germany's war effort, because the British Navy had cut off Germany's usual source of nitrates, imports from Chile. Haber reportedly said the gas would "settle the hash of the wicked English."

The Algerians took the rap for the British in the first gas attack. Two days later, the Canadians were the target of the second attack. On the 23rd, though, Canadian officers had identified the mysterious cloud as chlorine. Chlorine is soluble in water, so the Canadians tied wet cloths over their faces. That helped to mitigate the effects of the gas, and the Allies had moved more reinforcements up behind the Canadians. The line held, and Canadians, British, and French counterattacked. On May 1st, Haber's invention was finally used against "the wicked English," the First Battalion of the Dorset Regiment. Somehow, the Dorsets seemed not to have heard about the wet rag counter. When the men began to choke, many of them fled. A second lieutenant named Kestell-Cornish picked up a rifle one of the men of his platoon dropped and fired into the green cloud rolling toward him. The four men remaining from his platoon of 40 men joined him. Other British soldiers joined them. Once again, the Germans were beaten back, but the price the British paid was high. Ninety men died in the trenches. Some 207 were evacuated to the aid station. Of them, 46 died immediately; 12 others after long suffering.

Chlorine causes the lungs to fill with fluid, and the victim drowns. It was not the only gas in the German arsenal. The next one used was *phosgene*, a colorless gas that smells like new-mown hay and chokes its victim much more quickly than chlorine. Then there was *mustard gas*, a blistering agent. Mustard gas burns and blisters any tissue it touches—any exposed skin and also the lungs. It is extremely lethal, and many of the men it didn't kill were crippled for life. Basil H. Liddell Hart, the British military commentator, was invalidated out of the army as a result of injuries from mustard gas. The Allies quickly countered the German gas offensive with gases of their own. The United States entered the race late but produced Lewisite, a byproduct of a search for synthetic rubber that out-blistered the blistering mustard gas.

One product all these gases had in common was that they were heavier than air. Instead of billowing into the upper atmosphere, they flowed to the lowest points on the ground. A veteran of World War I once told the author that he was more afraid of gas than any other weapon. He was in the Signal Corps, and his job was to help operate a telephone switchboard deep underground. His dugout was so deep, he explained, that he might not hear the gas alarm. Even if he did, the alarm might be too late. He wouldn't have time to take off his headphone and put on his gas mask before phosgene laid him low.

Gas was a true terror weapon—one that can cause fear out of proportion to its effectiveness. Actually, of the deaths on the Western Front, only about 1.1 percent were caused by gas, but fear of gas terrified whole nations on the eve of World War II. Governments tried to issue gas masks to their civilian populations, but there were far too few gas masks. Fortunately, no belligerent tried to gas an enemy's civilians. Even if there were enough masks, they wouldn't solve the problem. Mustard gas and Lewisite burn on contact with the skin, and the new nerve gases can quickly kill without being inhaled. Of the three most common nerve gases, *Tabun* will cause death if 1,000 milligrams touches the victim's skin; *Sarin* takes 1,700 milligrams, but *VX* requires only 15 milligrams on the skin to kill, less than half a fatal dose if inhaled. A person attacked by any of these gases is a grave threat to would-be rescuers. Good Samaritans may get a fatal dose just touching the victim's clothing.

Gas masks, covering the face and allowing a potential victim breath through a filter, usually composed of activated charcoal, were issued to all soldiers, and those in especially hazardous areas got protective overalls as well. Poison gas was hazardous to everyone near it, especially when used as it was on April 22, 1915, being released into the wind from cylinders. The wind could always shift. As a result, all belligerents went back to using gas primarily in shells.

In World War II, the Allies, it has been said, were waiting for the Germans to use gas first. Then they would retaliate. The Germans, in spite of all their preparations for war, were not able to deal with poison gas. One reason, according to some experts, was that they had been unable to devise a gas mask for horses. Although when the war began, the German Army was believed to be the ultimate in mechanization, it still relied heavily on horses for towing artillery and general transport. It continued to do so until the end of the war. German officers complained during the Russian campaign that their "modern" horse-drawn wagons broke down on the awful Russian roads and they had to comandeer Russian peasant carts to carry supplies.

Poison gas did not entirely disappear in spite of its general non-use. The Japanese used mustard gas and other chemical agents against the Chinese in World War II, before the United States and other Western nations became involved, because the Chinese could not retaliate. Iran used poison gas in the Iran-Iraq War of 1980-1988. The Iranians, fanatical followers of the Shi'a Ayatollah Ruhollah Khomeini, were willing to use anything available in what they considered a holy war. The Iraqis, under the pragmatic and self-centered Saddam Hussein, retaliated with their own gas. That war ended in a stalemate, but Hussein then turned on the Iraqi Kurds, a minority that wanted independence, and slaughtered thousands of them with gas. The Kurds, of course, had no way to retaliate.

Poison gas was one of the "weapons of mass destruction" Iraq was supposed to be hoarding before the U.S. invasion of Iraq in 2002. The only gas found was one artillery shell filled with nerve gas that an Iraqi guerrilla tried to turn into a roadside bomb, apparently believing that it was filled with high explosive. The shell apparently had been scheduled to be disposed of with the rest of Saddam's gas but got lost among the hundreds of thousands of high explosive shells that seem to be buried every couple of square miles in Iraq.

The future use of gas is uncertain. As time goes on, the chemists are inventing ever more deadly gases—gases that kill quicker, that penetrate filters and protective gear, that kill with the merest touch. It is becoming as horrible as the other components of what the military calls CBR—chemical, biological, and radiological—warfare. Whether or not it is ever used again, it will influence the thinking and action of governments for years to come.

35

Artillery Up Close and Personal:
The Trench Mortar

National Archives from Army

U.S. troops use mortar to help establish a beachhead on the right bank of the Rhine in 1945.

Of all the war-changing weapons, this has to be one of the most unimpressive. It looks like a piece of plain pipe propped up on a couple of legs. And, to a large extent, that's what it is.

When trench warfare developed on a large scale, all armies felt a need for something that would lob explosives down into their enemy's trenches. That was not a brand-new need, of course. Mortars, which throw shells on a high trajectory, had been among the earliest of firearms. Small mortars for close-range work had been around since the 17th century, but nobody had ever used high-trajectory weapons on the scale they were wanted in World War I. All kinds of contrivances, such as *catapults*, were tried. The Russians had a cata-pult that consisted of a pivoted wooden arm that threw hand grenades. Instead of a skein of rope, it was powered by a modern steel coil spring attached to the short lower portion of the arm.

The Germans observed the use of small mortars during the Russo-Japanese War and began to build up their stock in preparation for the next war, which everyone in Europe assumed would happen sooner or later. By 1914, they had 2,000 *Minenwerfers* (mine throwers), as they called these small mortars. They came in a variety of calibers, from 3 to 9.8 inches. One type of shell had a tube at one end containing powder and a percussion cap. The tube was inserted in the short barrel of the small mortar and fired. This system allowed a small, portable gun to fire a comparatively heavy shell. Unfortunately, the shell, gy-rating end over end, wasn't very accurate. In the 1948 Israeli war for indepen-dence, the Israelis built a similar mortar from odds and ends and called it "Little David." Little David was hailed as a masterpiece of ingenuity by people who had never heard of its German prototype. Most German *Minenwerfers* were more complicated than Little David's ancestor, and heavier, too. All were muzzle-loaders, but they had recoil mechanisms like the field guns. Many were rifled, with driving bands engraved to fit the rifling. Because the shells now flew point-first, they could be fitted with ordinary percussion fuses. Previously, they had time fuses or a gadget called an "all ways" fuse—a rather dangerous device that would explode the shell no matter what part struck a solid object.

As it turned out, the 2,000 *Minenwerfers* were but a drop in a bucket of what was needed.

The British came up with a much simpler gun after gas was introduced. Called a Livens projector, it was merely an unrifled steel tube with a diameter of eight inches welded to a steel base plate. Groups of 25 projectors were dug into the ground, placed at a pre-determined angle facing the German trenches. Each gun was loaded with a powder charge wired for electrical ignition and a drum of poi-son gas 8 inches wide and 25 inches long. All 25 guns were then fired simulta-neously. The gas drums burst and the gas vaporized as soon as they landed.

It was just a short step from the Livens projector to the next British design, the Stokes or Newton-Stokes trench mortar. Versions of the Stokes mortar were adopted by every country in the world soon after its introduction because it was light, accurate, and versatile. And above all, it was cheap and easy to make in great quantities.

The new trench mortar was a smoothbore steel tube that rested on a separate steel base plate. The barrel was propped up on two legs, making the whole weapon a kind of tripod. On top of the legs was an elevating gear, making possible fine adjustments. Although it was a smoothbore, the mortar's projectiles flew point-first and accurately, because they were stabilized by fins on their tails. The firing mechanism was simply a fixed firing pin at the bottom of the tube. To fire the mortar, the gunner merely dropped a shell down the muzzle and snatched his hand out of the way immediately. The shell slid down the barrel, and a powder charge, contained in what looked like a shotgun shell, struck the firing pin. The pin ignited the percussion cap on the end of the "shotgun shell" and the mortar round went sailing off to the enemy. Later, it became possible to vary the power of the propelling charge by adding increments in the form of rings of smokeless powder to the tail of the mortar shell. That gave the gunners two ways to vary the range—changing the elevation or adding increments to the propelling charge.

The trench mortar gave the infantry a weapon that could be carried by one or two men and was capable of firing a shell of significant size at the enemy. The French in World War I also used a small, 37 mm cannon on a tripod, but that was a flat trajectory weapon mostly useful for countering machine gun nests, and its shell was far smaller than the trench mortar's. Trench mortars come in a variety of sizes. The British in World War II used a 50-mm (2-inch) mortar that one man could carry and operate. The Japanese had a similar gun with a curved base plate. Some GIs called it a "knee mortar," supposing that the curved base plate fit over the gunner's extended leg. One or two American soldiers tried to fire it that way and ended up with broken legs. U.S. trench mortars in World War II were in calibers 60 mm, 81 mm, and 4.2 inches (106.6 mm). The 4.2 inch mortar was not limited to short ranges. It could send a shell 6,000 yards, or about 3 1/2 miles. It took the shell about a minute to go that far. Using the 4.2 mortar, a good crew could put half a dozen shells in the air before the first one landed. The Warsaw Pact countries and some other nations used a 120 mm mortar. The Chinese and North Korean version was a superb weapon, as any veteran of the Korean War will affirm. NATO has since adopted a 120 mm mortar. Some modern mortars are rifled, a system that increases range and accuracy at the expense of simplicity and speed of fire.

The introduction of the trench mortar made it possible to lay unprecedentedly heavy fire on enemy positions. In World War I, the trench mortar was used extensively by German "storm troops" during Ludendorff's 1918 offensive. In World War II, mortars were everywhere. And the trench mortar's simplicity has made homemade mortars popular with guerrillas all over the world.

36

Traveling Forts:
Armored Vehicles

National Archives from Marine Corps

U.S. troops take cover behind a tank during a
firefight near Hongchon, Korea, in 1951.

German infantrymen were ready for another assault by the English. The English had been attacking almost continually for the last two and a half months. When they weren't sending swarms of men at the German line, their artillery was pounding the trenches. Not a tree was standing. Not even a blade of grass. Their guns had churned the fields of Flanders into a muddy morass. It looked like something Breughel might have dreamed up if he were painting a landscape of Hell. Then the Germans saw some things that looked as if they might have come from Hell. They were metal rhomboids with caterpillar tracks running all around them. They had no windows that anyone could see, but from a projection on each side, each of these monsters had machine guns or light cannons. They fired as they waddled and wobbled across the mud, rolled right over shell craters and trenches. After a few moments of shock, the German *landsers* recovered their wits and fired at the strange machines. Their bullets bounced off.

This day, September 13, 1916, would forever change the way war was waged. The tank had appeared.

It almost hadn't. And this premature appearance did nothing to enhance its chances for a future role in war. The tanks did drive back the Germans, who knew of no way to deal with them. But one by one, the machines broke down for a variety of reasons, and the British had no vehicles that could tow them back, few mechanics who could repair them, and fewer spare parts with which to repair them.

The tank was the most promising British effort to break the unholy deadlock that the Western Front had become. With their artillery, the Allies and Germans had been pounding each other to pieces. Infantry trying to break through the enemy trench lines had been hung up on barbed wire and mowed down by machine guns. Between attacking and repulsing attacks, the men in the trenches had to cope with such delights as poison gas and midnight raids. Worst of all, there seemed to be no way to end this horrible war. The tank was designed to mash down barbed wire, crush machine gun nests, straddle trenches, and cut down their defenders. If it could do those things, it could end the war.

In prewar days, when nobody thought pastures could be turned into cratered swamps and that the whole of Europe between the Alps and the North Sea could be divided by intricate trench lines, the more radical military thinkers advocated armored cars. (Most of the rest thought horses were still the essence of military mobility.) The Western Front, it turned out, became just about the worst possible terrain for anything with wheels. In some spots, horses sank into the mud up to their shoulders. It wasn't too good for them, either. Armored cars did turn in sterling performances in the deserts of Palestine and Mesopotamia, but not in France or Belgium.

Lieutenant Colonel Ernest Swinton was an official British combat historian (an "eye witness," was the Royal Army classification). In 1914, he saw tractors using an American invention, the caterpillar track, pulling artillery. The caterpillar tractors were not handicapped by the rough and muddy ground. Swinton proposed armored vehicles using caterpillar tracks to British headquarters in France. The generals there had the same reaction as King Archidamus of Sparta (see Chapter 9), although they didn't express their feelings so honestly. They fervently believed that battles were decided by human valor. Use of machines was unworthy, underhanded, and dastardly. They rejected Swinton's proposal. Swinton sent a copy of his paper to a friend, Lieutenant Colonel Maurice Hankey, who was secretary to the Committee of Imperial Defense. At that time, all matters concerning military motor vehicles were handled by the navy, so the proposal ended up with the first lord of the admiralty, Winston Churchill. Churchill was impressed and got the support of the prime minister. By this time, Swinton, still in France, had managed to get some interest from the GHQ in France for his "armored machine gun destroyer." There was more bureaucratic battling, especially after the resounding failure of the landing at Gallipoli. The Dardanelles expedition had been Churchill's brainchild. He was ousted from the cabinet and his influence became negative.

Some machines were eventually built and passed tests for serviceability. By this time, Douglas Haig (see Chapter 27), who had lost hundreds of thousands of men to German machine guns on the Somme, was desperate for something to counter the guns he had once scorned. He demanded the armored machine gun destroyers, which were now officially called *tanks*: to confuse the Germans, they were said to be mobile water tanks for use in the desert.

Colonel Swinton, who had been promoted to command of the Tank Corps, opposed the premature use of tanks. He wrote a memo on the conditions that should be met before tanks were introduced. Terrain, weather, the availability of reserve tanks, repair facilities were among the conditions. The Somme battlefield in September 1916 met none of them. And there were too few tanks.

Haig's staff appeared to have been delighted with the tanks' failure. They wrote a scathing report that result in an order cancelling future production of tanks. That might have buried the tank for a generation if it had not been for Major Albert Stern. Stern, an important financier in civilian life, believed in the tank and was a friend of the prime minister. Stern visited his friend, and the cancel order was cancelled.

Haig dealt the tanks another blow when he demanded them for this offensive at the Third Battle of Ypres in 1917. Shell fire and rain had turned the area into not only a swamp, but something just short of quicksand. The tanks were defeated by General Mud. Later, at Cambrai, the tanks, following a plan devised by a brilliant staff officer, J.F.C. Fuller, won a solid victory, although one infantry outfit, the 5th Highlanders, was not enthusiastic about tanks and did not follow them closely enough. Unfortunately, that sector was commanded by a General von Walter, an old artilleryman, who brought his field pieces close to the front and trained his gunners to hit moving targets. The Germans knocked out 11 British tanks before the Highland infantry arrived to silence their cannons.

Fortunately for the Allies, the German generals generally could see no value in the tank. The French, though, were enthusiastic. They built more tanks than the British. On August 8, 1918, 600 French and British tanks attacked the Germans. Ludendorff later called it "the black day of the German Army." It convinced Ludendorff and the kaiser that the war could not be won. They later changed their minds, but the rest of Germany did not. On November 11, 1918, the war ended. Germany lost.

One reason for that loss was the German contempt for the tank. The new generation of German officers changed that. When Germany rearmed, it concentrated on tanks, close air support, armored personnel carriers for infantry, and self propelled guns. These were grouped into *panzer* (armored) divisions. The German generals devised new tactics for them, based, ironically, on the writings of Fuller and a British military commentator, B.H. Liddell Hart. Fuller and Liddell Hart advocated "torrents" of tanks, which would bypass strong points, sweep into rear areas and disrupt supplies, communications and the whole command structure. Using these tactics and with the aid of its then-ally, the Soviet Union, Germany conquered Poland in about two months.

After a lightning campaign ("Blitzkrieg") in Denmark and Norway, the Germans turned on France, a nation reputed to have the best army in the world. France had been joined by Britain, its ally in the last war. The allies had more tanks than the Germans, and some of them were bigger and had heavier armor, but they kept them scattered among all their troops. The concept was that tanks were "mobile pillboxes." The German panzer divisions lanced through the allied armies on May 10, 1940. France surrendered on June 21st. Before that, the British evacuated their expeditionary force, which left most of its equipment on the beach.

The German Blitzkriegs were wars of movement, as far removed from the stalemate of the Western Front as could be imagined. The Blitzkrieg had to be modified, however. New weapons, the anti-tank land mine, infantry rocket launchers like the U.S. "bazooka," recoilless guns and fighter-bombers armed with rockets all ended the comparatively carefree life of the tankers. But tanks permanently changed warfare and are still a most important part of any army.

37

Air Power on the Sea:
The Aircraft Carrier

Navy dive bombers attack Japanese ships during Battle of Midway. Note smoke from burning Japanese ship.

Before the First World War, relations between Britain and Germany became strained when the two countries engaged in an arms race. The Germans felt that a great power had to have a great navy as well as overseas colonies. The British felt that survival on their islands required that they have a navy superior to any other in the world. So each began building more and better battleships.

Battleships, floating steel fortresses carrying guns far more powerful than any that could be used by a field army, were symbols of military might. They were called "capital ships."

The arms race ended with World War I. At the end of the war, the mighty German High Seas Fleet—which spent most of the war in the Baltic and never reached a higher sea than the North Sea—was no more. Britain had more battleships than any other country, but many of her "battle wagons" were old, slow and had only 12-inch guns. A new threat to British sea supremacy was shaping up far from Europe. Two Pacific powers, the United States and Japan, decided to build new battleships. Unlike Germany in the previous naval arms race, neither country was thinking about Britain. The Japanese worried about the Americans, and the Americans about the Japanese.

In 1915, Japan announced a program to build 16 battleships and battle cruisers. The battle cruiser was a ship, pioneered by the British and the Germans, that looked like a battleship but had thinner armor. It was faster than a battleship but carried the same heavy armament. The U.S. Congress passed a law authorizing creation of a navy "second to none." The United States began building 10 new battleships which, like those of the new Japanese ships, would carry 16-inch guns. In response, the British began building four enormous—48,000-ton—battle cruisers and started designing battleships with 18-inch guns. A new, three-runner naval arms race was beginning.

At this point, the United States took advantage of two facts. First, Britain was broke and exhausted by the late war and could not hope to out-build the American shipyards. Second, Japan just didn't have the industrial capacity to compete in an all-out arms race. The United States called on the other countries to join in a naval arms limitation treaty. The treaty, the Washington Treaty of 1921, imposed a moratorium on capital ship building and set limits for the world's major naval powers. Britain and the United States were allowed to have the largest navies, Japan, the next largest, and France and Italy somewhat smaller fleets. France and Italy, like Britain, had been impoverished by the war and were happy to have an excuse for not spending a lot of money on battleships. Japan, which had been one of the Allies, but which was untouched by the war, was less happy. The Japanese saw the terms, which let them have less than the Americans or British, as evidence of Anglo-American racial prejudice. They were right. But they couldn't hope to compete with the Americans in an arms race. So they accepted the treaty, and the long-simmering Japanese-American rivalry grew hotter.

When the treaty was signed, the United States was building two battle cruisers, which would be the first such ships in the American navy. Both battleships and battle cruisers were considered capital ships. To keep from exceeding its capital ship quota, the United States altered the construction of two battle cruisers to make them into a new type of ship—aircraft carriers. The projected battle cruisers would make excellent aircraft carriers because they were so big and so fast. Size was important, because the larger the ship, the more space planes would have to take off and land. There was no way a ship could be built that was as big as the average air field, so all navy planes but the big patrol bombers had to be constructed to have a maximum of lift. That was also why speed was important. During take-offs, the carrier headed into the wind and proceeded at full speed to enhance the plane's own take-off speed. The two former battle cruisers became the U.S.S. *Lexington* and the U.S.S. *Saratoga*, which for many years were the world's biggest, fastest, and most powerful aircraft carriers.

They weren't the first. In the U.S. Navy, the U.S.S. *Langley* (named after aircraft pioneer Dr. Samuel Langley), a converted collier, had preceded them. During World War I, the British had experimented with aircraft carriers. The H.M.S. *Furious* had a flight deck, but it was too short and located behind the funnels, which created too much turbulence. *Furious* could handle only amphibian planes that landed in the water and had to be winched aboard the ship. In the U.S. Navy, cruisers and battleships had been carrying seaplanes on catapults since 1912. These aircraft, too, landed on the water and were hauled up to the deck. The British then built the H.M..S. *Argus*, which had an unbroken flight deck, but *Argus* was not commissioned until after the war. Meanwhile, the Japanese had not been idle. Japan commissioned its first ship designed from the start to be an aircraft carrier in 1922. That ship, *Hosho*, entered the Imperial service 12 years before *Ranger*, the first purpose-built American carrier, was commissioned.

Aircraft carriers required specialized planes and highly skilled pilots because they provided such limited take-off and landing space. Arresting gear helped to slow landing planes, and carriers built during World War II had catapults to help their planes become airborne. Still, to a high-flying pilot, his carrier was a tiny dot that might be moving faster than most craft on the ocean. And if he were flying any kind of bomber, his target was usually even smaller. Carrier-based bombers were considerably smaller than their land-based counterparts. There were three kinds—*high-level bombers, dive bombers,* and *torpedo bombers*. Bombs dropped from high altitude had more penetration than those released at a lower level, but if dropped on ships that were under way, their chances of scoring a hit were extremely small. The U.S. Navy invented dive bombing so its planes could hit those small, fast-moving targets. Dive bombing was dangerous, because, to a gunner on the surface, the plane appeared immobile, only getting bigger as it approached the ship. Even more dangerous was torpedo bombing, because the plane appeared equally immobile while flying just above the water.

Aircraft carriers were now firmly established in the world's navies, but they weren't considered capital ships. Until 1937, the world's navies concentrated on rebuilding their old battleships—even battleships those that weren't so old. When the Japanese battleship *Nagato* was commissioned in 1920, she was the most powerful battleship in the world. *Nagato's* armor was increased, raising her displacement by 6,000 tons. Her speed stayed the same, because she received new engines. And the range of her 16-inch guns was increased by allowing them greater elevation. In 1937, limitations on capital ships ended and all naval powers resumed building battleships. The United States built the most, but Japan built the most powerful. *Musashi* and *Yamato* were two monsters each carrying nine 18-inch guns and displacing 72,908 tons when fully laden. Naval historian Admiral Samuel Eliot Morison wrote that the two ships "would have inaugurated a new standard for battleship construction—as H.M.S Dreadnought had done 40 years earlier."

But that was not to be. This was, to a large extent, because of something the proud owners of these super ships did December 7, 1941.

On that day, Admiral Yamamoto Isoroku carried out the attack he had planned over the opposition of the Naval General Staff—a surprise attack on the U.S. Pacific Fleet at Pearl Harbor. The Naval General Staff, the part of the Japanese navy responsible for plans, had no faith that mere airplanes could successfully cripple a whole battle fleet. But Yamamoto believed that immobile ships crowded into a harbor would make good targets. He called in specialists to develop shallow-running torpedoes, armor piercing bombs and tactics suitable for operations in a constricted space such as Pearl Harbor. Then he created the First Air Fleet—six aircraft carriers escorted by two battleships and a number of cruisers and destroyers.

At the last moment, the Naval General Staff ordered Yamamoto to send three of his carriers to the naval force about to begin operations in Southeast Asia. Yamamoto said that if he had to do that, he and his whole staff would resign. The Naval General Staff backed down. The First Air Fleet sailed under the command of Admiral Nagumo Chuichi, an old battleship admiral who was not convinced he could accomplish his mission.

Fortunately for the United States, all the aircraft carriers in its Pacific Fleet were elsewhere. Nagumo could hardly believe his success. His planes had sunk or crippled every battleship in the U.S. Pacific Fleet as well as many other smaller ships and a large number of land-based planes—most of them caught on the ground. From that day on, he was a fervent supporter of air power.

The U.S. Pacific Fleet was suddenly at war without battleships. Admiral Ernest J. King, commander-in-chief of the United States fleet, was hoarding all the newest battleships in the Atlantic, in line with the official policy that major enemy was Germany. It only gradually dawned on King that battleships were useless against Germany but would be most helpful fighting Japan. Admiral Chester W. Nimitz, commander of the Pacific Fleet, and his staff had to improvise. They created a new tactical formation, the carrier task force. It was modeled on Yamamoto's First Air Fleet. It was built around one or more carriers which were escorted by cruisers and destroyers.

The new formation got its first big test in the Battle of the Coral Sea, when American and Japanese fleets slugged it out without ever coming to within sight of each other. All the action was done by airplanes. The battle was a tactical draw but a strategic U.S. victory, because it turned back an attempted Japanese invasion of the south coast of New Guinea, which would put Japanese troops in place for an invasion of Australia. The heaviest American loss was the end of "Lady Lex," the big old U.S.S. *Lexington*.

The second test was the Battle of Midway. This was Yamamoto's attempt to finish off American power in the Pacific. The Japanese plan was complicated. A diversionary attack on the Aleutians was supposed to draw off the American ships. Meanwhile, a task force under Nagumo, which included all four of the large Japanese carriers now operational, would attack American forces on Midway Island. Then the main Japanese fleet, commanded by Yamamoto himself from his flagship, the enormous *Yamato*, would wipe out the American ships returning from the north and invade Hawaii.

The Americans didn't go to the Aleutians, because they had decoded enough of the Japanese radio transmissions to know that the Aleutians attack was a feint. They did not know, however, where the fleets of Nagumo and Yamamoto were. Scout planes then spotted Nagumo's ships about the time they launched their first aerial attack on Midway. Admiral Raymond Spruance launched the planes from his carriers, *Enterprise* and *Hornet*, in an attempt to get the Japanese carriers while their planes were refueling. Meanwhile, Nagumo had changed his course. The American planes could not find the Japanese ships. While they were searching, the Japanese planes returned and refueled. Admiral Frank Jack Fletcher, aboard the U.S.S. *Yorktown*, launched his planes.

Meanwhile, navy, marine, and army planes from Midway attacked Nagumo's fleet and were shot down or driven off without causing damage. U.S.S. *Nautilus*, a submarine, launched a torpedo at a Japanese carrier that missed. *Nautilus* was driven off by depth charges. Then *Hornet's* torpedo bombers spotted the Japanese. Every single plane was shot down. *Enterprise's* torpedo squadron then appeared, the Japanese shot down 10 of the 14 planes. *Yorktown's* torpedo planes attacked next and suffered the same fate.

At this point (at 10:24 a.m.), on June 4, 1942, Nagumo's carriers had defeated land-based air attacks and a submarine attack and shot down almost all of the Americans' most formidable aircraft—their torpedo planes. It looked as if Yamamoto's main fleet would have little to do.

At 10:26, Lieutenant Commander Clarence McClusky, leading the two dive bomber squadrons from *Enterprise* back to the carrier after an unsuccessful search, saw the carriers *Kaga* and *Akagi* through a break in the clouds. He signaled one squadron to follow him, and dived on *Kaga*. His second-in-command, Lieutenant W.E. Gallaher, led the second squadron on *Akagi*. The *Enterprise* dive bombers arrived while the Japanese Zeros were at a low altitude where they had been shooting down torpedo planes. *Kaga* was soon burning from stem to stern. *Akagi* took a hit on the flight deck and the explosion blew off the planes that were trying to refuel. Another bomb exploded in the torpedo magazine. Nagumo moved his flag from *Akagi* to a destroyer and the Japanese abandoned the ship. A Japanese destroyer sent *Akagi* to the bottom. A third Japanese carrier, *Soryu*, moved up and prepared to launch its Zeros. Just then, some of *Yorktown's* dive bombers under Lieutenant Commander Maxwell Leslie appeared. They dived on *Soryu*, and three hits turned the Japanese carrier into an inferno. Then *Nautilus* reappeared and shot three torpedoes into *Soryu*. The ship broke in two and went down in a sizzling mass of steam.

Nagumo had one carrier left: *Hiryu*. He sent its planes off to attack the American ships, wherever they were. They found *Yorktown*, which had just launched its remaining dive bombers. The Japanese planes crippled *Yorktown*, but, while they were doing that, *Yorktown's* second set of dive bombers found *Hiryu*. They attacked, refueled on *Enterprise*, and then returned with *Enterprise's* dive bombers. The crippled *Hiryu* began to sink and went to the bottom the next day.

Nagumo signaled to Yamamoto what had happened and recommended he call off the expedition. Yamamoto was beside himself with rage and relieved Nagumo of his command. He refused to turn back. But after a short time, he realized that, without air cover, he would be heading for a disaster. He turned back.

Yorktown, which had been severely damaged in the Coral Sea and hastily repaired, was towed back to Pearl Harbor for more repairs. But a Japanese submarine spotted her and her tow ship and sank them both. "Waltzing Matilda," as her crew called her, was a big loss, but it was nothing compared to what the Japanese had suffered.

In five minutes, with the destruction of *Kaga*, *Akagi*, and *Soryu*, Nagumo went from complete triumph to utter defeat. Then the destruction of *Hiryu* wiped out *all* of Japan's operational fleet carriers. Japan could never build enough carriers or train enough pilots to come near to matching the Americans.

The Japanese tried, however. They turned what was to be a sister ship of *Yamato* and *Musashi* into an aircraft carrier. The new carrier, *Sinano*, became the biggest and most powerful aircraft carrier in the world, dwarfing the mighty old *Saratoga*. *Sinano* made her maiden voyage in November of 1944. On November 29, 1944, the U.S. submarine *Archerfish* sank *Sinano* before she could send a plane into combat.

That may have been prophetic. Many naval analysts think that nuclear-powered submarines may really be the new capital ships. At the present, aircraft carriers have been invaluable in projecting American power to the far corners of the world. But the big, powerful, and highly vulnerable ships have not been used since World War II against a major naval or air power.

38

A Machine Gun for Every Man: Submachine Guns and Assault Rifles

West Point Museum

German *machinenpistole* 44—really an assault rifle, rather than a submachine gun, because it uses a rifle cartridge. The designation was later changed to *sturmgewehr*, assault rifle.

The landings of the 82nd and 101st Airborne Divisions and the other paratroop outfits in Normandy on D day were nothing like what happened on maneuvers. Each landing was mass confusion—almost chaos. The troops landed at night, a pitch-black night, scattered over a strange countryside. Some spent hours trying find another paratrooper. Many were unable to join all their regular units for quite a while.

Staff Sergeant Harrison Summers was at least able to join his battalion, the first battalion of the 502nd Regiment. Summers's battalion commander, desperately short of men, gave the sergeant 15 strangers and told him to capture a

German coast artillery barracks. Summers took his *Thompson submachine gun*, a basic load of ammunition, and the 15 strangers. Because the other men didn't know him and didn't trust him, Summers knew he'd have to lead them, not just tell them what to do.

The "barracks" was actually a number of buildings, strung out over almost half a mile. Summers ran up to the first building, kicked in the door, and mowed down four of the defenders with his tommy gun. The rest dashed out the back door. Summers looked around and saw that he was alone. "His" men were hiding in a ditch. He left them there and charged the second building. The Germans there saw him coming and fled. That encouraged one of the 15, a machine gunner, to set up his weapon and fire on the third building, covering Summers's next charge. The Germans in the third building opened fire on Summers. From somewhere, a lieutenant appeared and told Summers he would join him. The officer, though, was hit as he and Summers reached the door. Summers entered alone and sprayed the room with his submachine gun. He killed six Germans, and the rest fled.

While Summers was catching his breath, a captain appeared and offered to join him on his attack on the next building. They set out, but the captain caught a bullet in his heart. Once again, Summers broke into a building with his tommy gun blazing. He killed six Germans, and the rest surrendered. Summers's scratch platoon had moved up cautiously, and one of them volunteered to join him on his next attack. The machine gunner followed to give them fire support. Summers and his two companions killed 30 more Germans.

Summers kicked in the door of the next building and found 15 German soldiers eating breakfast, apparently never having noticed all the shooting that had been going on around them. With his tommy gun Summers shot them all down at the table.

Harrison Summers was a man of great courage and initiative. But he could not have accomplished what he did without his submachine gun. The submachine gun (often abbreviated SMG), a small machine gun that fired pistol ammunition, was born in World War I. It achieved maturity in World War II, where it became the most valuable weapon in every army for clearing buildings and urban fighting.

In the Soviet Union's Red Army, it was as important as the rifle. In a typical Red Army attack, submachine gunners in the first wave laid down a barrage of small arms fire from 200 yards and worked their way forward. Then the tanks, with "tank riders" advanced. Tank riders were soldiers with submachine guns and hand grenades who fired on any enemies they saw. They protected the tanks from antitank guns in the enemy front lines as well as from infantry with antitank grenades and *panzerfausts*. The *panzerfaust* was a very small recoilless gun, an ancestor of the Russian RPG-7 (erroneously called a rocket-propelled grenade launcher), which fired a shaped-charge shell considerably larger than its diameter. Tank riders led a life that was short and not at all merry. A single burst of machine gun fire could—and usually did—clear a tank of all its tank riders.

Towards the end of World War II, the submachine gun became obsolescent. The *U.S M-2 carbine*, a smaller, lighter, and more powerful automatic, indicated the trend of the future, but it was the German *sturmgewehr*, or assault rifle that revolutionized infantry small arms and introduced the weapon that would replace both rifle and the submachine gun.

Some authorities say the first submachine gun was the Italian Villar Perosa, a very strange weapon. The Villar Perosa was a pair of tiny machine guns firing the 9 mm Glisenti cartridge, an underpowered version of the 9 mm Luger. It was fired from a bipod or tripod, from a truck mount, and even from the handle bars of bicycles. Each barrel fired at the rate of 1,200 rounds per minute. Each barrel was fed from a separate 25-round magazine. With that rate of fire, the soldier with a Villar Perosa must have spent a lot of time changing magazines.

The idea of a pistol-caliber automatic may have reached Germany from the Italian front, or it may have occurred independently to Hugo Schmeisser, who designed a short, heavy automatic weapon for the 9mm Luger cartridge called the *Bergmann Musquete* or by German troops, the *Kugelspritz* (bullet squirter). The Bergmann gun, the MP (for *maschinenpistole*) 18, was carried by some of the "storm troopers," who spearheaded Ludendorff's 1918 offensive. It took the 32-round drum magazine that had already been developed for the Luger pistol and had a cyclic rate of 400 rounds a minute—much more reasonable than the Vilar Perosa's 2,400 a minute from both barrels. The German army planned to issue submachine guns to every infantry company officer and NCO as well as 10 percent of the privates. Each company was to have a submachine gun squad with six SMGs, six gunners, and six ammunition bearers. The six ammunition bearers would push three handcarts loaded with cartridges and magazines. Production of SMGs never reached a point that would allow the Germans to even begin that kind of distribution, however.

Meanwhile, Tulio Marengoni of Italy's Beretta factory separated the two barrels of the Villar Perosa, made each barrel a weapon for an individual soldier, added some other improvements, and, although the new gun was not ready for World War I, Beretta ended up with the Model 38, one of the best submachine guns of World War II.

In the United States, retired General John T. Thompson conceived the idea of a light automatic weapon that could be used by an individual soldier in the vicious, close-quarters fighting that characterized trench warfare. Before any news of European developments reached them, Thompson and his employees were working on a hand-held machine gun firing .45 auto pistol cartridges.

Oscar Payne of the Thompson organization came up with a workable gun. The war ended, though, before Thompson could offer the government his "trench broom."

The U.S. Army wasn't interested in Thompson's "trench broom" when the war ended, and the Allies outlawed all SMGs for the Germans and Austrians except for a few to arm the police. Most Thompsons went to police agencies. The Coast Guard used them in its campaign against rum runners, and the Marine Corps adopted the gun for its brush-fire wars in Central America and the Caribbean. Gangsters also used them, but not as many as the gangster movies of the 30s and 40s would have you believe. The Germans couldn't keep submachine guns, but they turned out several submachine gun designs and sold them around the world. Most of them were chambered for the 9 mm Luger cartridge, which is one reason why that is now the world's most popular cartridge for military pistols. The Finns produced their own submachine gun, the *Suomi*, which they considered their most important weapon in the Winter War of 1939-1940 against the Soviet Union. That war also stimulated Soviet interest in the little, pistol-caliber machine guns.

The American and British armies were among the last to adopt submachine guns on a large scale, but when they did, they came up with two of the most easily mass produced SMGs in history:the U.S. "grease gun," officially the *M 3*, and the British *Sten gun*.

Meanwhile German ordnance specialists were working on the problem of the rifle. They had started before the war. The problem was known to all ordnance men. The infantry rifle was too powerful. It was designed to kill enemy troops at more than 1,000 yards, but you seldom saw an enemy soldier that far away. And given the marksmanship training they had, few of the soldiers in World War II's mass armies would be able to hit a man at that distance. To get that power, the rifle used ammunition that was at least 50 percent heavier than it needed to be, and which gave the rifle a kick that recruits found disturbing and inhibited their marksmanship.

Most of the rifles in World War II had hand-operated bolt actions. Only the United States had generally issued a semiautomatic. The German ordnance people dreamed of giving every soldier a fully automatic rifle—or better, a selective fire rifle, capable of either automatic or semiautomatic, as with the best submachine guns. To produce a workable, handheld automatic rifle, the power would have to be greatly reduced in anything of around the weight of a standard infantry rifle. Otherwise the repeated recoil would make the rifle unmanageable.

So the Germans designed a new cartridge. It was the same 8 mm caliber as the standard round, but it had a lighter bullet—120 grains instead of 198 grains—and a lower velocity: 2,250 feet per second instead of 2564. The cartridge case was shorter and the whole round weighed about half the weight of the standard cartridge, so soldiers could carry more ammunition.

Then, they built a rifle to use the new cartridge. Legend has it (and it's probably true) that Hitler violently objected to reducing the power of the standard rifle cartridge—it would be unmacho, or whatever the German equivalent is. So ordnance specialists changed the designation of the experimental guns from *maschinen karabiner* to *maschinen pistole*. Hitler was not happy with a low-powered rifle, but he liked a high-powered submachine gun. Then some of the generals on the Russian front asked for more of those new MP 43s and MP 44s. The Nazi dictator decided that such a successful weapon should have a more macho name. It changed from *maschinen pistole* to *sturmgewehr*, or assault rifle. "Assault rifle" is the name now applied to all low-powered, selective fire (both full automatic and semiautomatic) military rifles. In spite of many American politicians, no semiautomatic-only rifle is an "assault rifle."

And the basic personal weapon of soldiers all over the world is now the assault rifle.

39

Hidden Death:
Land Mines

National Archives from U.S. Information Agency

American lieutenant, wounded by a Viet Cong land mine, is treated by a medic.

Land mines have been around for a long time, and it's only in the last few years that they have aroused public concern. A few land mines were used in the American Civil War, although they seem to have been mostly improvised devices—usually an artillery shell with a percussion cap arrangement where the time fuse would have gone. The public took a dim view of these "land torpedoes," calling them, as they did submarines, "infernal devices." The Turks used land mines on the beaches at Gallipoli, but they were not common on most of the major battle fronts. Barbed wire and the machine guns provided a pretty complete defensive system. Land mines would just have complicated things when it was time to advance.

It was the appearance of the tank that caused a quantum jump in land mine warfare. The Achilles' heel of the lumbering monsters was their caterpillar treads. A small amount of explosive could break a tread, leaving the tank immobile and almost helpless—certainly useless as a breakthrough weapon. Early land mines were do-it-yourself propositions, improvised from artillery shells or bulk explosives. Later, government-issue mines appeared, but, by that time, the war was almost over.

When the Second World War began, all belligerents had factory-made land mines. Some were antitank mines; some were antipersonnel mines. Antipersonnel mines were even simpler than antitank mines: it takes very little high explosive to blow a man's foot off. Most of the early mines had metal bodies. To locate them, members of antitank and mine platoons would sweep the ground with electronic metal detectors—ancestors of the gadgets hobbyists used to find coins in public parks and on beaches. The armies then switched to non-metallic mines. The Germans had a nasty little number the GIs called a "shoe mine." It was a wooden box the size of a shoe box with a loose lid. Any pressure on the lid ignited a percussion cap, which exploded a charge of TNT. The foot that stepped on the shoe mine never needed a shoe again—if its owner survived. The United States used a similar device, a small round plastic case that exploded if any pressure was put on its top. To locate these non-metallic mines, the infantry had to use their bayonets. They probed the ground ahead of them as they walked. The British even had a purpose-built bayonet probe—one of their cheap "spike" bayonets welded to a length of pipe.

The antitank mines needed far more pressure to make them explode. Men could walk across a field of antitank mines with complete safety, but any tanks attempting to follow them would be in serious trouble. Some mines, especially antitank mines, had two devices for setting them off. A plate on top would explode the mine if pressure were placed on it. Another device on the bottom would also explode the mine if it were lifted up and pressure removed from the bottom element.

One type of antipersonnel mine, the "claymore," was not buried, but placed above the surface, usually hidden by brush or high grass. It was used a lot in Vietnam. The claymore was a curved plastic case holding a slab of high explosive behind hundreds of steel ball bearings. When it exploded, it threw the ball bearings in a 60-degree arc to a range of 270 yards. It could be ignited by a trip wire or electricity.

Another antipersonnel mine using ball bearings was the "bouncing betty." When an enemy hit a trip wire, it would explode a small powder charge in the base of the mine. The mine would fly up, but it was attached to a wire anchored to the ground. When the mine reached waist height, the wire released a firing pin and the mine exploded and scattered ball bearings in all directions.

One thing few citizens who have not been in combat know is that armies frequently marked their minefields with wire and warning signs. Trying to find their way around a minefield could delay enemies almost as much as trying to cross it, and it could channel them into areas that have already been zeroed in on by the defenders's guns. It also helps avoid the chance of being blown up by your own mines. And, it greatly reduces the chance of civilians being killed by mines long after the fighting is over.

That's why one of the new methods of laying mines is particularly nasty. Helicopters now can scatter both antitank and antipersonnel mines over a wide area. A single Black Hawk helicopter can place 960 mines. Unless the mines are the self-destructing type, one may lie on the ground for years until someone, maybe a child, sets it off. Finding and collecting such randomly scattered mines in unmarked minefields after a war is a herculean task.

Cluster bombs, delivered by airplanes, helicopters, artillery shells, or rockets cause a similar problem. At a predetermined height, the bomb, shell, or rocket opens and scatters scores of bomblets, each less than four inches long and an inch-a-half in diameter, over an area known to contain enemy troops. The bomblets trail streamers that unscrew their arming devices. The problem is that these tiny bombs, each with the power of a hand grenade, may not explode when they strike, because the arming device may not have been fully unscrewed. If a curious child should pick up a bomblet, it might go off.

Antitank mines were one of the main means of taking the Blitz out of Blitzkrieg, and they were so successful they stimulated the use of antipersonnel mines. At one time, mines were individually dug in. Now, the work is often done with machinery. Even in marked minefields, the chances are that the weapons have been plowed in with a mechanical minelayer.

Clearing mines is also often done without hand work. One Russian general is reported to have sent his troops right across an undefended German minefield to save time. His reasoning: He wouldn't have lost any more men than if the area were defended by artillery. On D day in Normandy, the Allies used tanks pushing heavy rollers or cylinder that flailed the ground with chains to set off antitank mines ahead of them. That worked until the Germans began planting mines with delayed action fuses. Artillery and mortar barrages were a good way to eliminate minefields. So were "Bangalore torpedoes"—long pipes filled with explosives that were pushed over the minefields and exploded. A modern version of the "torpedo" used a rocket to pull an explosive filled hose across the minefield. The newest way to clear minefields is to use fuel-air explosives. The United States has a bomb containing three smaller bombs, each containing 71.8 pounds of ethylene oxide. The bomblets are ejected from the big bomb and arrive by parachute, open, and the gas vaporizes, forming a cloud about 50 feet in diameter and eight feet high. Then it detonates, exploding all the mines beneath it. Deep penetration bombs filled with ethylene oxide can also be used to fill underground fortifications, like those in Afghanistan with explosive vapor.

In the last half of the Korean War, the trench-and-bunker warfare environment resulted in all kinds of homemade mines. The *Husch flare*, named after the lieutenant who invented it, used by the 27th Infantry Regiment, was typical. It was a diesel oil drum buried in the mountainside and slanted toward North Korean lines. At the bottom of the drum was a half-pound block of TNT, a blasting cap and a firing pin. Leading from that were trip wires going in many directions. The drum was then filled with napalm and many hand grenades. The flare would not only cause great harm to anyone trying to sneak through the barbed wire at night, it would show the troops where the enemy soldiers were and illuminate the targets.

Today, a kind of mine called a *roadside bomb* is one of the principal weapons of the Iraqi guerrillas. Because of the huge number of artillery shells, bombs, and rockets apparently lying around everywhere in Iraq, making the bomb is simplicity itself. Get one or many shells, bombs, and so on, wire them together and set them off with a small charge of TNT or some other explosive. A favorite method of ignition involves a mobile telephone. Dial the phone's number and, instead of ringing, it sets off the bomb. The bomb doesn't have to be dug in, something that might attract attention on a paved road. Just hide it in a trash can, a wrecked vehicle, or the body of a dead animal—a dog, a donkey, or maybe a camel. A big bomb doesn't have to explode under a vehicle. A really big one can take out several vehicles in the area. You'll find more on this in Chapter 50 (on improvised weapons).

40

Less Is More—A Lot More: The Shaped Charge

Bazooka shell. Little rockets like this let one infantryman knock out a tank weighing many tons.

Back in 1883, an American engineer named Monroe exploded a slab of explosive against a steel plate. The explosive had letters impressed on it showing that it was the property of the U.S. Navy. After the explosion, Monroe was amazed to find that the impressions on the explosive had been reproduced on the plate. He published a paper describing the phenomenon, then everybody forgot about it. There were much easier ways to engrave inscriptions on steel plates.

Actually, Monroe didn't discover the effect named after him. The earliest reference to the fact that a depression in an explosive concentrates its force goes back to 1792. Further, there are indications that mining engineers had been using this phenomenon for 150 years without telling anybody about it. But the scientific community put the "Monroe effect" in the space reserved for useless knowledge and went on about its business. Von Neumann rediscovered the effect in 1911, but there still seemed to be no practical use for it.

In 1935, a Swiss chemical engineer, Henry Mohaupt, was on duty as a machine gunner in the Swiss Army. All men in Switzerland serve in the armed forces, take periodic military training and are active reservists until age 45. The tensions that would culminate in World War II were building up, and Mohaupt was disturbed at the ineffectiveness of antitank weapons available to the infantry. Switzerland, for example, was relying on the Solothurn antitank rifle—a semiautomatic 20 mm weapon that would have made hash of the tanks of World War I, but would not even dent such vehicles as Germany's Pzkw IV medium tank. When his active duty term was up, Mohaupt established a laboratory to develop an antitank weapon for the infantry soldier. He took the Monroe effect as a starting point. At first, he used hollowed-out explosive charges to propel metal disks against a steel target. That led him to line the hole in the explosive with a metal cone. That, he learned, multiplied the penetration of the steel— especially if he moved the charge back from the target for a short distance. At the optimum distance, the shaped explosive charge would drill a small hole in the steel about seven and a half times deeper than the diameter of the cone. Through that hole, a stream of fire and molten metal would cause horrible damage to people and machinery.

Mohaupt, knowing that Hitler was a threat to all of Europe, demonstrated his discovery to French and British military authorities. The French, in turn, passed on the information to the United States. U.S. Government officials invited Mohaupt to come to the United States after the invasion of France and the Low Countries on May 10, 1940. He finally got to the United States in October 1940, after delays caused by other U.S. Government officials because he was not an American citizen. He then took over direction of the "bazooka project"—the attempt to develop a handheld rocket that could penetrate tank armor. Britain was working on a similar weapon, the PIAT (for Projector Infantry Anti-Tank)—a strange-looking weapon that used an immensely heavy main spring to power a massive firing pin that ignited a small powder charge to toss a large shell with a shaped-charge filling at enemy tanks. The firing pin and its main spring absorbed most of the recoil, and the recoil cocked the main spring for another shot. Even so, the PIAT kicked like a blue-nosed mule and was even more unpleasant to fire than the .55 caliber Boys antitank rifle—the second least-popular weapon in the British Army. The bazooka, unlike the two British weapons, would have no recoil at all.

The U.S. Army Ordnance Department was skeptical about the whole idea of penetrating armor with an explosion, but the bazooka proved to be a success. In June 1941, the government labeled the bazooka *Secret*. Thereafter, its inventor, Mohaupt was excluded from the project because he wasn't an American citizen. That same month, Mohaupt had filed for a patent on his application of the Monroe effect. (He had previously patented it in Europe.) Because he was a Swiss, not an American, citizen, the Justice Department pursued him for violation of the War Secrets Act. Fortunately, someone with common sense in the government called off the Justice Department. Mohaupt then joined the U.S. Army and was assigned to the bazooka project. He perfected the weapon, which was introduced to the Germans in North Africa in 1943.

For the first time, the individual infantryman had a weapon that would reliably stop a tank. When tank armor got thicker, bazookas got bigger. In the Korean War, the 3.5-inch "super bazooka" made short work of the North Koreans' Russian-built T 34 tanks, which had defied not only older bazookas but also high explosive shells from the 105 mm howitzer.

The bazooka's shaped charge became the heart of a huge variety of antitank weapons. Most field artillery guns now use shaped charge shells, known as HEAT (for High Explosive Anti-Tank). All antitank rockets do, too. So do recoilless guns. Some of them use special ammunition that does not require the charge to spin. Spinning, the result of rifling, decreases the penetration of a shaped charge. There's more on that in Chapter 41.

The Germans adopted a very unusual recoilless gun that used a shaped charge shell. Called a *Panzerfuust*, it looked like nothing more than a length of pipe. Its shell looked like a trench mortar shell with a long tail. The tail contained its propelling charge. Some of the gas generated by the propelling charge pushed the shell forward, the rest exited through a venturi at the rear of the gun. Gas leaving the venturi blasted out at extremely high velocity—high enough to balance the effect of the low velocity shell leaving the front of the gun. Recoil momentum equals mass times the velocity of what is shot from the muzzle, divided by the inert weight of the gun. The gas had little mass but lots of velocity. Ian Hogg, the British artillery expert, has called recoilless guns like the *panzerfaust* and more conventional guns "Newton's artillery," because balancing recoil by escaping gas is based on Isaac Newton's discovery that every action has an equal reaction.

The *panzerfaust* was not the German grunt's favorite weapon. Firing a big shell from a little gun on your shoulder would make anyone nervous, but it was the *panzerfaust's* short range that bothered its users. They had to get close to their targets to use it. Getting close to an enemy tank is not comfortable, and anyone who gets too close could be done in by the explosion of his own shell. The *panzerfaust* was effective, though—effective enough to make the Russians adopt an imitation, a gadget they called the *RPG 2*. They improved the early model enormously by giving the shell a rocket assist. This improved model, the RPG 7, fires the shell from a recoilless gun, like the German and early Russian models. But when it's a safe distance from the gunner, a rocket motor takes over and carries the shell to a much greater range. With all rocket weapons, a main concern is arranging things so the gunner does not get incinerated by the backblast of his own rocket. The recoilless gun part of the RPG 7 process takes care of this nicely and allows a much more powerful rocket motor than can be used on a bazooka.

RPG 7s have been sold and made all over the world. The weapon is as popular as that other Russian product, the AK 47. It's particularly popular with Iraqi guerrillas. The United States and its partners in Iraq have far more sophisticated and more powerful antitank weapons than the RPG 7, but the guerrillas don't have any tanks, so our antitank superiority means nothing.

The *panzerfaust* was dangerous because its user had to get close to an enemy tank, but it was by no means the worst in that respect. Every belligerent had a version of the antitank hand grenade, most of them using the shaped charge. The Germans had the *Panzerwurfmine*, a grenade with four canvas fins to keep it flying point-first so the shaped charge would be effective.

The Soviet Union had the RPG 43, which had a long streamer that popped out when thrown to keep it head-on. And Japan had the Type 3, which had a tail of hemp fibers to insure that the point struck first. Japan also had the ultimate up-close-and-personal antitank weapon: a large shaped charge on the end of a pole. To use it, the soldier ran up to the tank and rammed the charge into it.

In Normandy, the Americans and British used another type of antitank grenade, the *Gammon grenade*, a sort of bag filled with a plastic explosive. The grenade spreads itself out on the tank, covering any angles, before it explodes. When the Gammon grenade explodes, it is supposed to detach "scabs" of steel from the inner surface of the armor to kill or wound the tank crew, ignite fuel lines and do other damage. It worked quite well on some of the World War I tanks the Germans used in the defense of Normandy. British and Americans have used artillery shells based on this principle. The British call theirs HESH (for High Explosive Squash Head) shells; the Americans use the less colorful HEP (High Explosive Plastic). HESH and HEP shells are seldom used on tanks now. They are more commonly shot at concrete fortifications.

The shaped charge, even more than the land mine, took the Blitz out of Blitzkrieg. Tankers have been able to use a number of defenses against it. Dangling additional armor plates outside the regular tank armor was an early try. That, in effect, moved the charge back from the optimum distance so that full strength of the lethal jet from the exploding charge would not reach the regular armor. The plates, though, added a lot of extra weight and were quickly blown off or askew. Another addition is "reactive armor." Slabs of explosive are hung on the tank. When a shaped charge explodes, so does the reactive armor. The reactive explosion blocks the effect of the shaped charge. That kind of armor defends against only the first shot. If a second shell hits the tank, there is no more reactive armor to react. And, it has been reported, on some lightly armored vehicles, the reactive explosion crushed the machine that was carrying it. A third, and apparently more effective, defense is laminated armor. This has a layer of ceramic material between layers of armor plate. The ceramic resists the burning effect of the jet of gas and molten metal caused by the shaped-charge explosion. It also dampens the shock waves caused by the explosion of an HEP shell and makes less able to break pieces off the interior of the armor.

But with all these defenses, shaped charges and still being used. And, regrettably, even relatively primitively shaped charge weapons are still putting holes in our tanks.

41

Red Glare Everywhere: Small Rockets

Nineteenth-century rocket battery firing.

T he rocket is one of the oldest of explosive weapons. The Chinese were using rockets before they—or anyone else—had guns. Rockets appeared in Europe around 1250—again, before any Europeans had guns. Rockets may have been even more useful than guns for scaring horses (the chief effect of the earliest guns). They could also set fires. But rockets weren't worth a hoot for knocking down stone walls, which was what interested most belligerents at that time, so they were soon dropped by most armies.

They came back into fashion in the early 19th century when an Englishman named William Congreve, impressed by rockets the Indians were using, invented an improvement. Congreve's rockets were iron and carried a warhead of either gunpowder or incendiary material. He built several sizes, and all were stabilized by a long pole fastened to the body of the rocket. They were launched from a long ramp and used by both armies and navies. Ships using rockets had sails set back from the front of the ship, which was reserved for rocket launching, and some had chains, instead of rope, for rigging. The rocket's back blast as always been a factor that must be reckoned with. During the Napoleonic Wars, British ships used rockets to burn down Copenhagen, and in the War of 1812, they used rockets in the unsuccessful bombardment of Fort McHenry.

Later, rockets were stabilized by either propellant gases pushing vanes at the rear of the rocket, which set it spinning, or by tail fins. Rockets were easier to move than artillery, but they were much less accurate, so they remained a secondary weapon until World War II. Changed conditions combined with improvements in rocket engines made rockets important weapons. Continued improvement after the war has led to rockets replacing guns in many situations. This trend is particularly noticeable in navies. All the world's huge 16-inch-gun battleships are now out of service, and their places have been taken by smaller ships armed principally with rockets and guided missiles. In the Iraq War, Coalition naval forces included four carrier battle groups, including four of the giant nuclear Nimitz class carriers, each displacing more than 93,000 tons, as well as slightly smaller carriers like the 81,990 Kitty Hawk class. There were scores of smaller ships: cruisers, destroyers and frigates. None carried many guns, and those were comparatively light antiaircraft or dual purpose guns, fast-firing lightweights for which shore bombardment was little more than an afterthought. Instead of heavy guns, the fleet carried hundreds of antiaircraft, anti-ship, and other surface-to-surface rockets in addition to cruise missiles.

For ground fighting, rockets turned out to the perfect antitank weapon for infantry. A rocket launcher has no recoil, because it's just a hollow tube. There's no internal pressure, as there is in a gun. All the internal pressure is in the rocket itself, so the launcher can be quite light. The bazookas, short-range point-and-shoot weapons, were fired from one man's shoulder. There are still modernized forms of the bazooka in service, but there are also much longer ranged antitank rockets, which are guided by signals coming over a thin wire (the Brennan torpedo—see Chapter 26—was a century ahead of its time). Other antitank rockets home in on reflected laser light. All of them are much lighter and more mobile than any kind of artillery.

World War II produced many situations that required a sudden, intensely heavy bombardment for a short period. For this, the rocket was ideal. Landing craft equipped with masses of rockets delivered more explosives on enemy beaches in a shorter time than any battleship could. Both the Germans, with their *Nebelwerfer,* and the Russians, with their *Katyusha*, laid down massive rocket bombardments on the Eastern Front. Rockets were especially important for air defense in World War II. Planes were flying higher and faster, only rockets could reach the necessary altitude, and only rockets could be programmed to home on the planes. After the war, rockets also gave the infantry a way to cope with low-flying enemy planes attempting to strafe them. Shoulder-fired rocket launchers as the United States's Stinger now allows the dogface to fight back effectively. Unfortunately, they also give terrorists something to use against civilian airliners.

Aircraft, too, found rockets essential. German night fighters, confronted with Allied bombers flying in tight formation for mutual defense, simply launched their rockets at the formations as if the rockets were torpedoes and they were submarines attacking a convoy. In dogfights, fighter pilots on both sides used rockets extensively. A rocket packed a much heavier punch than a .50 caliber bullet or a 20 mm shell. Rockets could also be made to home in on enemy planes—to turn with them, dive with them, outrun them and blow them up.

For strafing ground targets, the rocket was also ideal. World War II ground fighting saw the obsolescence of dive bombers such as the German Stuka. Dive bombing was an extremely hazardous occupation if the enemy had any decent ground fire capability, because the bomber appeared to be almost motionless to those immediately below it. The only reason for dive bombing was that it was the most accurate way to drop an unguided bomb. Rockets had accuracy built in. The fighter-bomber (pure fighters were also becoming obsolete) would approach its target at high speed in a rather shallow dive and fire rockets when the target was in range. Rockets for antitank use, of course, had shaped-charge fillings.

During the Cold War, all the nations of the world feared the nuclear-armed intercontinental ballistic missile. They still do. Witness the flap over nuclear programs in North Korea and Iran. Although the ICBM has strongly affected nations' political and military strategy, it has never been used. That's not true of its smaller cousins. They have already changed the nature of war on land, sea, and air.

42

Firing a Cannon Like a Rifle:
Recoilless Guns

National Archives from Army

U.S. troops fire 75 mm recoilless gun at North Koreans in 1951.

Ⅰn the armies of Napoleon and Gustavus Adolphus, cannoneers and their guns fought right up in the front lines as the infantry. That had many advantages. Front line commanders didn't have any trouble getting fire support from the artillery. But when rifles were adopted, standing up in the front line loading a cannon meant that you probably would not get a chance to tell your grand-children any war stories.

There were some attempts to rectify the situation. Until World War II, the most successful was the *trench mortar*. In the First World War, French and American infantry troops used a light, low-power 37 mm gun. It was good for knocking out machine gun nests, but very little else. In the Second World War, the American Army experimented with "cannon companies," artillerymen who dragged a 105 mm howitzer up to the front and used it to give direct fire sup-port. The trouble was that the gun was a magnet for enemy fire, and life in a cannon company tended to be short.

The greatest disadvantages of modern artillery pieces is their weight and bulk. The carriage has to be massive and heavy to withstand the stress of recoil, even though the guns are equipped with a recoil-absorbing mechanism, which artillerymen call a *recuperater*. The recuperator also adds weight and bulk. If recoil could be eliminated, the gun could be smaller and lighter. The first man to eliminate recoil from a cannon was a U.S. Navy officer —a Commander Davis. A gun recoils because, as Isaac Newton stated, every action has an oppo-site and equal reaction. A shell is much lighter than the gun that fires it, so it travels at high speed and goes a great distance. The gun does not recoil at the same speed and, even without a recuperater, it doesn't travel anything like the distance the shell goes. If the gun fired a missile of the same weight from each end of the barrel, there would be no recoil at all. That's what Davis did. The missile from the rear end of his gun was mixture of lead shot and grease so, unlike the shell fired from the front end, it quickly dispersed. Davis sold his gun to the British, who used some of them on naval aircraft during World War I.

Recoil depends on the mass of the missile being fired times its velocity. If the Davis gun could fire a rear missile weighing half the "business" missile but at twice the velocity, recoil would still be eliminated. In calculating recoil, you have to figure the mass of the gas, as well as the mass of the missile. The mass of the gas is roughly the same as the weight of the powder charge. Some of the powder does not leave the gun in the form of gas but remains as residue. With smokeless powder, however, this is negligible, so it would be possible to elimi-nate recoil by ejecting only gas from the rear of the gun, provided the gas could be ejected at a high enough velocity to balance the force of the shell being fired. Because it's gas that's ejected, the danger zone behind the gun is much shorter than if any kind of solid were ejected. Still, there is a fan-shaped danger zone behind these guns that may extend more than 100 feet. The gas jet also kicks up a huge cloud of dust, which makes it easy for enemies to locate the gun.

The first to put this principle to practical use was the German firm, Krupp. In 1940, Krupp produced a 75 mm light gun for airborne troops. The gun used fixed ammunition, but the base of the cartridge case was plastic. When fired, the plastic shattered and blew out a hole in the breechblock. The hole was a venturi, a tube with a narrow center section and widened, tapered ends designed to increase the speed of gas ejected through it. That speed was carefully calculated to equal the action of the shell being fired from the muzzle. The light gun had a carriage of light alloy and motorcycle wheels. It weighed only 321 pounds, compared to 1.1 tons for the regular 75 mm field gun, but had velocity and range only a little less than that of the regular gun. The Germans used the light gun during their invasion of Crete, and it was such a success they ordered two more recoilless guns, a 105 mm and a 150 mm.

The British also produced a recoilless gun design, invented by Sir Dennis Burney. The biggest difference between the Burney and Krupp guns were the ammunition they used. The Burney gun had a cartridge case with a few large holes punched in it. These were covered by thin brass sheets that blew out when the gun was fired. The escaping gas traveled to the rear around the cartridge case and was ejected from several venturis. Burney also invented a projectile for his gun, something he called a "wallbuster," intended for use against fortifications. The wallbuster developed into the HESH or HEP shell (see Chapter 39) and turned out to be a good antitank round. It is less effective with modern layered armor, because that type does not transmit shockwaves through the metal so well, and the explosion of a HEP shell is less likely to break off significant "scabs" of metal.

Neutral Sweden got into recoilless gun design early, bringing out a 20 mm antitank gun in 1942. It used fixed ammunition with a plastic base cartridge case similar to the Krupp gun. It followed this rather ineffectual weapon with a much more formidable 105 mm gun.

The United States developed a different recoilless gun. As the others did, it used fixed ammunition, but the cartridge case was punctured with many small holes, instead of a few big ones, as in the Burney gun. It was nicknamed the *Kromuskit* from the names of its designers, Kroger and Musser. The shell's driving band was pre-engraved to fit the gun's rifling. That meant that less gas pressure was needed to send the shell on its way at a decent velocity, and that meant that the barrel of the gun could be lighter. Also, a larger proportion of the propelling charge would actually be pushing the shell. Earlier recoilless guns needed a powder charge five times heavier than used in a standard gun—most of the burning gasses being ejected through the venturi rather than pushing the shell.

The first Kromuskit was a 57 mm gun weighing only 35 pounds. It could easily be fired from one man's shoulder. The next one, a 75 mm, weighed 115 pounds—a bit heavy for shoulder firing, but usable on a machine gun tripod.

All of these recoilless guns fired shaped charge as well as ordinary high explosive shells. The Kromuskit guns also fired white phosphorus shells, which were both antipersonnel and smoke shells, and canister shot, which turned them into giant shotguns for use against personnel at close range.

Most of the recoilless guns lost some of the efficiency of their shaped charge antitank shells because they were rifled. Spinning decreases the power of the jet blast of a shaped-charge explosion. The Swedes avoided that trouble with their 84 mm *Carl Gustaf* recoilless gun. The shell is fitted with rotating bearings. The rifling spins the bearings, imparting enough gyroscopic stability to keep the projectile on course, but the core, containing the shaped charge, does not spin. At 38 pounds, the Carl Gustaf is light enough to fire from the shoulder and is able to penetrate 15.75 inches of homogeneous armor at a range of 500 yards. A second Swedish recoilless gun, called the *Miniman*, is disposable. Fire the one shell packed in it and throw it away. It's a smoothbore, firing a shell stabilized by tail fins, has a range of 250 yards and can penetrate 11.8 inches of homogenous armor. It weighs only 6.31 pounds.

Germany also has a disposable recoilless gun. Like the Swedish model, it's a smoothbore firing a finned shell. But no gas escapes from either the muzzle or the rear end. The propelling charge moves two pistons to the front and to the rear. The front piston throws out the shell and the rear pistol ejects a solid counterweight that is designed to rapidly disperse. Presumably, this makes the gun less visible on firing than the traditional recoilless gun. The German gun, called the Armbrust, is also light enough to fire from the shoulder.

Recoilless guns give the infantry direct fire artillery for the first time in centuries. They are available for any job that calls for something heavier than rifle or machine gun fire. Especially, they are available for antitank and—although the situation has not yet occurred—anti-helicopter work.

43

Eyes and Ears :
Sonar and Radar

National Archives from Coast Guard

Coast Guardsmen drop depth charges on German submarine located by sonar in 1943.

In the early years of the submarine, it seemed that the only problems the undersea craft would have would be its own mechanical deficiencies. There was no way anyone on the surface could detect the presence of a submerged boat. In the first part of World War I, the object of the British Navy was to catch German U boats on the surface. The main anti-submarine weapons were the destroyer and the "Q ship," a converted merchant ship, often carrying a cargo of lumber to inhibit sinking, with hidden deck guns. The former cruised the waters haunted by submarines and tried to catch one on the surface. Because the early subs had to spend most of their time on the surface, that task is not as hopeless as it sounds. The latter was a seagoing booby trap. To save on torpedoes and to comply with accepted standards of decency, subs in the early days of the war often approached freighters on the surface, told the crews to abandon ship and then sank them with gunfire. The Q ships aimed to attract these surfaced submarines and sink them with its guns. But after a few Q ship mishaps, submarine commanders just torpedoed all ships while submerged.

The first step toward the detection of a submerged U boat was the hydrophone. Hydrophones could pick up the sound of a submarine's engines, but there were two big drawbacks. First, the hunter ship had to shut down its own engines so it could hear the subs. Second, one ship could not locate the sub by itself. Several ships working together were needed to get a rough approximation of the sub's location. Once that was found, the navy ships would attack with depth charges.

The best anti-submarine measure in the First World War was the convoy system, but not because convoys made it easier to locate or destroy U boats. It was because the convoy system bunched freighters up. Previously, the U boats waited for a freighter to come along. If its torpedoes missed, another ship would be along soon. A submerged submarine was about the slowest craft at sea. It couldn't catch up with or even keep up with the slowest freighter. Convoys eliminated the steady stream of ships steaming across the Atlantic. U boats had to wait a long time between targets, and when a convoy appeared, it was guarded by naval ships. If the U boat were not positioned just right, it might miss all the ships in the convoy, and it was too slow to make up for poor positioning.

In the next war, the submarines were bigger, faster, and sturdier, but their enemies had something new, too. The British called it asdic; the Americans called it sonar. Basically, sonar sends beeping sounds into the water and listens for echoes caused by other objects in the water. An experienced sonar operator could distinguish between the echoes from a U boat or a whale. The convoy escorts also had better hydrophones, and whales don't make engine and propeller noises.

Locating subs was also helped by another, more sophisticated method of detection: radar. Radar used radio waves instead of sound waves, but it, also, relied on echoes. The first important use of radar was in the Battle of Britain. Britain had radar stations all along its shore. They were able to locate German planes long before they were in sight, allowing the British fighter command to concentrate its interceptors to meet the threat. The Germans had a primitive form of radar and had no idea that the British had any, much less the more advanced form they were actually using.

British scientists continually improved their radar devices. They made some small enough to be installed on ships. That further complicated life for submariners. Radar could "see" in the dark, and it could "see" at much longer distances than human eyes. Submarines could no longer travel on the surface at night in safety, as they once did. It got worse. Radars became precise enough to "see" periscopes; they became small enough to install on airplanes. In daylight, unseen planes swooped out of the clouds and bombed surfaced submarines. At night, a surfaced submarine could be located by a plane and bombed before its crew even knew they were under attack. Airborne radar became operational in 1943, the year a German writer called "the year of the slaughter of the U boats."

The miniaturization of radar went on. One result was the greatest advance in artillery in the 20th century: the proximity fuse (see Chapter 19). For the first time in history gunners could explode their shells, whether for antipersonnel ground fighting or for antiaircraft fire, at the optimum distance from the target, and do it without failure.

Radar and sonar were the first of a great array of detection devices that are at the heart of many of our modern "smart" weapons (see Chapter 50).

44

The Fires of War:
Thermite, Napalm, and
Other Incendiaries

French soldiers repel German attack with flamethrowers.

On the night of March 9, 1945, as the B 29s took off from Guam, war was raging everywhere. In Europe that day, American forces had taken the Ludendorff Bridge at Remagen, crossing the border of Germany for the first time. The Red Army had entered Germany and had trapped half a million German troops in a pocket against the Baltic Sea, but there were still months of fighting ahead. In the United States, the American Office of War Information was desperately trying to perpetuate the myth, based on Roosevelt's promise to Churchill, that American forces were concentrating on defeating Germany first, after which they would turn to Japan.

Actually, there was no such concentration on Germany by American forces. That propaganda line, politically correct at the time, has unfortunately been accepted by some later writers. That makes it sound as if Japan was a paper tiger that collapsed like a punctured balloon as soon as we were able to turn away from Germany. And that supposition ignores all the toil, blood, and heroism of the American forces that pushed Japan almost to the breaking point while their contemporaries were helping to defeat Germany. The British forces did concentrate on Germany, certainly. Germany was a near, clear-and-present danger. But, although the largest part of the U.S. Army was in the European and Mediterranean theaters, almost all of the major ships of the U.S. Navy— aircraft carriers, battleships, cruisers, and submarines, and most of the Marine Corps—were in the Pacific and had been for three years. Guam itself, the base of these super-heavy B 29 bombers, had been retaken from the Japanese less than a year before this. At the same time, at the Battle of the Philippine Sea (also known as the Great Marianas Turkey Shoot), the U.S. Navy had broken the back of Japanese naval air forces and dealt a heavy blow to the Imperial Navy. A few months later, on October 24 and 25, 1944, the United States struck an even heavier blow at the Battle of Leyte Gulf. Japan lost four aircraft carriers, three battleships, 10 cruisers, and nine destroyers as well as 500 planes, and U.S. forces began the reconquest of the Philippines. They had gone from there to Iwo Jima on the doorstep of Japan—almost, in fact, one of the Japanese home islands. By this time, Japan had no airframe factories, almost no shipping, hardly any oil, and hardly any planes on the home islands.

The B 29s soared over the Pacific on a route that had been used many times before. They were heading for a target so far away such a bombing mission would have been unthinkable early in the war. Enough 29s had already flown this route, though, to have wiped out some of Japan's strategic industries such as airframe factories and oil refineries. The Japanese had managed to disperse other industries all around their country, but that didn't matter now. The Americans were after cities. Tonight's target was the huge Tokyo-Yokohama metropolitan area.

The bombers swooped to low altitude as they approached the Japanese coast and unloaded their deadly cargo over the port city of Yokohama and the Japanese capital, Tokyo, then returned to Guam after experiencing hardly any resistance. Behind them, 16 square miles of homes and businesses were ablaze. They had created a fire storm—the biggest one in history.

A *fire storm* occurs when a conflagration becomes so big and hot that it creates a powerful updraft over the center of the fire, consumes all the oxygen in the affected area, and draws so much cool air to the center of the fire that winds reach gale force. The winds make the fire more intense. The heat in Tokyo was so intense that the water in the city's canals boiled. In places, the fire took all the oxygen out of the air. Many of those caught in the firestorm, even though sheltered from the flames, suffocated for lack of oxygen. In this raid, some 86,000 people—almost all civilians (men, women, and children)—died.

In June 2004, John Yoo, a law professor explaining some memos (which he helped write) defending the use of torture on prisoners in the Iraq War, said, "This is an unprecedented conflict with a completely new form of enemy that fights in unconventional ways that violate the very core principles of the laws of war by targeting civilians."

The weapon that made possible conflagrations such as the Tokyo-Yokohama fire and the fires that destroyed all of the largest cities of Japan was based on an incendiary substance known and used by every American: gasoline. It was jellied by mixing it with aluminum naphthenate, a naphtha-based soap, and aluminum palmate, a palm-oil-based soap. The thickened gasoline clings to whatever it touches and burns more fiercely. It was also used in American flamethrowers during World War II. Because of the thickening, flamethrowers projected in a narrow stream with greater range than would have been possible with gasoline. The jet of fire could be made to ricochet around corners. Newer fire bombs use a liquid, not a gel, called napalm B, composed of polystyrene, benzine, and gasoline. It is said to burn three times longer than the older mixture and cause more destruction.

The idea of napalm bombs came from fighter-bomber pilots who discovered that if one of their auxiliary gas tanks were dropped while still loaded, it ignited spontaneously. That made it a potentially deadly weapon, and substituting napalm for aviation gas made it even more deadly. Most napalm bombs were quite large, in contrast to the thermite bombs that initiated this horrible form of warfare, first by the Germans, then by the British.

Thermite, too, is a combination of common materials—powdered aluminum and ferric oxide—better known as rust. Neither component, though, is generally considered a fire-starter. Thermite had been used to an extent in the First World War when German zeppelins bombed cities. At that time, it formed the center of a cone of resinous material bound with tarred rope. In the Second World War, the Germans used thousands of 2-pound bombs that looked like a magnesium rod with tail fins. Each consisted of a thick-walled casing of magnesium with a core of thermite. The thermite ignited the magnesium, which burned so intensely it could not be extinguished with water. Water only made it burn more fiercely, because the hot magnesium took oxygen from the water, which, of course, is a compound of hydrogen and oxygen. Air raid wardens were encouraged to cover the burning bombs with sand or else spray them with a fine spray of water to make them burn themselves out more quickly without spreading the fire. The longer the bomb burned, the more likely it was to cause a bigger fire. Thermite and magnesium burned hot enough to melt any metal and pulverize several inches of concrete.

When the British began bombing German cities, they turned thermite against its former users and added some refinements. One was a bomb that parachuted to Earth. When it landed, the tail blew off, then it forcibly ejected seven thermite bombs over a period of 10 minutes while thermite in its nose burned where it landed.

Artillery use a variety of incendiary shells. Some contain thermite, some white phosphorus, some other chemicals. Small arms also shoot incendiary ammunition. Tracer bullets are incendiaries, so were what the British called "Buckingham bullets," which had small amount of white phosphorus or an explosive in the nose. One high-tech incendiary is *depleted uranium* solid shot, widely used by U.S. forces against armor. DU, as it's called, gives off sparks when it strikes something hard, such as armor plate. The sparks have an extremely high temperature, which makes them likely to ignite anything inflammable, such as gasoline vapor in the interior of a tank (see Chapter 49).

Fire has been a weapon of war for long before Greek fire, probably for as long as there has been war, but it never gained the importance it did in World War II with the advent of thermite and napalm aerial bombs.

45

Jumping and Coasting Into War: The Parachute and the Glider

National Archives from Army

Paratroopers jump at Munsan, Korea, in an unsuccessful attempt to cut off retreating enemy troops.

The Belgian government was resolved that 1914 would not be repeated. Overlooking the Albert Canal, a little north of Liege, the Belgians built Fort Eben-Emael. Eben-Emael incorporated all of the technology used in the famous French Maginot Line. It had armored rotating gun cupolas whose low, curved shape made a direct hit impossible, and that could be lowered beneath the surface of the Earth. These cupolas mounted five 60 mm, 16 75 mm, and two 120 mm guns—all quick-firers. The fort was surrounded by an antitank wall and barbed wire. It had armored positions for searchlights, grenade throwers and many, many machine guns. Everything was underground, protected by a thickness of reinforced concrete that would have defied Big Bertha. Some 700 trained soldiers made up its garrison.

At 5:20 a.m.,on May 10, 1940, seven gliders landed on the top of Eben-Emael. The Belgian stronghold had practically no antiaircraft defenses. Out of the gliders climbed 55 Germans equipped with flamethrowers and shaped demolition charges as well as the usual infantry arms. They used the shaped charges to blast the cupolas and other armored positions or they burned the defenders out of them with flamethrowers. They tossed explosive charges down the air vents. The defenders fought from tunnel to tunnel when the Germans entered the underground fortress. Some of them even managed to fire on the regular German troops who were trying to cross the canal. The Germans got across, however, and when they brought up reinforcements the next day, the garrison surrendered. The garrison commander shot himself.

While glider troops were attacking Eben-Emael, paratroopers dropped into Holland and seized bridges, making the vaunted Dutch water-defenses useless. Even earlier, during the German invasion of Norway, a long narrow country broken up by fjords and mountains, the Germans dropped paratroops to seize key airfields. They were quickly reinforced by troops arriving on transport planes. These attacks of troops from the sky seemed to many at that time like something from a science-fiction tale. For years, there had been reports of paratroopers of the Soviet Union's Red Army and how they would change warfare. But the publications that printed these stories also had articles on how the Japanese-owned fishing boats in Los Angeles Harbor would cover that immense body of water with oil and ignite it, roasting everyone in the Pacific Fleet. Then came the Soviet Union's fumbling effort against Finland in the Winter War of 1939-1940. No paratroopers appeared, and the Red Army's campaign was distinguished mostly by its ineptitude. The paratroop threat seemed on a par with the martian threat.

The aerial component of the Blitzkrieg was a shock, but worse was to come.

On May 20, 1941, the remnants of the British force that had been driven out of Greece were holed up on Crete with some 10,200 Greek allies. Soon after dawn, the defenders saw an enormous fleet of aircraft. Suddenly, parachutes blossomed behind the planes, thousands upon thousands of parachutes. Behind the parachutes came planes towing gliders that held artillery, more heavy equipment and more soldiers. On May 26th, Major General Bernard Freyberg of New Zealand, commander of the Allied forces on Crete, radioed his commander, General Archibald Wavell, that Crete could not hold out. On June 1, the Royal Navy evacuated 18,000 men. Some 12,000 of the British force had been captured, and 2,000 had been killed. The British and Americans put new emphasis on developing airborne divisions of their own.

The Allies used their paratroopers for the first time in the invasion of Sicily in 1943. The airborne troops avoided the main German mistake on Crete: dropping directly on enemy troops, something that caused them extraordinarily heavy losses. They landed away from enemy troop concentrations, then attacked outposts, bridges, road intersections, and made it almost impossible for Axis forces to reach the beaches being attacked from the sea.

D day, June 6, 1945, saw the greatest parachute and glider assault in history—one that will probably still be the greatest in history a thousand years from now. Four divisions, two American and two British, parachuted onto Normandy in the dead of the night. It was hardly a flawless operation. Most of the paratroopers landed at a distance from their intended drop zones, and wind scattered them so far that many did not return to their own units for 24 hours. That wasn't all bad. The troopers were scattered so widely that the Germans were utterly surprised to find enemy troops among them. The paratroopers took advantage of that surprise and captured many of the Germans' rear installations. The landings greatly disrupted attempts to reinforce the German troops being attacked on the beaches.

One of the big factors in the success of the airborne assault was that much of Normandy, except for the front-line troops on the beaches, was defended by second-line troops with third-line equipment. Some of the German units were equipped with French tanks left over from the First World War and with under-powered artillery from the same war. Antiaircraft guns were in short supply. A mass jump, such as those on Normandy with troops wearing static-line parachutes, requires transport planes to fly in a fairly dense formation at a rather low altitude and continue on course until the last trooper has jumped. And *that* is the answer to an antiaircraft gunners' prayer. Before conditions that permit that kind of jump occur again, troops may be wearing antigravity boots or rocket belts. The glider forces did not have the luck of the Germans at Eben-Emael. Landing at night in a land of hedgerows and swamps, many of them crashed, and large numbers of troops were killed or suffered disabling injuries.

The German invasion of Crete had breathed new life into the concept of airborne operations, but enthusiasts overlooked a few facts. First, German losses at first were so great that General Karl Student, chief of the Luftwaffe's airborne troops, thought his men had lost the battle on the first day of the invasion. They dropped directly on the airfields, and the defenders began killing them before they touched the ground. The slaughter was especially heavy at airfields held by New Zealand troops. German General Erwin Rommel said the New Zealanders were the best troops he fought in his North African campaigns. Most of them were farmers, and they had been using rifles since childhood. They shot a large proportion of the airborne invaders as they hung helplessly beneath their parachutes. Second, in spite of their skill, the defenders were refugees from the defeat in Greece. They had machine guns without tripods, mortars without shells, almost no motor transportation, absolutely no air cover, and, especially, they had a great shortage of radios. Freyberg was unable to coordinate his troops' movements; his subordinate commanders didn't know what other units were doing or where they were. When one New Zealand commander pulled back to regroup, he left a corner of the airfield he was defending uncovered. By a sinister coincidence, Student had just at that time dispatched a fleet of transport planes loaded with regular—not airborne—troops to that airfield. If the New Zealanders had been in their former position, the Germans would have been slaughtered. As it was, they gained a foothold and were able to continue to pour in reinforcements. Nevertheless, German deaths were more than twice those of the British: 5,000 to 2,000. This was largely because of losses the first day.

The Allies conducted more successful parachute drops after D day, seizing bridges just ahead of the ground forces and preventing their demolition by the enemy. These, though, were small scale jumps in territory held by forces whose top priority was getting away from there. One parachute drop was a disaster. The British "Red Devils" jumped at Arnhem in the Netherlands "One Bridge Too Far," as Cornelius Ryan's bestseller put it, ahead of the British ground forces. They were all killed or captured. In Burma, the maverick British General Orde Wingate used gliders to successfully bring troops and artillery to his "strongholds" in the jungle, pioneering what later developed into the "air mobile" tactical doctrine of such outfits as the U.S. First Air Cavalry Division.

Paratroopers jumped twice in the Korean War. Both times, the 187th Airborne Regiment tried to cut off retreating North Korean troops. But each time, the enemy had already retreated farther north than the drop zone. After Korea, troop-carrying helicopters made both parachutes and gliders largely obsolete. Special Forces troops use steerable parachutes for small-scale special operations, but the mass jump of paratroopers with static cord chutes is a thing of the past. Some Special Forces troops jumped to secure airstrips in northern Iraq at the beginning of the Iraq War, but the jump itself seemed to be mainly for exercise. The airfields were undefended.

Still, just about every country in the world has paratroopers, even countries with hardly any airplanes. Paratroopers are considered elite troops. They are much like the grenadiers in the late 18th century—that is, highly trained masters of a military skill no longer needed. In combat, all other things being equal, including leadership, airborne outfits have proven to be neither better nor worse than ordinary infantry. That statement may anger paratroopers or former paratroopers who have been brainwashed to believe that they are superior to all "straight-legs," but combat records permit no other conclusion.

Politicians and much of the public—and certainly Hollywood—want to believe it is possible to field mini-supermen. President John F. Kennedy believed that the Special Forces, the "Green Berets," were the answer to troubles in Vietnam, but it didn't turn out that way. Achilles is out of date. The strongest and toughest man ever born can be killed instantly by a bullet from a .22 short—the least-powerful cartridge generally available. Beyond a certain reasonable limit, strength and toughness are irrelevant. Courage still counts, of course. So does confidence and skill with weapons. But no one became braver by doing 100,000 push-ups. No one became confident by listening to some leather-lunged jackass with stripes on his sleeve call him a maggot. And few people became notably better marksmen because of the crash course they got in basic training. The really skilled are those such as the New Zealanders in Crete, who had the skill before they enlisted. Courage is inborn, but it can be developed by confidence. Confidence comes from trusting the other soldiers in your unit. You trust them, and you know they trust you. Because they trust you, you don't want to let them down. So you don't, even though terrified. That's courage.

Another name for this is morale. And morale is what makes a good unit. Colonel David H. Hackworth, America's most decorated living soldier, summed up what makes a good outfit when writing about one of his former regiments, the 27th Infantry (Wolfhound) Regiment. He said, "They weren't a special unit, just a group of guys who *thought* they were good, so they *were* good."

46

From Sea to Shore:
Landing Craft

National Archives from Coast Guard

Hundreds of drums of gasoline are brought ashore by Coast Guard landing craft to supply U.S. troops in the Philippines.

World War II introduced a long string of firsts. One of these was the first modern amphibious war. The American Civil War included a few, very small-scale landings from seagoing ships or river boats. The ordinary whale boat, rowed ashore by sailors, was sufficient to get soldiers or marines to the beach. It also sufficed in the Spanish-American War, especially as most landings then were made where the enemy was not. In the many U.S. forays into Caribbean brush fires, including the Vera Cruz expedition in 1914, the overwhelming gun power of the U.S. Navy discouraged any attempt to bring troop-carrying rowboats or motor boats under fire. The United States did have some specialized landing craft, including some rowboats mounting cannister-firing cannon on the bow.

World War II was different. Japanese strategists envisioned a huge number of landings on Pacific islands and the southern shores of East Asia. They prepared for it by building scores of flat-bottomed boats that could be run right up on the beach, or at least to where the water was shallow enough for men to wade ashore. Some of the boats could carry small tanks and light artillery. They had ramps to allow vehicles to be run right off the boat.

The Japanese used these boats all over the far (from the United States) end of the Pacific following their attack on Pearl Harbor. They landed on the Philippines and the Dutch East Indies in several places. In Malaya, Japanese troops outflanked stronger British forces continually by landing behind their lines. They drove the British back to Singapore, then landed on that British fortress and added it to their explosively growing empire.

By May of 1942, six months after Pearl Harbor, Japan controlled French Indo-China, Thailand (Siam at that time), Malaya, the Philippines, the Marianas, Wake Island, almost all of Burma, and all of the Dutch East except the southern shore of New Guinea. It controlled the northern shore of the other half of New Guinea, mandated to Australia. (The interior of New Guinea was controlled—as it always had been—by stone-age head-hunters.) The Japanese were attempting more landings—on southern New Guinea and the Solomon Islands—when the Pacific war suddenly began to change.

The first check to Japanese plans was the air-sea Battle of the Coral Sea. That was followed quickly by another air-sea fight: the decisive Battle of Midway. After those two battles, America's "island hopping" campaign began.

The U.S. Marine Corps, whose main function was landing troops from ships, had been experimenting with light, specialized landing craft since the 1930s. The Japanese sea-borne Blitzkrieg shocked the United States and its ship-building industry into concentrating on bigger and better landing craft. The result was thousands of troop carriers, ranging from inflatable rubber boats for small-scale surprises to ponderous LSTs (*Landing Ship Tanks*)—flat bottomed but sea-worthy (although notably rough-riding) ships that could carry up to 20 tanks. The LST would run right up to the shore; its bow would open up like a mammoth garage door; a ramp would run down and the tanks would roll up on the beach, firing as they moved. The LCT (*Landing Craft Tank*) was smaller than the LST and had a flat front, like a modern Boston Whaler. The front would drop down and become a ramp for the tank or tanks to run down. The LCI (*Landing Craft Infantry*) was similar to the LCT, although, as its name indicates, it carried people but not tanks. It came in various sizes, the largest being able to hold 200 soldiers.

The largest of these boats were armed with machine guns or light automatic cannons. One type of LCT, however, the LCT (R) [Landing Craft Tank (Rocket)] carried only weapons—not troops or tanks. The largest had 1,080 five-inch rockets mounted on its deck ready for firing. The rockets were fired in a continuous stream, a spectacular (and spectacularly deadly) fireworks display. Any but the strongest enemy fortifications were pulverized. The Japanese, however, routinely built bunkers that resisted anything but a direct hit from a 16-inch naval gun. Bigger than the LCT (R) and less specialized was the LSM (Landing Ship Medium) which was armed with guns as well as rockets and could also carry troops.

Some landing craft were truly amphibious. One of these was the DUKW or *Duck* (nobody today is sure what the initials originally stood for). The Duck was a three-quarter-ton truck—an amazingly surefooted vehicle itself—surrounded by a boat hull. The Duck could take equipment, supplies or infantry from ship to beach and continue on to the firing line. A few Ducks are still running. One of them takes sightseers on the roads and waterways of Washington, D.C.

Even more impressive was the LVT (*Landing Vehicle Tracked*), better known as the *Alligator*. It was a modification of the original Alligator, a swamp rescue vehicle developed in 1935. The Alligator was an amphibious tank and the star of many U.S. Marine Corps landings in the Pacific. It was propelled by scores of small paddles on it tractor treads. Alligators performed a variety of chores. Some carried infantry, some carried supplies, some acted as light tanks, and others as self-propelled guns. Some were armored, some were equipped with turrets and the 37 mm gun of the M 3 light tank (Stuart tank to the British) , and others carried a 75 mm howitzer. All of them, in spite of the guns and armor, were light enough to float and seaworthy enough to make a sometimes lengthy trip from an anchored troop ship to the beach of a Pacific atoll.

The expertise and weapons the United States had been developing in the Pacific were applied to the Mediterranean and Europe between the end of 1942 and 1944. The landings in Vichy French North Africa, being practically unopposed, presented no big problem. The landings on Sicily the next year, though, brought a demonstration of amphibious warfare technology new to the European continent. There had been sea landings there before, of course. The Germans had landed in several places in Norway in 1940, but given their overwhelming air superiority, they had no need for anything fancy. The British had been working on specialized landing craft for some time, but their raid on the French port of Dieppe in August 1942 was a disaster. More than half of the attacking force was killed or captured and they were never able to achieve their objective—taking and holding the port for a limited time.

June 6, 1944 saw The Big One—the D-day landing in Normandy. In addition to the aerial bombardment and bombardment by both U.S. and British naval ships, the landing craft were supported by four LCGs (*Landing Craft Gun*) firing 4.7 inch guns and 17 LCT(R)s blasting the beach with rockets.

D day in Normandy saw the largest amphibious operation in history, made possible by the swarm of specialized landing craft that had been developed. It seems unlikely that a larger such operation will be needed in the foreseeable future.

47

Shooting Across Oceans: ICBMs and Cruise Missiles

National Archives from U.S. Information Agency

V-1, the world's first cruise missile, in flight over a London roof top.

On June 13, 1944, people in London heard a peculiar buzzing sound. When they looked up, they saw a small airplane traveling across the sky at high speed. Then the plane's engine stopped and it plunged to the ground. There was a terrific explosion. People were still wondering where the plane came from and what happened to it, when another plane just like the first appeared, and as the first did, crashed into the city and exploded. That was followed by another, then another, then several of the little planes. All crashed and exploded.

The V 1 attack had been launched.

For the first time, it was possible to bombard a target at distances beyond the range of even such hopped-up artillery as the 1918 "Paris gun." The German were using unpiloted planes—really flying bombs powered by pulse-jet engines (the only time that type of engine has ever been used in combat). The Germans called the "buzz bombs" (British nickname) *Vergelstungwaffe eins*. To the rest of the world, the flying bomb was the V 1—Hitler's first "vengeance weapon." It was also, although the name had not yet been invented, the world's first *cruise missile*.

The V 1 caught the British public by surprise and inflicted heavy damage at first. The flying bombs directed at England destroyed 25,000 houses and killed 6,184 people, almost all in London. It was, however, hardly the ultimate weapon. It had to be launched from a catapult—the only way its pulse-jet engine could be made to start. It cruised at about 3,000 feet, easily within range of antiaircraft guns as well as fighter planes. It was fast for a plane of those days—559 miles per hour. It was a jet, after all. But it flew in a straight line and wasn't so fast that slightly slower (about 100 mph slower) fighter planes couldn't shoot it down. By August 1944, Allied fighters and antiaircraft guns were shooting down 80 percent of the V 1s.

The next month, Londoners got another surprise—a nastier one than the first. The V 2s arrived. They arrived without warning. No noise announced their coming, and there was nothing to see. The first notice of their coming was a terrific explosion. The V 2 (the Germans called it the A 4) was a quantum leap ahead, technologically, of the V 1. It was a liquid-fueled rocket with a programmable guidance system—a product of years of research into both space travel and weaponry. It was launched straight up, into outer space and described a high arc. Then its rocket engine stopped and it fell toward its target, powered only by gravity. That was enough to give it far more than supersonic speed, so there was no warning sound as there was with the "buzz bomb." And it arrived so fast it was practically invisible.

The main brain behind the V 2 was a scientist named Werner von Braun, who had been fascinated by the idea of space travel as a youth and built rockets as a teenager. Von Braun, it seems, had little interest in anything but rocket technology. Politics meant nothing to him. He just wanted to build rockets. What was done with them did not concern him. In 1932, he met an old artilleryman named Walter Dornberger. Dornberger, too, had an interest in rockets, but his reasons were different from von Braun's. The Treaty of Versailles had forbidden Germany from having any heavy artillery, but it said nothing about rockets. Dornberger saw that rockets could substitute for artillery. One result was Germany's profusion of traditional solid-fuel rockets like the *Nebelwerfer*. Braun was not particularly interested in short-range solid fuel rockets. He had been working on liquid-fuel rockets, using an inflammable liquid combined with liquid oxygen—a systemAmerican, Robert Goddard, had pioneered a little earlier.

Dornberger, too, was interested in long-range rockets—at least, rockets with a longer range than the "Paris gun." The Paris gun, the ultimate long-range artillery piece, he said, would throw 25 pounds of high explosive 80 miles. He wanted the first rocket to throw a ton of high explosive 160 miles. But it would be a rocket that was militarily useful. It had to be accurate: it could not deviate from the target more than 2 or 3 feet for each 1,000 feet of range. And it had to be mobile: it could not be too large to transport by road.

The prototype V 2 was successfully test fired in October 1942. By the end of that year, however, British intelligence learned of the V 2 program, and the next April it learned of the Luftwaffe's development work on a flying bomb. Both projects were underway on the island of Peenemunde. Thereafter, the RAF bombed Peenemunde so heavily that neither weapon was ready until the summer of 1944.

By the time the V 2 was ready, the Luftwaffe V 1 batteries had been driven out of any launching site within range of England, and the V 2s never got a chance to fire from the chosen sites in France. Germany produced 35,000 V 1s, but only 9,000 were launched against England, and of these 4,000 were destroyed before they got there. The Germans continued flying buzz bombs, though. Their main target was Antwerp, the principal Allied supply base. The V 2s continued to bombard London between September 8, 1944, and March 29, 1945, when Allied troops captured their base.

While all this was going on, von Braun and other German scientists were working on a couple of projects that were really scary. Von Braun and Dornberger had written the specs for a new missile, the A 10, which would have more than one motor and would drop off each as it became exhausted. It would have a range of 2,800 miles—long enough to reach New York. At the same time, others in Germany had been working feverishly on a radically new payload: a nuclear bomb. Time ran out on the "thousand-year Reich," and neither project was able to help Hitler.

The ideas, of course, did not go away. One day short of three months after Germany surrendered on May 7, 1945, the United States dropped the first nuclear bomb on Hiroshima. As soon as possible, the United States brought Werner von Braun and many of his fellow rocket scientists to the United States. Russian officials brought other German scientists to the Soviet Union. Soon the U.S. and the U.S.S.R. were building ultra-long-range rockets and testing nuclear bombs. The super-rockets were called *Intercontinental Ballistic Missiles* (ICBMs) because, like the V 2s, when their engines stopped, they were guided by nothing but the laws of ballistics. They could not be turned back. Similar to the ICBMs are the IRBMs (Intermediate Range Ballistic Missiles).

Since then, guidance systems and other features of these rockets have greatly improved. The latest intercontinental missiles have multiple warheads. The first of these were *Multiple Reentry Vehicles* (MRVs), which scatter warheads around a single large target to multiply the destruction. A later development was *Multiple Independently-targeted Reentry Vehicles* (MIRVs). As this rocket descends, warheads and perhaps some decoys are ejected at different points to hit a number of targets. Most diabolical is the MARV system (for *Maneuverable Alternative-target Reentry Vehicle*. With this system, each warhead has its own rocket, and the warheads can change course to an alternative target if anti-ballistic missile defenses appear.

At present, all of these ICBMs are designed for nuclear warheads. They are far too expensive to waste on mere high-explosive warheads. None of them have ever been used. And the world hopes, they may never be used. All wars and all foreign policy, however, have been conducted with fear of the nuclear-armed ICBM in the background influencing every decision.

Superpowers and even great powers refuse to be stymied because they can't use the long-range nukes. They do avoid conflict with each other because of the nuclear danger, and they do not even use their nukes on small powers for fear that such action might provoke others to use nuclear weapons. They do, however, use long-range missiles. These missiles, carrying high explosive warheads are much cheaper than ICBMs. They are a development of the old V 1.

Cruise missiles were a major U.S. weapon in both the Gulf War of 1991 and the Iraq War of 2002. There were two types: the *Tomahawk* and the *CALCM* (for Conventional Air Launched Cruise Missile). In both wars, the Tomahawk was launched from both surface ships and submarines. Some subs are equipped to launch the missiles through the deck the same way the Polaris ballistic missiles are, others are merely shoot out of the torpedo tubes, after which they rise to the surface and fly away. The CALCMs are launched from B 52 bombers. They have less range than the Tomahawks, because their launching vehicles can get closer to most targets, but they carry a bigger warhead.

In one way the modern cruise missiles are similar to their V 1 ancestor. They're also powered by jet engines (turbofan jets in this case), and they both have a maximum speed of around 590 miles per hour. Their range and accuracy has vastly improved, though. The Tomahawk can travel 1,550 miles and, even at maximum range, it can hit "within meters" of its target. Tomahawks in the Gulf War were guided by a radar system which noted terrain features of the land it was flying over and electronically compared them with topographical information programmed into it. In the Gulf War, this was largely replaced by a global positioning satellite system that was even more accurate.

Tomahawks were the weapon of choice not only in the two Mesopotamian conflicts but in such other situations as during the Clinton administration when U.S. Navy cruise missiles flattened a Sudanese chemical plant that was believed to be producing nerve gas for Al Qaeda and some public buildings in Baghdad in reprisal for an attempt to assassinate former president George H. W. Bush.

Long-range missiles, even without nuclear warheads have changed modern warfare considerably.

48

Straight Up:
The Helicopter

National Archives from Navy

Marine infantry attack from a helicopter in Korea, September 20, 1951, one of the first times a helicopter was used as an offensive weapon.

"The helicopter," said the famous pioneer, "does with great labor only what a balloon does without labor." He concluded: "The helicopter is much easier to design than the aeroplane but it is worthless when done." That was Wilbur Wright in 1906.

Mr. Wright had a point. People had been trying to build helicopters for centuries, and their efforts had produced hardly any results. In 1935, airplanes had reached the altitude of 47,352 feet, attained the speed of 440 miles per hour and had flown non-stop for 5,657 miles. At the same time, the helicopter altitude record was 518 feet, a chopper had reached the speed of 60 miles per hour and another had flown 27 miles.

This was in spite of the fact that Europeans had been making toy helicopters since the 12th century, and the Chinese had been making them even earlier. The toy helicopter was a stick with rotor blades. The stick fitted into a cylinder that was wound up with a string. The operator pulled the string, and the little 'copter flew straight up. Powering the rotor was an early problem. One bright soul in renaissance times suggested that the helicopter pilot pull a rope wound around the rotor the way a child pulled the string of the toy. Aside from the fact that Superman, or his ancestors, was still on the planet Krypton and rope-pulling propulsion awaited his coming, the author of this idea could not explain how the pilot would rewind the rope to continue his flight. Leonardo da Vinci, who did so much futurist thinking, took a shot at helicopter design. His machine had two counter-rotating rotors and was powered by clockwork. Clockwork appeared in many inventions of the 15th and 16th centuries—everything from clocks to wheel lock rifles.

About the only power source available in the 18th and most of the 19th centuries, other than muscle power, was steam. And nobody was able to design a steam engine with a high enough power-to-weight ratio. In 1842, an Englishman named W.H. Phillips flew a jet-powered helicopter, perhaps the first man-carrying jet aircraft in history. Phillips's machine had jet nozzles on the tips of his rotors. The fuel he burned was an alarming mixture of potassium nitrate, charcoal, and gypsum. Substitute sulfur for gypsum, change the proportions a bit, and you have gunpowder. That early jet carried Phillips several hundred yards, but it was a technological dead end.

Until the internal combustion engine appeared, powered flight in either helicopter or airplane appeared hopeless. But, after the Wright brothers showed the way, the development of airplanes was phenomenally fast, although helicopters were barely able to get off the ground. The trouble was that helicopters had some problems that never occur in airplanes.

One was torque. The huge rotor blades spinning above the helicopter had a tendency to twist the whole ship and drive it off course. If this tendency could not be cured, the helicopter could only fly in a giant circle. The chopper pioneers tried two methods to neutralize torque. One method was to have counter-rotating rotors (like Leonardo's plan), another was to put a small propeller on the tale. The rotors could also cause another type of twisting—one considerably more dangerous.

Each rotor blade is a kind of wing, generating lift the same way a wing does. The faster air passes over a wing, the greater the lift it generates. On a helicopter, the blades moving forward generate more lift, because the speed of the air over the blade equals the speed of the blade plus the speed of the craft's forward motion. The speed of the air over the retreating blade equals the speed of the blade *minus* the speed of the helicopter's forward motion. As a result, the helicopter without compensation would roll over. So helicopter progress depended on finding a way to vary the pitch of the rotor blades depending on their direction of motion.

While engineers were working on that problem, a Spaniard named Juan de Cierva invented a new type of rotor plane: the *autogyro*. The rotors were attached with flapping hinges that let them automatically change their pitch. The rotors were unpowered. The autogyro was propelled by an ordinary aircraft engine and propeller. As the plane gained speed, the rotors turned freely and provided the lift. Some autogyros had a clutch that let the engine supply power to the rotors for a brief time, making possible a straight-up takeoff. Autogyro air mail planes were actually flown from the roofs of large post offices. Several air forces adopted them, and the Soviet Union's autogyros strafed the German invaders during World War II.

While de Cierva was working on his autogyro, an Argentine, Marquis de Petraras Pescara, invented cyclic pitch control on a helicopter with powered rotors spinning around a tilting rotor head, which made possible a practical helicopter. That was in 1924—21 years after the Wright brothers' flight, which made possible a practical airplane. From there, progress was rapid. In 1936, Heinrich Focke of Germany produced a twin rotor helicopter that flew successfully. Two years later, it traveled 143 miles, reached a speed of 76 miles per hour and climbed to 11,243 feet.

Also in 1938, a Russian immigrant, Igor Sikorsky, who had earlier designed and flown groundbreaking large passenger and military planes in Russia, settled in the United States and started designing helicopters. In 1941, his single rotor 'copter smashed all records and became the basis of all modern helicopters.

The Germans had a few helicopters in World War II, but too few to accomplish anything noteworthy. In the Korean War, the small helicopters of the time were used extensively for reconnaissance, transporting generals, and, especially, evacuating wounded. Almost 80 percent of all the wounded airlifted to field hospitals got there by helicopter. Helicopters grew in size during that war, and in the next war, Vietnam, they were big enough to carry significant numbers of troops and artillery. They were used for reconnaissance; directing battles from the air; and taking part in battles with machine guns, automatic cannons, and rockets. They were still used for medical evacuation, and were the basis for all the tactics of the First Cavalry Division, the U.S. Army's first "air mobile" division.

A deal between the U.S. Army and the U.S. Air Force gave all fixed-wing planes to the Air Force and all helicopters to the Army. Today, every U.S. Army division includes helicopters. Helicopters have replaced all airborne divisions' gliders and usurped most of the functions of their parachutes. Equipped with the wire-guided TOW rockets, they fight tanks; with the six-barreled modern Gatling guns, they mow down infantry; with other special equipment, they lay mines. In Iraq, they have taken part in street fighting. In Israel, and to a lesser extent in Iraq, they have been used to assassinate suspected terrorists.

Most helicopter successes have been against foes lacking effective antiaircraft fire. Even in Vietnam, where neither the Viet Cong nor the North Vietnamese Army was strong in antiaircraft weapons, helicopter losses were heavy. A weapon like the Carl Gustaf recoilless gun (see Chapter 44) would be deadly against a hovering helicopter. A shell from a recoilless gun has far more velocity than a rocket, especially one of the guided rockets now used for antitank work. The chances of the helicopter evading the shot after it's been fired are virtually nil.

Nevertheless, the "chopper's" ability to take off and land on a postage stamp, to hover at will, to hide behind hills and other terrain features, to climb beyond the range of most ground fire, and to travel faster than any other vehicle except an airplane insures that it will continue to influence warfare for a long time.

49

The Ultimate Weapon?
Nuclear Weapons

National Archives from Office of War Information

Atomic bomb explodes over Nagasaki
August 8, 1945.

At 8:15 a.m. on August 6, 1945, an American B 29 bomber flew over the city of Hiroshima, Japan and released something on a parachute. Hiroshima was a medium-size city, largely untouched by the war because it contained no military objectives worth touching. The object floating earthward under the parachute was the first nuclear weapon to be used in war. When the bomber was far away, but the parachute still above the ground, the bomb exploded. Between 70,000 and 80,000 people in the city below died instantly or almost instantly. As many as 125,000 more died later as a result of injuries incurred by the blast. Three days later, a similar bomb exploded over Nagasaki, killing from 40,000 to 70,000 more people at once and 50,000 to 100,000 later from radiation sickness, cancer, or other illnesses caused by the explosion. Six days later, Japan surrendered.

The possibility of nuclear weapons had been known in the scientific community for years. All matter is composed of atoms, which have a nucleus composed of protons and neutrons around which electrons orbit. The number of atomic particles in the nucleus of an element's atom determines its atomic weight, which is expressed in numbers that have bedeviled generations of high school chemistry students. When neutrons, protons, deuterons, and other particles strike a nucleus of high atomic weight, they are absorbed and the nucleus splits into two, forming two lighter atoms. The process releases a million volts of energy per atom. This process goes on continually in radioactive material but causes no trouble, because the released energy simply bypasses the other atoms in a block of material and passes into space.

However, by forming certain radioactive materials in a large enough and dense enough block, you have so many atoms in such limited space that a released neutron simply has to strike another nucleus, and particles released by that splitting of that atom will strike another nucleus. Then you have a chain reaction, with the energy in those trillions and trillions of atoms released all at once. Of the kinetic energy released in the chain reaction, about 50 percent forms a shock wave that flattens buildings, trees, and so on, the way a conventional explosion would. The main difference from conventional explosives is in the strength of the shock wave. The power of atomic bombs is measured in kilotons, each the equivalent of 1,000 tons of TNT, or megatons, the equivalent of a million tons of TNT. Thirty-five percent of the kinetic energy appears as heat, light, and ultraviolet radiation. The heat is radiated heat—infrared radiation—and travels at the speed of light. At the center of the explosion, the heat reaches 10,000,000 degrees centigrade. Conventional explosives may produce 5,000 degrees. The remaining 15 percent of the kinetic energy forms various nuclear radiations such as neutron rays and gamma rays, which are extremely destructive to living tissue. Some of this radiation kills or injures people in the initial spurt. More of it—about two thirds—is in radioactive dust that falls to earth. Some of this "fallout" may appear a few hours after the explosion, but fallout from a single explosion may continue falling for months or years, depending on how high it was blown into the atmosphere. It may be carried by the wind for thousands of miles.

Weapons using this "fission" reaction are commonly called "atomic bombs." There's another process—fusion—that can produce even more powerful bombs. This consists of combining the nuclei of two light elements. That forms an element that is lighter than the sum of the two elements that were combined. The difference in mass is released as energy. The fusion of two light elements may release less energy than the fission of a heavy element such as uranium 235, but a chain reaction is different. Because light atoms are much smaller, there are far more of them in a given volume of material. A fusion bomb may release four times as much energy and six times more neutron rays than a fission bomb of the same size.

Fission bombs were the first kind developed. The most common fissionable materials are U-235 and U-233, unstable isotopes of uranium, and plutonium—a man-made element created by bombarding neptunium by deuterons or by performing other atomic hocus-pocus on uranium 238.

To reach a critical mass of plutonium 239, you need a lump of about 15 kilograms; for uranium 235, the critical mass is about 50 kilograms. There are two ways to make a critical mass in a bomb. One uses two pieces of the fissionable material, machined to extremely close tolerances to fit tightly together. These are driven together in the bomb by explosive charges. When they meet, they form a critical mass and a nuclear explosion occurs. The second method uses a spongy ball of the fissionable material—full of holes so a fair proportion of the atoms are not in contact with other atoms. In this kind of bomb, explosives outside the fissionable material squeeze it together to form a critical mass.

Fusion bombs use light elements that fuse only when subjected to enormous heat. Hence they are called thermonuclear bombs. In these bombs, the heat is supplied by a fission explosion.

Much research on nuclear explosions has been directed at miniaturization. The United States developed an enormous 280 mm howitzer, nicknamed the "atomic cannon," to shoot nuclear shells. It was just barely road-transportable. But it was hardly out of its testing before the U.S. had a shell that could be fired from an ordinary 8-inch gun or howitzer. Then there was a still smaller atomic shell that fit the 155 mm cannons. Innumerable rockets, bombs, and shells have been designed for nuclear explosions. There are even nuclear depth charges. One that seemed to arouse particular horror was a weapon the news media called the "neutron bomb" and the U.S. military called an "enhanced radiation device." The neutron bomb will explode, but the explosion is, for a nuclear weapon, nothing much. What it does is project massive amounts of neutron rays that would kill everyone and everything in an area while leaving buildings, vehicles, and all man-made property unscathed and uncontaminated with radiation. It was probably this single effect—killing without destroying property—that led the public to view the neutron bomb with such horror.

None of these weapons have ever been used, and everyone in the world devoutly hopes that they never will be. One reason is that even use of the small "tactical" nuclear weapons might induce an enemy to respond with something bigger, like an ICBM. The other is the largely unknown danger of the fallout from a number of tactical nukes.

Although they have been used only twice in history, nuclear weapons have decisively influenced both warfare and all international relations.

50

High Tech and Low:
The Future of Warfare?

Sky Crane helicopter, capable of lifting enormous loads,
was one of the many high-tech devices the enemy could
not match in Vietnam.

In 2003, U.S. and British forces invaded Iraq with an array of weapons that the troops of World War II would have considered miraculous. There were planes that couldn't be seen, even with radar; bombs that could see a dot of laser light and steer themselves into it; and bombs that could fly hundreds of miles without a pilot and—more amazing—land right on the building they were aimed at. There were planes that needed no pilots and could send television pictures of what a pilot would have seen, making themselves the eyes of people in a headquarters hundreds, even thousands, of miles away. Those Remotely Piloted Vehicles, or "drones," could act as well as see. One of them in Yemen identified a terrorist suspect and killed him with a rocket.

Individual grunts in Iraq could see in the dark, using night vision goggles that enormously amplify any ambient light. Thermal imaging equipment let them see would-be ambushers from inside tanks and other vehicles in the darkest dark. Sensors picking up vibrations in the ground let them locate any enemy attempting to sneak up on an encampment.

There are a host of guided antitank missiles—some guided by wire or fiber optic, others that fly towards reflected laser light. One type has its own laser in its nose that searches an area of 328 square yards for a tank, locates it, and steers toward it. This particular system, the British MERLIN, is not a rocket, but a mortar shell. Most of the wire-guided missiles merely require the operator to keep the target in his sights: the missile automatically steers itself into the target. Others, though, once fixed on the target, follow it like a bloodhound while the operator takes cover. One rocket, the Swedish BILL system, flies above a tank and dives into the vehicle's thin top armor at the appropriate time. The American Javelin does that, too. The javelin is carried and fired by one man, and it's a "shoot and scoot" type. The operator puts the tank in his sights, fires the rocket and the missile does the rest, following the tank if it tries to take evasive action. Then there's the French antitank weapon that picks a target and fires itself. It's really a modern version of the "trap guns" that 18th-century landowners used to discourage poachers. The weapon is set up to cover a gap in a minefield, a bridge, or some other key point. When a vehicle of the proper bulk enters the space being covered, it fires an antitank rocket.

Antitank weapons do not rely entirely on the shaped charge, which has been made less effective by laminated armor. The ancient solid shot is back, but with improvements. There's discarding sabot shot: a dart-shaped piece of very sharp depleted uranium (DU) that is much smaller than the bore of the gun that shoots it. It is encased in a "sabot" of the proper diameter for the gun. The shot, therefore is much lighter than a regular shell of the proper diameter. Because it is so light, it leaves the gun with a terrific muzzle velocity. As soon as it leaves the muzzle, the sabot drops off so wind resistance does not hinder the flight of the DU shot. In some versions, the sabot, traveling through a rifled barrel, imparts its stabilizing spin to the shot. In others, fired from smoothbore guns that also fire shaped charge shells, the shot is fin-stabilized. Depleted uranium, the metal American solid shot is made of, is harder than tungsten and so heavy a piece the size of a golf ball weighs 2 pounds. When it strikes something hard, it throws off extremely hot sparks that have an incendiary effect.

The Coalition forces have, as we've seen (see Chapter 40) several types of improved armor for tanks and other vehicles. In the Iraq War, the troops themselves have vastly improved body armor—what the news media erroneously call "flak jackets." Flak jackets were worn by flight crews in World War II. As the name indicates, the jackets—fabric covering metal plates—were designed to protect the wearer from antiaircraft shell fragments. "Flak" is an abbreviation of *Fliegerabwehrkanone*, German for "antiaircraft gun." Flak jackets would stop shell fragments but not bullets. In the latter part of the Korean War, infantry got armor jackets. These were made of nylon and were lighter than the aircrew armor. They would stop shell fragments and bullets from a .45 caliber pistol, but they wouldn't stop bullets from an M 1 carbine or any more powerful rifle— and all other military rifles were more powerful. The new armor will stop bullets from the AK 47 and its modifications—the universal weapon of the Iraqi guerrillas.

Stopping enemy fire is good. Becoming invisible to the enemy is even better. "Stealth" fighters and bombers are designed to present a minimum profile to enemy radar and are covered with material that greatly reduces radar reflection. In the Gulf War of 1991, some U.S. planes carried radar jamming equipment, forcing the Iraqi radar operators to turn their radars up to full power. That made it easy for other planes to release radar homing missiles from a considerable distance. The missiles then rode down the radar beams and destroyed the radars. In the Gulf War, in spite of all the television footage showing missiles flying into buildings, only about 7 percent of the munitions were "smart" weapons. In the Iraq War, about 70 percent were. Ordinary aerial bombs—the archetypical dumb weapons—became smart by adding a global satellite positioning navigation device and connecting it with movable tail fins.

Some planes, notably the British Harriers, are able to take off straight up and land almost straight down by using movable jet nozzles. Helicopters, of course could always do that, and in the Iraq War there were more and bigger helicopters than ever. One division in that war, the 101st Airborne, is built around helicopters. Parachutes in the 101st had gone the way of gliders. Helicopters carried the 101st troopers, artillery, and vehicles. They fought enemy tanks, destroyed enemy artillery, and strafed enemy infantry. The helicopters carried standard machine guns, the variable-rate chain guns, modern Gatling guns, automatic cannons, and rockets. Helicopter pilots have an aiming device built into their helmets: they can train their weapons on a target just by looking at it.

In the Iraq War, the Iraqis had neither planes nor helicopters, but Coalition forces had antiaircraft guns ranging from the shoulder-fired Stinger to rockets that could knock down enemy aircraft scores of miles away.

The formal part of the Iraq War was over in three weeks. The American forces, which made up the overwhelming majority of the Coalition troops and did by far most of the fighting, lost only 122 troops. The formal war was followed by the guerrilla war. Because of that, as this book went to press American losses approached 1,400.

That calls for a look at "dumb" weapons—the kind guerrillas use.

In 1962, a young officer serving as an adviser to Vietnamese troops stepped on a punji stick smeared with excrement. The sharpened bamboo spike penetrated the sole of his boot and passed entirely through his foot and the instep of the boot. As a result, Captain Colin L. Powell was laid up quite a while in an army hospital. Some men who had the same experience died of the infection incurred.

The punji stick was a favorite improvised weapon of the guerrillas in Vietnam. Some were placed behind trip wires so a victim would fall on them and receive multiple wounds. Others were planted in pits hidden under a rotating platform covered with leaves. Flexible steel spikes in a wooden frame over a pit were another variation. Called a "venus flytrap," it was almost impossible for a victim to pull his leg out. Jungle warfare made it possible for guerrillas to use a wide variety of deadfalls and other man traps. Another favorite was a poisoned arrow launched by elastic bands made from inner tubes and triggered by a trip wire. Poisoned arrows shot from crossbows, weapons that in east Asia have been used since prehistoric times, killed 20th century soldiers in Vietnam.

Improvised weapons ranging from punji sticks to roadside bombs are weapons American troops may be facing in increasing numbers. United States superiority in "smart" weapons and other high-tech devices makes it unlikely that American forces will be seriously challenged by conventional military organizations. Anyone who thinks that these primitive devices do not constitute a serious challenge should study the Vietnam War.

The simple fact is that while weapons have increased in sophistication and lethality for thousands of years, human beings are still put together the same way. An arrow—arrows will penetrate some forms of body armor that will stop a bullet—can kill an American soldier today just as it could kill a French knight in 1346. A roadside bomb consisting of old artillery shells detonated by a small explosive charge—a weapon that is about as dumb as they come—will kill a person just as dead as the most sophisticated cruise missile.

It is true that few places have the abundance of unguarded caches of artillery shells, bombs, and rockets as Iraq. Every country in the world, however, uses explosives in construction and mining. Any guerrilla organization can steal this material without exerting itself. Gasoline and diesel oil are even easier to obtain. These can be used for a variety of weapons, ranging from the lowly Molotov cocktail to anfo (ammonium nitrate and fuel oil) bombs like the one Timothy McVeigh exploded in Oklahoma City. Ammonium nitrate, the other component, besides fuel oil, of McVeigh's bomb, is a commonly used fertilizer. It can easily be obtained in it pure form or leached from brand-name fertilizers. Ordinary flour can be used to make a bomb that purposely reproduces the kind of explosion that accidentally occurs in grain elevators. The list of household products that can be used to make explosives is amazing. It includes granulated sugar, Vaseline, auto battery acid, swimming pool cleaner, and common matches. Matchheads alone can make a dangerous explosive. All of these explosives can be used in mines and booby traps; many can also be used as propellants in improvised guns.

Information on making explosives, as well as making improvised guns and rockets has been widely disseminated. There are at least 40 books in print on the subject, one of which is published by the United States Army. This training manual also includes directions for making a slew of homemade weapons.

Guerrillas using such primitive weapons will, of course, try to obtain better ones. The classic way to obtain better weapons is to get them from the enemy. In Vietnam, early in the war, many of the Viet Cong carried M 1 and M 2 carbines that they had apparently obtained from South Vietnamese troops, either by sale or capture. Iraqi guerrillas apparently have not obtained many, if any, American weapons, but the Russian-built weapons they have—especially the

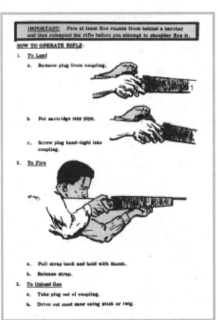

Reprint of an item in the U.S. Army's Improvised Munitions Handbook, which tells how to make a wide variety of weapons.

Kalashnikov rifles and RPG 7s—make pretty good guerrilla weapons. The biggest handicap the Iraqis have is their generally dreadful marksmanship.

Superior weapons mean that just about any regular force can defeat just about any guerrilla force in a formal battle. That's why guerrillas don't fight formal battles. Guerrillas ambush troops on the move, plant mines and other *IEDs* (improvised explosive devices) on supply routes, and attack isolated bases.

They kill supporters of an occupying power. (Most guerrilla enemies are occupying powers.) Guerrillas gave Napoleon's armies a terrible time in Russia and Spain. And over time, they've gradually become more effective. In South Africa, the British had to flood the Orange Free State and the South African Republic (sometimes called the Tranvaal) with more troops than the entire enemy population. And even then, they didn't win until they had incarcerated virtually the whole civilian population in concentration camps. A few years later in Africa, the guerrillas of Abd el Krim, with weapons considerably inferior to those of the Afrikaners, drove the Spanish army out of Morocco and came close to doing that to the French. French air power proved to be too effective against guerrillas in an open desert.

In modern times, those within the memory of most living people, guerrillas have gone from success to success. Consider Africa. Almost every nation on that continent, from Algeria to Zambia, is independent because of a successful guerrilla war. In Malaya, the British put down a guerrilla movement, but that was because the movement was limited to members of a despised minority, the Chinese. Most of the population opposed the guerrillas. Mao Zedong, the most successful guerrilla in modern times, compared guerrillas to fish and the population to the sea. The population shelters the guerrillas and keeps them supplied and informed. Until that human "sea" dries up, the guerrillas are a potent force. They have become more potent in recent years because of three things: (1) instant, world-wide communications; (2) the growth of nationalism; and (3) the development of weapons adapted to guerrilla warfare.

Today guerrillas use television and computers to transmit their propaganda and influence global public opinion. The Irish, in their war of independence made international public opinion their most potent weapon, and modern communications have given propaganda even more potential. In the early years of the last century, colonial powers had a relatively easy time because nationalism was largely confined to Europe and the Americas. In other places loyalty was primarily to the tribe or clan. Today, nationalism is visible everywhere, and in many Muslim lands it's allied with religious zeal. And early in the century, the "Boers" of South Africa didn't have trench mortars or rockets to fire at British bases, and Abd el Krim's Berbers had no anti-aircraft missiles. That's no longer true of most guerrillas.

All of this means that to fight guerrillas, the major powers are going to have to concentrate on drying up the "sea" in which the guerrilla "fish" swim—convincing the populations of enemy countries that it's in their interest to join us.

Honorable Mentions

Whenever you choose the most important of anything, be it battles (as in *50 Battles that Changed the World*), or weapons, or ice cream, other people will have other ideas. That's the reason for elections and the existence of horse races. So here are some weapons that had been suggested or otherwise considered as possibilities and the reasons they didn't make this list. As in the main list, they are presented more or less chronologically.

- **The Ax:** The ax was probably an important hand-to-hand weapon in the Stone Age. One large prehistoric European group is even called the Battle Ax People. But we have no record of whether or not the Battle Ax People actually used their stone axes in battles or, if they did, how they used them or how much they depended on them. Until recent times, the ax was an important weapon to many people in central Africa, but it was never as important as the spear, which is the first item on the list of 50 weapons. Scandinavian, Anglo-Saxon, and Russian warriors used axes extensively, but those axes were never more important than swords, spears, and bows. Nor did use of the ax result in any change in the tactics of these northern fighters

- **The Sling:** Although this weapon proved to be quite decisive for young David and was widely used in antiquity, it was never as decisive as the bow was for either the Eurasian nomads or the English yeomen.

- **The Spear-Thrower:** This weapon, called a *woomera* in Australia and an *atlatl* in ancient Mexico, was a major weapon for many primitive hunting peoples. It's basically a stick with a hook or notch at one end. The user fits the butt of his spear into the hook or notch. When he throws the spear, he flips up the end of the spear-thrower, which adds velocity to the spear. Most people who used the spear-thrower were hunter-gatherers such as the Australian aborigines or the Eskimos, people who lived in small groups and seldom engaged in what we would call war. The Aztecs of Mexico used spear-throwers in war, but their primary weapons were bows and obsidian-edged clubs. They used their atlatls to throw harpoons to collect victims for sacrifice and cannibal feasts.

➧ **The Siege Tower and the Battering Ram:** These devices were used in sieges since before history was written. They were still in use after the introduction of gunpowder, but they were usually ineffective. Mining was much more effective if the enemy stronghold were not built on solid rock or surrounded by water, as many of them were. Until the invention of gunpowder, the outcome of most sieges depended on who got hungry first.

➧ **The Halberd:** The halberd, a combination of ax, spear, and sharpened hook, was a major weapon in the Swiss struggle for independence. The Swiss phalanx used a wall of pikes (very long spears) to stop enemy cavalry so their halberdiers could move up through the ranks to pull the enemy knights off their horses and chop them up. In the chopping-up process, the Swiss halberdiers were assisted by other infantry with two-handed swords, some of which were more than 6 feet long. On the flanks of the Swiss phalanx were crossbowmen who softened up the enemy before contact. The crossbow, incidentally, was greatly esteemed by the Swiss, as can be seen in the legend of William Tell.

➧ **The Crossbow:** This weapon is a favorite of mine and I have owned a couple of crossbows. It is far more powerful than the highly publicized longbow and far more accurate. It can be shot from cover or from the prone position—something extremely difficult with a longbow. It can also be reloaded while the shooter is prone or under cover. Try that with a muzzle-loading musket! The Chinese invented a repeating crossbow that could shoot 10 arrows in 10 seconds or less. Crossbowmen shared, with armored knights and infantry spearmen, credit for the Crusader victories in the Holy Land. But if an inanimate object can be said to have had bad luck, the crossbow had it. Neither the Chinese (who had, in some respects, the best crossbows) nor the Europeans ever used enough crossbows to be decisive. Longbows were far cheaper and could shoot arrows faster (except for the low-powered Chinese repeating crossbow), although with less range, accuracy, or penetration. Even the recurved bows of the nomads—which required great skill to manufacture—were cheaper than crossbows. By the late 14th and early 15th centuries, Europeans finally began making enough crossbows to make a difference, but by that time, they were also making guns, which were cheaper than crossbows and even more powerful.

➡ **The Wagenburg:** This item is somewhat marginal, because the wagenburg is really a formation rather than a weapon. It was a ring of armored wagons containing soldiers manning very small cannons, crossbows, and primitive hand guns. It was a decisive factor in the Hussite Wars of the 15th century, but was little used outside of central Europe. Mobile artillery quickly made it obsolete.

➡ **The Horse Pistol:** When the Swiss phalanx of pikemen was adopted throughout western and central Europe, mounted lancers quickly learned that their favorite weapon had become obsolete. The pike was longer than any spear a cavalryman could manage on horseback. So the horsemen adopted the pistol. This was a gun you could manage with one hand and had a much longer reach than any pike. The cavalrymen created the caracole—a long column of horsemen, each carrying from two to six large pistols. The pistols used the newly invented wheel lock, which fired the priming charge with sparks caused by the abrasion of a spinning wheel on iron pyrites. The column of cavalry trotted forward, and, as the front rank neared the enemy pikemen, they fired their pistols and rode to the rear, while succeeding ranks were firing. The caracole kept up continuous fire on one point of the pike phalanx. The new formation was an early success. Then armies increased the proportion of musketeers in their ranks. The musket outranged the pistol the way the pistol outranged the pike, and a dense column of horsemen made a splendid target. The horsemen were armored, but the big heavy muskets, which had to be fired from a rest, could penetrate any armor a man could carry.

➡ **Percussion Ignition:** Using a small explosive pill to ignite a powder charge instead of sparks caused by the collision of steel and stone greatly improved the reliability of guns. It did not, however, require a change of tactics. When that percussion lock was attached to a rifled barrel, as happened shortly after the introduction of percussion ignition, a change of tactics become necessary. The need for a change was bloodily demonstrated in the American Civil War.

➡ **The Battleship:** The battleship is an armored ship, a classification already on the list. Like the U.S.S. *Monitor*, it has armored sides and a revolving turret—actually multiple turrets, like some Civil War *Monitor*-class ships. Like the U.S.S *New Ironsides* of the Civil War, it has a high freeboard. It's also powered by engines rather than wind. But, although the battleship is merely a development of ships introduced in the 1860s, it does rate some consideration. One strange thing about it is that, although the most powerful weapon of the late 19th and early 20th centuries, it turned out to be more important politically than militarily. The Battle of Manila Bay in 1898 caused the United States to be internationally recognized as a great power, but no U.S. battleships were involved in that fight. The Battle of Tsushima Strait in the Russo-Japanese War was a great and decisive battleship clash, but the war itself had already been decided by the land battle of Mukden. What made Tsushima Strait decisive was that it showed east Asian people, most of them colonized (or, as in China, semi-colonized) that an east Asian people could use modern ships to defeat a European power with a much larger navy. Still, every country considered battleships the ultimate expression of military power. The race between Britain and Germany to see which could build the most battleships greatly increased the tensions that contributed to World War I. When that war came, its greatest battleship fight, the Battle of Jutland, was thoroughly indecisive. Still, battleship construction continued, and the Washington naval treaty, followed by Japan's construction of the super dreadnoughts, *Yamato* and *Musashi,* built up tension between the United States and Japan. But when the two Pacific powers came to blows in World War II, the aircraft carrier, not the battleship, proved to be the new capital ship.

➡ **The Dirigible:** Dirigibles, ranging from the huge Zeppelins of World War I to the little blimps of World War II, played important parts. German Zeppelins were the world's first strategic bombers, and one of them taking supplies to German colonial troops in East Africa made a mind-boggling flight of more than 4,000 miles at a time when few airplanes could travel much more than 100 miles. During World War II, U.S. Navy blimps contributed heavily to the defeat of the German U boats. But Zeppelins proved too vulnerable to attack by fighter planes, and a series of horrendous accidents after the war discouraged any more development of big dirigibles. Blimps are still around, but they are slow, clumsy, and unable to do anything that cannot also be done by helicopters.

➡ **The Molotov Cocktail:** The Molotov cocktail, a bottle of gasoline, or gasoline and motor oil, with a burning cloth wick, was an important weapon in the Spanish Civil War, when Loyalist militia used them against tanks. Tanks in that war were thin-skinned and primitive. Molotov cocktails have not been of much use since then—except when, in World War II, U.S. troops used them against Japanese troops holed up in caves. These gasoline bombs have been widely used since the Spanish Civil War, however, and are still being used. That's because they are dirt cheap. Anyone using a Molotov cocktail against a modern tank would be just as effective if he put a gun to his own head and pulled the trigger. Actually, a Molotov cocktail is no more than a reproduction—not a development—of an ancient and medieval naphtha bomb.

➡ **The Shotgun:** Small arms enthusiasts rate the shotgun as the deadliest close-quarters weapon ever developed. Since World War I, shotguns have played a part in U.S. infantry tactics. They were "trench guns" in World War I and widely used in the jungle fighting in World War II and Vietnam. In mountainous Korea, where ranges tended to be long, they were mostly used for guarding prisoners, but in the street fighting common in Iraq, the shotgun again plays an important role, but in no war has the shotgun ever been a decisive weapon.

➡ **The Rocket Propelled Grenade:** The rocket-propelled grenade does not make the list for a number of reasons. The first is that the name is a misnomer. It has been applied to a Russian-invented weapon called in Russia the RPG 7. RPG does not stand for rocket-propelled grenade, because the weapon is *not* a grenade. A grenade is a missile, usually hand propelled. The RPG 7 is a combination recoilless gun and a rocket launcher. It's a development of the Russian RPG 2, which was a small recoilless gun pattered after the German *panzerfaust* of World War II. The RPG 7's missile is a rocket-assisted shell. Early shoulder-fired rocket launchers, like the U.S. bazooka, fired a rocket with a quick-burning motor. The rocket fuel was consumed inside the launcher tube so the firer would not be burned to a crisp by the back blast of the rocket. What the RPG 7 does is shoot the missile far enough before the rocket motor ignites so there's no danger of the rocket burning the firer. The rocket is then capable of a prolonged blast, giving it far more range than the bazooka. The RPG 7 (RPG is a designation the Russians applied to a number of antitank weapons, including the RPG 43, a World War II hand grenade) is basically an antitank weapon. The Russians claimed it could penetrate 11 inches of homogeneous armor, though, today, most tanks are not protected by homogeneous armor. Tanks have laminated armor, with materials other than steel sandwiched in to reduce the acetylene-torch effect of a shaped charge blast. They have reactive armor—slabs of explosive which neutralize the directed jet of a shaped-charge explosion, and they have steel mesh work outside the armor to make shaped charges explode before they reach the optimum distance for penetration. The RPG 7 is widely used today, possibly because its big bang impresses its users, but it is not very effective in the role it was designed for.

➡ **The Humvee:** Humvees seem to be everywhere in Iraq. But the humvee does not make the list for the same reason that jeep of World War II, Korea, and Vietnam did not, nor did the superb, but little-publicized, three-quarter-ton truck of those wars. The humvee and those other vehicles are trucks, basically a means of transportation rather than a weapon. All of them have, of course, been adapted to function as fighting vehicles, but that use has not resulted in a major change in tactics.

➡ **The Neutron Bomb:** The neutron bomb, also called an "enhanced radiation device," is a nuclear bomb that produces a relatively mild blast but fills a wide area with deadly radiation. Supposedly, it could kill every living thing in a city but leave the buildings largely intact. It has been the subject of horror stories by antiwar activists, who seem to think destruction of life without destruction of property is especially immoral. The neutron bomb, however, has never been built, and its effects are purely theoretical.

Bibliography

Adcock, F.E. *The Greek and Macedonian Art of War*. Berkeley, C.A.: University of California Press, 1962.

Axelrod, Alan. *America's Wars*. New York: Wiley & Sons, 2002.

———.*Chronicle of the Indian Wars*. New York: Prentice Hall, 1993

Barrow, Clyde. *The Poor Man's Armorer*. Eureka, C.A.: Atlan Formularies, 1978.

Billings, Malcolm. *The Cross and the Crescent*. New York: Sterling, 1988.

Bonds, Ray, ed. *Advanced Technology Warfare*. New York: Crescent, 1985.

Boxer, C.R. *Four Centuries of Portuguese Expansion*. Johannesburg: Witwatersrand University Press, 1961.

Bradford, Ernle. *The Sword and the Scimitar: The Saga of the Crusades*. New York: G.P Putnam's Sons, 1974.

Brice, Martin. *Forts and Fortresses*. New York: Facts on File, 1990.

Brownstone, David and Irene Franck. *Timelines of War: A Chronology of Warfare from 100,000 BC to the Present*. Boston: Little, Brown, 1994.

Bury, J.B. *The History of the Later Roman Empire*. New York: Dover, 1958.

———. *The Invasion of Europe by the Barbarians*, New York: Norton, 1967.

Carter, Anthony. *World Bayonets: 1800 to the Present*. London: Arms and Armour, 1996.

Childe, V. Gordon. *New Light on the Most Ancient East*. New York: Grove, 1957.

———. *Man Makes Himself*. New American Library, 1960.

Cipolla, Carlo M. *Guns, Sails and Empires*. New York: Minerva Press, 1965.

Clark, Sir George. *Early Modern Europe*. New York: Oxford University Press, 1960.

Coffin, Howard. *Nine Months to Gettysburg*. Woodstock, Vt.: Countryman Press, 1997.

Coe, Michael D., Peter Connolly, Anthony Harding, Victor Harris, Donald J. Larocca, Thom Richardson, Anthony North, Christopher Spring, and Frederick Wilkinson. *Swords and Hilt Weapons*. New York: Barnes and Noble, 1994.

Cohen, Richard. *By the Sword*. New York: Random House, 2002.

Cottrell, Leonard. *The Anvil of Civilization*. New York: New American Library, 1960.

Cowley, Robert and Geoffrey Parker. *The Reader's Companion to Military History*. Boston: Houghton Mifflin, 1996.

Danvers, F.C. *The Portuguese in India*. London: W.H.. Allen, 1894.

Delbruck, Hans. *History of the Art of War*. Lincoln, NE: University of Nebraska Press, 1990.

Derry, T.K. and Trevor I. Williams. *A Short History of Technology*. New York: Oxford University Press, 1961.

Diagram Group. *Weapons*. New York: St. Martins, 1990.

Duffy, Christopher. *Siege Warfare: The Fortress in the Early Modern World, 1494-1660*. New York: Barnes & Noble, 1979.

Dunnigan, James F. and Albert A. Nofi. *Dirty Little Secrets*. New York: William Morrow, 1990.

————. *Dirty Little Secrets of World War II*. New York: William Morrow, 1994..

Eggenberger, David. *An Encyclopedia of Battles*. New York: Dover, 1985.

Ellis, John. *The Social History of the Machine Gun*. New York: Pantheon, 1975.

Emery, W.B. *Archaic Egypt*. Baltimore: Penguin, 1961.

Ezell, Edward Clinton. *Small Arms of the World*. New York: Barnes & Noble, 1983.

Fairservis,Jr., Walter A. *The Ancient Kingdoms of the Nile*. New York: New American Library, 1962.

Fitzsimons, Bernard. *The Big Guns: Artillery 1914-1918*. London: BPC Publishing, 1973.

Frankfort, Henri. *The Birth of Civilization in the Near East*. Garden City, N.Y.: Doubleday, 1956.

Fuller, J.F.C. *A Military History of the Western World*. New York: DaCapo, 1987.

————. *The Conduct of War, 1789-1961*. New Brunswick, N.J.: Rutgers University Press, 1961.

Greenwood, John T., ed. *Milestones of Aviation*. New York: Crescent, 1989.

Gurney, O.R. *The Hittites*. Baltimore: Penguin, 1969.

Hackworth, Colonel David H. and Julie Sherman. *About Face*. New York: Simon & Schuster, 1989.

Hatcher, Julian S. *Textbook of Pistols and Revolvers*. Plantersville, S.C.: Small Arms Technical Publishing Co., 1935.

Helmer, William J. *The Gun that Made the Twenties Roar*. Highland Park, N.J.: Gun Room Press, 1969.

Herodotus. *The Histories*. Baltimore: Penguin, 1960.

Hogg, Ian. *Barrage: The Guns in Action*. New York: Ballantine, 1970

——————. *The Complete Machine Gun*. New York: Exeter, 1979.

——————. *The Guns 1939-45*. New York: Ballantine, 1970.

Hogg, Ian V. and John Weeks. *Military Small Arms of the Twentieth Century*. Northbrook, IL: DBI, 1999.

Jobe, Joseph, ed. *Guns: An Illustrated History of Artillery*. Greenwich, CT: New York Graphic Society, Ltd., 1971.

Joinville and Villehardouin. *Chronicles of the Crusades*. Baltimore: Penguin, 1963.

Keegan, John. *The First World War*, New York: Knopf, 1999

——————. *A History of Warfare*. New York: Random House, 1993.

——————. *The Illustrated Face of Battle*. New York: Viking, 1988.

——————. *The Iraq War*. New York: Knopf, 2004.

——————. *The Second World War*. New York: Penguin, 1989.

——————. *Six Armies in Normandy*. New York: Viking, 1982.

Keegan, John and Andrew Whewatcroft. *Who's Who in Military History*. New York: William Morrow, 1976.

Kershaw, Andrew, ed. *Weapons of War*. London: BPC Publishing, 1973.

Kramer, Samuel Noah. *History Begins at Sumer*. Garden City, NY: Doubleday, 1959.

Liddell Hart, Basil H. *The Real War: 1914 to 1918*. Boston: Little, Brown, 1930.

——————. *Strategy*. New York: Praeger, 1960.

McNeill, William H. *The Pursuit of Power*. Chicago: University of Chicago Press, 1982.

——————. *The Rise of the West*. Chicago: The University of Chicago Press, 1963.

McPherson, James M. *Battle Cry of Freedom: The Civil War Era*. New York: Ballantine, 1988.

Marsden, E.W. *Greek and Roman Artillery: Historical Development*. Oxford, England: Oxford University Press, 1969.

——————. *Greek and Roman Artillery: Technical Treatises*. Oxford, England: Oxford University Press, 1971.

Messenger, Charles. *The D-Day Atlas*. New York: Thames & Hudson, 2004.

Montross, Lynn. *War Through the Ages*. New York: Harper & Row, 1960.

Morrison, Sean. *Armor*. New York: Crowell, 1963.

Morris, Eric, Curt Johnson, Christopher Chant, and H.P. Willmott. *Weapons and Warfare of the Twentieth Century*. Secaucus, N.J.: Derbibooks, 1974.

Moscati, Sabatino. *Ancient Semitic Civilizations*. New York: Putnam's, 1960.

Norman, A.V.P. and Don Pottinger. *English Weapons and Warfare, 449-1660*. New York: Dorset Press, 1979.

Oakeshott, R. Ewart. *The Archaeology of Weapons*. New York: Praeger, 1960.

Oakley, Kenneth P. *Man the Toolmaker*. Chicago: The University of Chicago Press, 1957.

O'Toole, G.J.A. *The Spanish War*. New York: W.W. Norton, 1984.

Payne-Gallwey, Sir Ralph. *The Crossbow*. London: Holland Press, 1986.

Peterson, Harold L. *American Knives*. New York: Scribners, 1958.

————. *Arms and Armor in Colonial America*, 1526-1783. New York: Bramhall House, 1956.

————. *The Book of the Continental Soldier*, Harrisburg, Pa.: Stackpole, 1958.

————. *Round Shot and Rammers*. New York: Bonanza, 1959.

Pigott, Stuart, ed. *The Dawn of Civilization*, New York; McGraw-Hill, 1961.

Edge, David and John Miles Paddock. *Arms and Armor of the Medieval Knight*. New York: Crescent, 1988.

Pitt, Barrie and Frances. *The Month-by-Month Atlas of World War II*. New York: Summit, 1989.

Powell, William. *The Anarchist Cookbook*. Secaucus, NJ: Lyle Stuart, 1976.

Pope, Dudley. *Guns*. London: Spring Books, 1970.

Pope, Saxton T. *Bows and Arrows*. Berkeley, Ca.: University of California Press, 1962.

Preston, Richard A., Sidney F. Wise, and Herman O. Werner. *Men in Arms: A History of Warfare*. New York: Praeger, 1962.

Prestwich, Michael and Charles Coulson. Poole, England: Blandford Press, 1980.

Reid, William. *Weapons Through the Ages*. New York: Crescent, 1976.

Robinson, H. Russell. *Oriental Armor*. New York: Walker, 1967.

Rodgers, W.L. *Greek and Roman Naval Warfare*. Anapolis, MD: U.S. Naval Institute, 1964.

Rodgers, W.L. *Naval Warfare Under Oars*: 4th to 16th Centuries. Anapolis, MD: U.S. Naval Institute, 1967.

Saxon, Kurt. *The Poor Man's James Bond*. Eureka, CA: Atlan Formularies, 1972.

————. *The Survivor*, vol. 1. Eureka, Ca.: Atlan Formularies, 1976.

Simkins, Michael. *Warriors of Rome*. London: Blandford, 1988.

Smith, W.H.B and Joseph Smith. *Small Arms of the World*. Harrisburg, PA: Stackpole, 1960.

Snodgrass, *Arms and Armour of the Greeks*. Ithaca, N.Y.: Cornell University Press, 1967.

Stone, George Cameron. *A Glossary of the Construction, Decoration and Use of Arms and Armor in All Countries and in All Times*. New York: Jack Brussel, 1961

Sulzberger. C.L. *The American Heritage Picture History of World War II*. New York: American Heritage.

Tarassuk, Leonard and Claude Blair. *The Complete Encyclopedia of Arms and Weapons*. New York: Bonanza Books, 1979.

Taylor, A.J.P. *The Second World War*. New York: Putnam, 1983l

Taylor, Michael J. *History of Flight*. New York: Crescent, 1990/

van Creveld, Martin. *Technology and War: From 2000 BC to the Present*. New York: Free Press, 1989.

Vernadsky, George. *Ancient Russia*. New Haven, Ct.: Yale University Press, 1969.

Weir, William. *50 Battles that Changed the World*. Franklin Lakes, NJ: Career Press/New Page, 2001.

—————. *Fatal Victories*. New York: Avon, 1995.

—————. *Soldiers in the Shadows*. Franklin Lakes, N.J.: Career Press/New Page, 2002.

—————. *Written With Lead*. New York: Cooper Square Press, 2003.

Wheal, Elizabeth-Anne, Stephen Pope, and James Taylor. *A Dictionary of the Second World War*. New York: Peter Bedrick, 1990.

Wilkinson, Frederick. *Edged Weapons*, Garden City, N.Y.: Doubleday, 1970.

—————. *Arms and Armour*. London: Chancellor Press, 1996.

Yost, Graham. *Spy-Tech*. New York: Facts on File, 1985.

Young, Brigadier Peter, ed. *Great Battles of the World on Land, Sea and Air*. New York: Bookthrift Publications, 1978.

Periodicals

Guns and Ammo, October, 1976, "Tommy Guns," by William Weir

World War II, May 1989, "The Greatest Guns of the War," by William Weir

New York Times, February 24, 2004, "How Catapults Married Science, Politics and War," by John Noble Wilford.

Index

About the Author

William Weir, an army MP, became an army combat correspondent and photographer with the 25th Infantry Division and the 27th "Wolfhound" Regiment during the Korean War. After leaving the army, he was a newspaper reporter in Missouri and Kansas and was, among other things, the military editor of the *Topeka State Journal*. Later, as a public relations specialist with a large telephone company, he became a freelance writer. He has written more than 50 articles, mostly on crime, weaponry, and military affairs, and has written eight previous books, two of which, *50 Weapons that Changed the World* and *Soldiers in the Shadows*, have been published by New Page Books. He and his wife, Anne, live in Guilford, Connecticut, where they proudly watch the achievements of their three children: Alison, an Air Force lieutenant colonel now serving as a U.S. Supreme Court fellow; Joan, a special education teacher and the mother of their granddaughter, Emma; and Bill, a reporter for the *Hartford Courant*.